The Ultimate

The
Business
Start-Up
Toolkit

The Ultimate Guide to Starting Your Business

The Business Start-Up Toolkit

DANIEL SITARZ, ATTORNEY-AT-LAW

Nova Publishing Company
Small Business and Consumer Legal Books
Carbondale Illinois

ISBN 13: 978-1-892949-43-1
Book w/CD-Rom   price: $39.95

Cataloging-in-Publication Data
       The business start-up toolkit / Daniel Sitarz. -- 1st ed. -- Carbondale,
       Ill. : Nova Publishing, c2008.
       p. ; cm. + CD-ROM (4 3/4 in.)
       (Legal toolkit series)
       ISBN: 978-1-892949-43-1
       At head of title: The ultimate guide to starting your business.
       Includes index.
       1. New business enterprises--United States--Popular works.
       2. Small business--United States--Popular works. 3. New business
       enterprises--United States--Forms. 4. Small business--United
       States--Forms.
       I. Title. II. Title: Ultimate guide to starting your business.
       III. Series.
              KF1649 .S58 2008
              346.73/0652--dc22 0807

Nova Publishing Company is dedicated to providing up-to-date and accurate legal information to the public. All Nova
publications are periodically revised to contain the latest available legal information.

1ˢᵗ Edition; 1ˢᵗ Printing / July, 2008

This publication is designed to provide accurate and authoritative information in regard to the subject matter covered.
It is sold with the understanding that the publisher and author are not engaged in rendering legal, accounting, or other
professional services. If legal advice or other expert assistance is required, the services of a competent professional person
should be sought.

—From a Declaration of Principles jointly adopted by a Committee of
the American Bar Association and a Committee of Publishers

DISCLAIMER

Because of possible unanticipated changes in governing statutes and case law relating to the application of any information
contained in this book, the author, publisher, and any and all persons or entities involved in any way in the preparation, publication, sale, or distribution of this book disclaim all responsibility for the legal effects or consequences of any document prepared
or action taken in reliance upon information contained in this book. No representations, either express or implied, are made or
given regarding the legal consequences of the use of any information contained in this book. Purchasers and persons intending
to use this book for the preparation of any legal documents are advised to check specifically on the current applicable laws in
any jurisdiction in which they intend the documents to be effective.

Nova Publishing Company
Small Business and Consumer Legal Books and Software
1103 West College St.
Carbondale, IL 62901
Tech Support: (800) 748-1175
Editorial: (618)457-3521

Distributed by:
National Book Network
4501 Forbes Blvd., Suite 200
Lanham, MD 20706
Orders: (800) 462-6420 or
www.novapublishing.com

Nova Publishing Company Green Business Policies
Nova Publishing Company is committed to preserving ancient forests and natural resources. Our company's policy is to print
all of our books on recycled paper, with 100% post-consumer waste, de-inked in a chlorine-free process. In addition, all Nova
books are printed using soy-based inks. As a result, for the printing of this book, we have saved:
              26.1 trees • 7,561 gallons of water • 4,428 kilowatt hours of electricity • 65 pounds of pollution
Nova Publishing Company is a member of Green Press Initiative, a nonprofit program dedicated to supporting publishers in
their efforts to reduce their use of fiber obtained from endangered forests. For more information, check out www.greenpressin
itiative.org. In addition, Nova uses all compact fluorescent lighting; recycles all office paper products, aluminum and plastic
beverage containers, and printer cartridges; uses 100% post-consumer fiber, process-chlorine-free, acid-free paper for 95% of
in-house paper use; and, when possible, uses electronic equipment that is EPA Energy Star-certified. Finally, all carbon emissions
from office energy use are offset by the purchase of wind-energy credits that are used to subsidize the building of wind turbines
on the Rosebud Sioux Reservation in South Dakota (see www.nativeenergy.com).

Table of Contents

CHAPTER 9: Starting Business as a Corporation

List of Forms (in book and on CD)

All Forms on CD are in both PDF and text format unless noted

Chapter 2: Business Start-up Checklists

Sole Proprietorship Start-up Checklist (PDF only)
Partnership Start-up Checklist (PDF only)
Corporation Start-up Checklist (PDF only)
S-Corporation Start-up Checklist (PDF only)
Limited Liability Start-up Checklist (PDF only)

Chapter 3: Developing a Business Plan

Business Plan Worksheet
Executive Summary

Chapter 4: Developing a Marketing Plan

Business Marketing Worksheet

Chapter 5: Developing a Financial Plan

Business Financial Worksheet
Estimated Profit and Loss Statement (PDF only: 2 versions—fillable and non-fillable)
Current Balance Sheet (PDF only: 2 versions—fillable and non-fillable)

Chapter 6: Business Paperwork

Sole Proprietorship Paperwork Checklist (PDF only)
Partnership Paperwork Checklist (PDF only)
Corporation Paperwork Checklist (PDF only)
S-Corporation Paperwork Checklist (PDF only)
Limited Liability Company Paperwork Checklist (PDF only)

Chapter 7: Starting Business as a Sole Proprietorship

Sole Proprietorship Pre-Start-up Worksheet
Sole Proprietorship Pre-Start-up Checklist (PDF only)
Sole Proprietorship Plan Checklist (PDF only)
Sole Proprietorship Plan
Statement of Intention to Conduct Business Under an Assumed or Fictitious Name

Chapter 8: Starting Business as a Partnership

Pre-Partnership Worksheet
Pre-Partnership Checklist (PDF only)
Partnership Agreement Checklist (PDF only)
Partnership Agreement (Text only)
Amendment to Partnership Agreement
Partnership Termination Worksheet
Termination of Partnership Agreement
Statement of Partnership Authority
Amendment to Statement of Partnership Authority
Cancellation of Statement of Partnership Authority
Statement of Intention to Conduct Business Under an Assumed or Fictitious Name

Chapter 9: Starting Business as a Corporation

Pre-Incorporation Worksheet
Pre-Incorporation Checklist (PDF only)

Chapter 10: Starting Business as an S-Corporation

Chapter 11: Starting Business as a Limited Liability Company

DETAILS of APPENDIX of STATE BUSINESS LAWS

Details of the following are provided on the Forms-on-CD:

For All Businesses: Address of state business department, State website address: Website for Downloading state forms.

For Limited Liability Companies: State Lawbook reference; Title of filing; Forms available online; Forms provided on CD; Filing Fees; Name requirements; Organizer requirements; Articles of Organization requirements; Annual report requirement; Publication requirement; Effective date of limited liability company organization; Membership requirements; Other Provisions.

For Corporations: State Lawbook reference; Title of filing; Forms available online; Forms provided on CD; Filing Fees; Other fees; Name reservation; Name requirements; Incorporator requirements; Corporate purpose requirements; Director requirements; Paid-in-capital requirements; Annual report requirement; Publication requirements; Other provisions.

For Partnerships: State lawbook reference for partnership regulation; Statement of Partnership Authority registration; Partnership Authority statute listing; Partnership Authority online form; Partnership Authority registration fee.

For Partnership and Sole Proprietorship—Business Name Registration: State law reference for name registration; Registration of business name requirements; Business name online form; Business name registration fee; Term of registration; Name requirements; Registration application requirements; Publication requirements.

Introduction to the Business Start-Up Toolkit

This book is designed to assist its readers in understanding the general aspects of the law as it relates to starting your own business. Regardless of whether or not a lawyer is ultimately retained in certain situations, the legal information in this handbook will enable the reader to understand the framework of law in this country as it relates to business start-up. To try and make that task as easy as possible, technical legal jargon has been eliminated whenever possible and plain English used instead. When it is necessary to use a legal term which may be unfamiliar to most people, it will be shown in *italics* and defined when first used. There is a glossary of most legal terms used in the process of starting your business at the end of this book. Lawyers often caution people that such antiquated language is most important and that, of course, only they, the lawyers, can properly prepare and interpret legal documents using such language. Naturally, plain and easily-understood English is not only perfectly proper for use in all legal documents, but in most cases, leads to far less confusion on the part of later readers.

> **Toolkit Tip!**
>
> This book will allow you to set up any type of business: a sole proprietorship, partnership, corporation, S-corporation, or limited liability company.

Chapter 1 of this book contains information regarding the advantages and disadvantages of the various types of business entities that are available to new businesses. In Chapter 2, easy-to-use checklists are provided as outlines to use in starting the type of business that you have decided upon. The mechanics of developing and preparing a business plan and its executive summary are provided in Chapter 3. Chapter 4 outlines the development

> **☼Toolkit Tip!**
>
> Check your state's listing in the Appendix (which is contained on the enclosed CD) to see any specific state laws for your type of business entity.

of your business marketing objectives. The details of preparing a financial plan, estimated balance sheet, and estimated profit and loss statement are outlined in Chapter 5. The importance of business recordkeeping is explained in Chapter 6. Chapters 7-11 provide all of the information, instructions, and paperwork necessary for you to set up the type of business entity that you have chosen, whether it is a sole proprietorship, partnership, corporation, S-corporation, or limited liability company. Chapter 12 provides various forms for use if you will have any employees in your new business. The basics of financial recordkeeping and accounting are explained in Chapter 13. Chapter 14 provides details for setting up an employee payroll. The taxation of each type of business entity is detailed in Chapter 15. The Appendix (contained on the CD) provides a comprehensive listing of the individual state business laws for each of the 50 states and the District of Columbia. Finally, a glossary of legal terms most often encountered in business is included.

Installation Instructions for Installing Forms-on-CD

Installation Instructions for PCs

1. Insert the enclosed CD in your computer.
2. The installation program will start automatically. Follow the onscreen dialogue and make your appropriate choices.
3. If the CD installation does not start automatically, click on START, then RUN, then BROWSE, and select your CD drive, and then select the file "Install.exe." Finally, click OK to run the installation program.
4. During the installation program, you will be prompted as to whether or not you wish to install the Adobe Acrobat Reader® program. This software program is necessary to view and fill in the PDF (potable document format) forms that are included on the Forms-on-CD. If you do not already have the Adobe Acrobat Reader® program installed on your hard drive, you will need to select the full installation that will install the program on your computer.

Installation Instructions for MACs®

1. Insert the enclosed CD in your computer.
2. Copy the folder "Forms for Macs" to your hard drive. All of the PDF and text-only forms are included in this folder.
3. If you do not already have the Adobe Acrobat Reader® program installed on your hard drive, you will need to download the version of this software that is appropriate for your particular MAC operating system from www.adobe.com. Note: The latest versions of the MAC operating system (OS-X) has PDF capabilities built into it.

⚓ Toolkit Tip!

MAC users will need to download Adobe Acrobat Reader directly from www.adobe. com.

Instructions for Using Forms-on-CD

All of the forms that are included in this book have been provided on the Forms-on-CD for your use if you have access to a computer. If you have completed the Forms-on-CD installation program, all of the forms will have been copied to your computer's hard drive. By default, these files are installed in the C:\Business Toolkit\Forms folder which is created by the installation program. (Note for MAC users: see instructions above). Opening the Forms folder will provide you with access to folders for each of the topics corresponding to chapters in the book. Within each chapter, the forms are provided in two separate formats:

Text forms may be opened, prepared, and printed from within your own word processing program (such as Microsoft Word®, or WordPerfect®). The text forms all have the file extension: .txt. These forms are located in the TEXT FORMS folders supplied for each chapter's forms. You will use the forms in this format if you will be making changes to any of the text on the forms.

PDF forms may be filled in on your computer screen and printed out on any printer. This particular format provides the most widely-used format for accessing computer files. Files in this format may be opened as images on your computer and printed out on any printer. The files in PDF format all have the file extension: .pdf. Although this format provides the easiest method for completing the forms, the forms in this format can not be altered (other than to fill in the information required on the blanks provided). To access the PDF forms, please see below. If you wish to alter the language in any of the forms, you will need to access the forms in their text-only versions. To access these text-only forms, please also see page 18.

To Access PDF Forms

☼ Toolkit Tip!

Use the 'PDF' forms that are provided on the CD if you wish to simply fill in and print out the form that you select.

1. You must have already installed the Adobe Acrobat Reader® program to your computer's hard drive. This program is installed automatically by the installation program. (MAC users will need to install this program via www.adobe.com).

2. On your computer's desktop, you will find a shortcut icon labeled "Acrobat Reader®" Using your mouse, left double-click on this icon. This will open the Acrobat Reader® program. When the Acrobat Reader® program is opened for the first time, you will need to accept the Licensing Agreement from Adobe in order to use this program. Click "Accept" when given the option to accept or decline the Agreement.

3. Once the Acrobat Reader® program is open on your computer, click on FILE (in the upper left-hand corner of the upper taskbar). Then click on OPEN in the drop down menu. Depending on which version of Windows or other operating system you are using, a box will open which will allow you to access files on your computer's hard drive. The files for estate planning forms are located on your computer's "C" drive, under the folder "Business Toolkit." In this folder, you will find a subfolder "Forms." (Note: if you installed the forms folder on a different drive, access the forms on that particular drive).

4. If you desire to work with one of the forms, you should then left double-click your mouse on the sub-folder: "Forms." A list of form topics (corresponding to the chapters in the book) will appear and you should then left double-click

your mouse on the topic of your choice. This will open two folders: one for text forms and one for PDF forms. Left double click your mouse on the PDF forms folder and a list of the PDF forms for that topic should appear. Left double-click your mouse on the form of your choice. This will open the appropriate form within the Acrobat Reader® program.

To Fill in and Use PDF Forms

1. Once you have opened the appropriate form in the Acrobat Reader® program, filling in the form is a simple process. A 'hand tool' icon will be your cursor in the Acrobat Reader® program. Move the 'hand tool' cursor to the first blank space that will need to be completed on the form. A vertical line or "I-beam" should appear at the beginning of the first space on a form that you will need to fill in. You may then begin to type the necessary information in the space provided. When you have filled in the first blank space, hit the TAB key on your keyboard. This will move the 'hand' cursor to the next space which must be filled in. Please note that some of the spaces in the forms must be completed by hand, specifically the signature blanks.

> ☼ Toolkit Tip!
> Filled-in PDF forms can be printed out but not saved in the Adobe Acrobat Reader ® software program.

2. Move through the form, completing each required space, and hitting TAB to move to the next space to be filled in. For details on the information required for each blank on the forms, please read the instructions in this book. When you have completed all of the fill-ins, you may print out the form on your computer's printer. (Please note: hitting TAB after the last fill-in will return you to the first page of the form.)

3. IMPORTANT NOTE: Unfortunately, the Adobe Acrobat Reader® program does NOT allow you to save the filled-in form to your computer's hard drive. You can only save the form in a printed version. For this reason, you should complete a form only when you have all of the information necessary to complete a form in one session. You may, of course, leave the Acrobat program open on your computer and leave a partially-completed form open in the program. However, if you close the file or if you close the Acrobat Reader® program, the filled-in information will be lost.

To Access and Complete Text Forms

☀ Toolkit Tip!

Text forms are the forms you should use if you will be making changes to any of the text on the forms.

For your convenience, all of the forms in this book (except certain state-specific forms and IRS forms) are also provided as text-only forms which may be altered and saved. To open and use any of the text forms:

1. First, open your preferred word processing program. Then click on FILE (in the upper left-hand corner of the upper taskbar). Then click on OPEN in the drop down menu. Depending on which version of Windows or other operating system you are using, a box will open which will allow you to access files on your computer's hard drive. The files for estate planning forms are located on your computer's "C" drive, under the folder "Business Toolkit." In this folder, you will find a sub-folder: "Forms."

2. If you desire to work with one of the forms, you should then left double-click your mouse on the sub-folder: "Forms." A list of form topics (corresponding to the chapters in the book) will appear and you should then left double-click your mouse on the topic of your choice. This will open two folders: one for text forms and one for PDF forms. Left double-click your mouse on the text forms folder and a list of the text forms for that topic should appear. Left double-click your mouse on the form of your choice. This will open the appropriate form within your word processing program.

3. You may now fill in the necessary information while the text-only file is open in your word processing program. You may need to adjust margins and/or line endings of the form to fit your particular word processing program. Note that there is an asterisk (*) in every location in these forms where information will need to be included. Replace each asterisk with the necessary information. When the form is complete, you may print out the completed form and you may save the completed form. If you wish to save the completed form, you should rename the form so that your hard drive will retain an unaltered version of the original form.

Technical Support

Please also note that Nova Publishing Company cannot provide legal advice regarding the effect or use of the forms in this book or on the CD. For questions about installing the Forms-on-CD and software, you may call Nova Technical Support at 1-800-748-1175 or access the Nova Publishing Website for support at www.novapublishing.com.

For any questions relating to Adobe Acrobat Reader®, please access Adobe Technical Support at www.adobe.com/support/main.html or you may search for assistance in the HELP area of Adobe Acrobat Reader® (located in approximately the center of the top line of the program's desktop).

Note regarding legal updates: Although business law is relatively stable and the information provided in this book is based on the most current state statutes, laws regarding business start-up are subject to constant change. In the Appendix of this book on the enclosed CD are provided internet addresses for each state's legislature and statutes. These sites may be accessed to check if any of the laws have changed since the publication of this book. In addition, the Nova Publishing website also provides legal updates for information that has changed since the publication of any Nova titles.

> **Toolkit Tip!**
>
> Check online at *www.nova publishing. com* for any updates to the legal information in this book.

Chapter 1

Deciding to Start Your Own Business

One of the first decisions that potential business owners must confront is how their business should be structured and operated. This crucial decision must be made even before the business has actually begun operations. The legal documents that will generally accompany the formation of a business can follow many different patterns, depending on the particular situation and the type of business to be undertaken.

Initially, the type of business entity to be used must be selected. There are many basic forms of business operating entities. The five most common forms are:

- Sole proprietorship
- Partnership
- Corporation
- S-corporation
- Limited liability company

The choice of entity for a particular business depends on many factors. Which of these forms of business organization is chosen can have a great impact on the success of the business. The structure chosen will have an effect on how easy it is to obtain financing, how taxes are paid, how accounting records are kept,

☼Toolkit Tip!

The type of business organization that you choose can have a great impact on the success of your business. Take time to read all of the advantages and disadvantages of each entity.

whether personal assets are at risk in the venture, the amount of control the "owner" has over the business, and many other aspects of the business. Keep in mind that the initial choice of business organization need not be the final choice. It is often wise to begin with the simplest form, the sole proprietorship, until the business progresses to a point where another form is clearly indicated. This allows the business to begin in the least complicated manner and allows the owner to retain total control in the important formative period of the business. As the business grows and the potential for liability and tax burdens increase, circumstances may dictate a re-examination of the business structure. The advantages and disadvantages of the five choices of business operation are detailed below.

Sole Proprietorship

A sole proprietorship is both the simplest and the most prevalent form of business organization. An important reason for this is that it is the least regulated of all types of business structures. Technically, the sole proprietorship is the traditional unincorporated one-person business. For legal and tax purposes, the business is the owner. It has no existence outside the owner. The liabilities of the business are personal to the owner and the business ends when the owner dies. On the other hand, all of the profits are also personal to the owner and the sole owner has full control of the business.

Disadvantages

Perhaps the most important factor to consider before choosing this type of business structure is that all of the personal and business assets of the sole owner are at risk in the sole proprietorship. If the demands of the creditors of the business exceed those assets which were formally placed in the name of the business, the creditors may reach the personal assets of the owner of the sole proprietorship. Legal judgments for damages arising from the operation of the business may also be enforced against the owner's personal assets. This unlimited liability is probably the greatest drawback to this type of business form.

21

⌁Toolkit Tip!

As the business grows and the potential for liability and tax burdens increase, circumstances may dictate a re-examination of the business structure.

Of course, insurance coverage of various types can lessen the dangers inherent in having one's personal assets at risk in a business. However, as liability insurance premiums continue to skyrocket, it is unlikely that a fledgling small business can afford to insure against all manner of contingencies and at the maximum coverage levels necessary to guard against all risk to personal assets.

A second major disadvantage to the sole proprietorship as a form of business structure is the potential difficulty in obtaining business loans. Often in starting a small business, there is insufficient collateral to obtain a loan and the sole owner must mortgage his or her own house or other personal assets to obtain the loan. This, of course, puts the sole proprietor's personal assets in a direct position of risk should the business fail. Banks and other lending institutions are often reluctant to loan money for initial small business start-ups due to the high risk of failure for small businesses. Without a proven track record, it is quite difficult for a small business owner to adequately present a loan proposal based on a sufficiently stable cash flow to satisfy most banks.

A further disadvantage to a sole proprietorship is the lack of continuity that is inherent in the business form. If the owner dies, the business ceases to exist. Of course, the assets and liabilities of the business will pass to the heirs of the owner, but the expertise and knowledge of how the business was successfully carried on will often die with the owner. Small sole proprietorships are seldom carried on profitably after the death of the owner.

Advantages

The most appealing advantage of the sole proprietorship as a business structure is the total control the owner has over the business. Subject only to economic considerations and certain legal restrictions, there is total freedom to operate the business however one chooses. Many people feel that this factor alone is enough to overcome the inherent disadvantages in this form of business.

Related to this is the simplicity of organization of the sole proprietorship. Other than maintenance of sufficient records for tax purposes, there are no legal requirements on how the business is operated. Of course, the prudent businessperson will keep adequate records and sufficiently organize the business for its most efficient operation. But there are no outside forces dictating how such internal decisions are made in the sole proprietorship. The sole owner makes all decisions in this type of business.

> **⚡ Warning!**
> If the owner of a sole proprietorship dies, the business ceases to exist.

As was mentioned earlier, the sole proprietorship is the least regulated of all businesses. Normally, the only license necessary is a local business license, usually obtained by simply paying a fee to a local registration authority. In addition, it may be necessary to file an affidavit with local authorities and publish a notice in a local newspaper if the business is operated under an assumed or fictitious name. This is necessary to allow creditors to have access to the actual identity of the true owner of the business, since it is the owner who will be personally liable for the debts and obligations of the business.

Finally, it may be necessary to register with local, state, and federal tax bodies for I.D. numbers and for the purpose of collection of sales and other taxes. Other than these few simple registrations, from a legal standpoint little else is required to start up a business as a sole proprietorship.

A final and important advantage to the sole proprietorship is the various tax benefits available to an individual. The losses or profits of the sole proprietorship are considered personal to the owner. The losses are directly deductible against any other income the owner may have and the profits are taxed only once at the marginal rate of the owner. In many instances, this may have distinct advantages over the method by which partnerships are taxed or the double taxation of corporations, particularly in the early stages of the business.

Partnership

A partnership is a relationship existing between two or more persons who join together to carry on a trade or business. Each partner contributes money, property, labor, and/or skill to the partnership and, in return, expects to share in the profits or losses

⊘ Definition:

Partnership:
A partnership is a relationship existing between two or more persons who join together to carry on a trade or business.

of the business. A partnership is usually based on a partnership agreement of some type, although the agreement need not be a formal document. It may even simply be an oral understanding between the partners, although this is not recommended.

A simple joint undertaking to share expenses is not considered a partnership, nor is a mere co-ownership of property that is maintained and leased or rented. To be considered a partnership for legal and tax purposes, the following factors are usually considered:

- The partners' conduct in carrying out provisions of the partnership agreement
- The relationship of the parties
- The abilities and contributions of each party to the partnership
- The control each partner has over the partnership income and the purposes for which the income is used

Disadvantages

⚡ Warning!

Each partner is liable for all of the debts of the partnership, regardless of which partner may have been responsible for their accumulation.

The disadvantages of the partnership form of business begin with the potential for conflict between partners. Of all forms of business organization, the partnership has spawned more disagreements than any other. This is generally traceable to the lack of a decisive initial partnership agreement that clearly outlines the rights and duties of the partners. This disadvantage can be partially overcome with a comprehensive partnership agreement. However, there is still the seemingly inherent difficulty many people have in working within the framework of a partnership, regardless of the initial agreement between the partners.

A further disadvantage to the partnership structure is that each partner is subject to unlimited personal liability for the debts of the partnership. The potential liability in a partnership is even greater than that encountered in a sole proprietorship. This is due to the fact that in a partnership the personal risk for which one may be liable is partially out of one's direct control and may be accrued due to actions on the part of another person. Each partner is liable for all of the debts of the partnership, regardless of which partner may have been responsible for their accumulation.

Related to the business risks of personal financial liability is the potential personal legal liability for the negligence of another partner. In addition, each partner may even be liable for the negligence of an employee of the partnership if such negligence takes place during the usual course of business of the partnership. Again, the attendant risks are broadened by the potential for liability based on the acts of other persons. Of course, general liability insurance can counteract this drawback to some extent to protect the personal and partnership assets of each partner.

Again, as with the sole proprietorship, the partnership lacks the advantage of continuity. A partnership is usually automatically terminated upon the death of any partner. A final accounting and a division of assets and liabilities is generally necessary in such an instance unless specific methods under which the partnership may be continued have been outlined in the partnership agreement.

Finally, certain benefits of corporate organization are not available to a partnership. Since a partnership cannot obtain financing through public stock offerings, large infusions of capital are more difficult for a partnership to raise than for a corporation. In addition, many of the fringe benefit programs that are available to corporations (such as certain pension and profit-sharing arrangements) are not available to partnerships.

Advantages

A partnership, by virtue of combining the credit potential of the various partners, has an inherently greater opportunity for business credit than is generally available to a sole proprietorship. In addition, the assets which are placed in the name of the partnership may often be used directly as collateral for business loans. The pooling of the personal capital of the partners generally provides the partnership with an advantage over the sole proprietorship in the area of cash availability. However, as noted above, the partnership does not have as great a potential for financing as does a corporation.

As with the sole proprietorship, there may be certain tax advantages to operation of a business as a partnership, as opposed

> **♡ Toolkit Tip!**
> The pooling of the personal capital of the partners generally provides the partnership with an advantage over the sole proprietorship in the area of cash availability.

to a corporation. The profits generated by a partnership may be distributed directly to the partners without incurring any "double" tax liability, as is the case with the distribution of corporate profits in the form of dividends to the shareholders. Income from a partnership is taxed at personal income tax rates. Note, however, that depending on the individual tax situation of each partner, this aspect could prove to be a disadvantage.

> **:ϙ: Toolkit Tip!**
>
> A partnership is usually based on a partnership agreement of some type, although the agreement need not be a formal document. It may even simply be an oral understanding between the partners, although this is not recommended.

For a business in which two or more people desire to share in the work and in the profits, a partnership is often the structure chosen. It is, potentially, a much simpler form of business organization than the corporate form. Less start-up costs are necessary and there is limited regulation of partnerships. However, the simplicity of this form of business can be deceiving. A sole proprietor knows that his or her actions will determine how the business will prosper, and that he or she is, ultimately, personally responsible for the success or failure of the enterprise. In a partnership, however, the duties, obligations, and commitments of each partner are often ill-defined. This lack of definition of the status of each partner can lead to serious difficulties and disagreements. In order to clarify the rights and responsibilities of each partner and to be certain of the tax status of the partnership, it is good business procedure to have a written partnership agreement. All states have adopted a version of the Uniform Partnership Act, which provides an outline of partnership law. Although state law will supply the general boundaries of partnerships and even specific partnership agreement terms if they are not addressed by a written partnership agreement, it is better for a clear understanding of the business structure if the partner's agreements are put in writing.

Corporation

A corporation is a creation of law. It is governed by the laws of the state where it was incorporated and of the state or states in which it does business. In recent years, it has become the business structure of choice for many small businesses. Corporations are, generally, a more complex form of business operation than either a sole proprietorship or partnership. Corporations are also subject to far more state regulations regarding both their formation and operation. The following discussion is provided in order to allow the potential business owner an understanding of this type of business operation.

> **Toolkit Tip!**
> There are two basic types of corporations: C-corporations and S-corporations. These prefixes refer to the particular chapter in the U.S. Tax Codes that specify the tax consequences of either type of corporate organization.

The corporation is an artificial entity. It is created by filing Articles of Incorporation with the proper state authorities. This gives the corporation its legal existence and the right to carry on business. The Articles of Incorporation act as a public record of certain formalities of corporate existence. Preparation of Articles of Incorporation is explained in detail in Chapter 9. Adoption of corporate bylaws, or internal rules of operation, is often the first business of the corporation, after it has been given the authority to conduct business by the state. The bylaws of the corporation outline the actual mechanics of the operation and management of the corporation. The preparation of corporate bylaws is also explained in Chapter 9.

There are two basic types of corporations: C-corporations and S-corporations. These prefixes refer to the particular chapter in the U.S. Tax Codes that specify the tax consequences of either type of corporate organization. In general, both of these two types of corporations are organized and operated in similar fashion. There are specific rules that apply to the ability to be recognized by the U.S. Internal Revenue Service as an S-corporation. In addition, there are significant differences in the tax treatment of these two types of corporations. These differences will be clarified later in this chapter under the heading "S-Corporations." The basic structure and organizational rules below apply to both types of corporations, unless noted.

C-Corporation

In its simplest form, the corporate organizational structure consists of the following levels:

- Shareholders: who own shares of the business but do not contribute to the direct management of the corporation, other than by electing the directors of the corporation and voting on major corporate issues
- Directors: who may be shareholders, but as directors do

not own any of the business. They are responsible, jointly as members of the board of directors of the corporation, for making the major business decisions of the corporation, including appointing the officers of the corporation

- Officers: who may be shareholders and/or directors, but, as officers, do not own any of the business. Officers (generally the president, vice president, secretary, and treasurer) are responsible for day-to-day operation of the corporate business

Disadvantages

Warning!

Corporations are subject to a greater level of governmental regulation than any other type of business entity.

Due to the nature of the organizational structure in a corporation, a certain degree of individual control is necessarily lost by incorporation. The officers, as appointees of the board of directors, are answerable to the board for management decisions. The board of directors, on the other hand, is not entirely free from restraint, since it is responsible to the shareholders for the prudent business management of the corporation.

The technical formalities of corporation formation and operation must be strictly observed in order for a business to reap the benefits of corporate existence. For this reason, there is an additional burden and expense to the corporation of detailed recordkeeping that is seldom present in other forms of business organization. Corporate decisions are, in general, more complicated due to the various levels of control and all such decisions must be carefully documented. Corporate meetings, both at the shareholder and director levels, are more formal and more frequent. In addition, the actual formation of the corporation is more expensive than the formation of either a sole proprietorship or partnership. The initial state fees that must be paid for registration of a corporation with a state can run as high as $900.00 for a minimally capitalized corporation. Corporations are also subject to a greater level of governmental regulation than any other type of business entity. These complications have the potential to overburden a small business struggling to survive. The forms and instructions in this book are all designed to lessen the burden and expense of operating a business corporation.

Finally, the profits of a corporation, when distributed to the shareholders in the form of dividends, are subject to being taxed twice. The first tax comes at the corporate level. The distribution of any corporate profits to the investors in the form of dividends is not a deductible business expense for the corporation. Thus, any dividends that are distributed to shareholders have already been subject to corporate income tax. The second level of tax is imposed at the personal level. The receipt of corporate dividends is considered income to the individual shareholder and is taxed as such. This potential for higher taxes due to a corporate business structure can be moderated by many factors, however. Information dealing with taxation of corporations are contained in Chapter 15.

> **💡Toolkit Tip!**
>
> Information for dealing with taxation of all business entities are provided in Chapter 15.

Advantages

One of the most important advantages to the corporate form of business structure is the potential limited liability of the founders of and investors in the corporation. The liability for corporate debts is limited, in general, to the amount of money each owner has contributed to the corporation. Unless the corporation is essentially a shell for a one-person business or unless the corporation is grossly under-capitalized or under-insured, the personal assets of the owners are not at risk if the corporation fails. The shareholders stand to lose only what they invested. This factor is very important in attracting investors as the business grows.

> **💡Toolkit Tip!**
>
> The often complex details of corporation formation and operation must be strictly observed in order for its owners to retain their limited liability for corporate debts and obligations.

A corporation can have a perpetual existence. Theoretically, a corporation can last forever. This may be a great advantage if there are potential future changes in ownership of the business that are imminent. Changes that would cause a partnership to be dissolved or terminated will often not affect the corporation. This continuity can be an important factor in establishing a stable business image and a permanent relationship with others in the industry.

Unlike a partnership, in which no one may become a partner without the consent of the other partners, a shareholder of corporate stock may freely sell, trade, or give away his or her stock unless this right is formally restricted by reasonable corporate decisions. The new owner of such stock is then a new owner of the business in the proportionate share of stock obtained. This freedom offers potential investors a liquidity to shift assets that is not present in the partnership form of business. The sale of shares by the corporation is also an attractive method by which to raise needed capital. The sale of shares of a corporation, however, is subject to many governmental regulations on both the state and federal levels.

Taxation is listed both as an advantage and as a disadvantage for the corporation. Depending on many factors, the use of a corporation can increase or decrease the actual income tax paid in operating a corporate business. In addition, corporations may set aside surplus earnings (up to certain levels) without any negative tax consequences. Finally, corporations are able to offer a much greater variety of fringe benefit programs to employees and officers than any other type of business entity. Various retirement, stock option, and profit-sharing plans are only open to corporate participation.

S-Corporation

☼Toolkit Tip!

Unlike a standard corporation, shareholders of S-corporations can personally deduct any corporate losses.

The S-corporation is a certain type of corporation that is available for specific tax purposes. It is a creation of the Internal Revenue Service. S-corporation status is not relevant to state corporation laws. Its purpose is to allow small corporations to choose to be taxed, at the Federal level, like a partnership, but to also enjoy many of the benefits of a corporation. It is, in many respects, similar to a limited liability company. The main difference lies in the rules that a company needs to meet in order to qualify as an S-corporation under Federal law.

In general, to qualify as an S-corporation under current IRS rules, a corporation must meet certain requirements:

*   It must not have more than 100 shareholders

*   All of the shareholders must, generally, be individuals and U.S. citizens

*   It must only have one class of stock

- Shareholders must consent to S-corporation status

- An election of S-corporation status must be filed with the IRS prior to the 16th day of the 3rd month of the tax year, that the election is to take effect, or any time during the year before the tax year that the election is to take effect

- It must be a domestic U.S. corporation

The S-corporation retains all of the advantages and disadvantages of the traditional corporation except in the area of taxation. For tax purposes, S-corporation shareholders are treated similarly to partners in a partnership. The income, losses, and deductions generated by an S-corporation are "passed through" the corporate entity to the individual shareholders. Thus, there is no "double" taxation of an S-corporation. In addition, unlike a standard corporation, shareholders of S-corporations can personally deduct any corporate losses.

Limited Liability Company

The limited liability company is a hybrid type of business structure. It contains elements of both a traditional partnership and a corporation. The limited liability company form of business structure is relatively new. Only in the last few years has it become available as a form of business in all 50 states and Washington D.C. Its uniqueness is that it offers the limited personal liability of a corporation and the tax benefits of a partnership. A limited liability company consists of one or more members/owners who actively manage the business of the limited liability company. There may also be nonmember managers employed to handle the business.

> **☼ Toolkit Tip!**
>
> A limited liability company offers the limited personal liability of a corporation and the tax benefits of a partnership.

Disadvantages

In as much as the business form is still similar to a partnership in operation, there is still a potential for conflict among the members/owners of a limited liability company. Limited liability companies are formed according to individual state law, generally by filing formal Articles of Organization of a Limited Liability Company with the proper state authorities in the state of formation. Limited liability companies are, generally, a more complex form of business operation than either the sole proprietorship or the standard partnership. They are subject to more paperwork requirements than a simple partnership but somewhat less than a corporation. Limited liability companies are also subject to far more state regulations regarding both their formation and their operation than either a sole proprietorship or a partnership. In all states, they are also required to pay fees for beginning the company, and in some states, annual franchise fees of often hundreds of dollars are assessed for the right to operate as a limited liability company.

Similar to traditional partnerships, the limited liability company has an inherent lack of continuity. In recent years, however, an increasing number of states have allowed limited liability companies to exist for a perpetual duration, as can corporations. Even if the duration of a limited liability company is perpetual, however, there may be difficulties if the sole member of a one-member limited liability company becomes disabled or dies. These problems can be overcome to some extent by providing, in the Articles of Organization of the limited liability company, for an immediate reorganization of the limited liability company with the deceased member's heirs or estate becoming members of the company. In addition, similar to partnerships, it may be difficult to sell or transfer ownership interests in a limited liability company.

Advantages

The members/owners in such a business enjoy a limited liability, similar to that of a shareholder in a corporation. In general, the member's risk is limited to the amount of their investment in the limited liability company. Since none of the members will have personal liability and may not necessarily be required to personally perform any tasks of management, it is easier to attract investors to the limited liability company form of business than to a traditional partnership. The members will share in the potential profits and in the tax deductions of the limited liability company, but will share in fewer of the financial risks involved. Since the limited liability company is generally taxed as a partnership, the profits and losses of the company pass directly to each member and are taxed only at the individual level.

A further advantage of this type of business structure is that it offers a relatively flexible management structure. The company can be managed either by members (owners) themselves or by managers who may or may not be members. Thus, depending on needs or desires, the limited liability company can be a hands-on, owner-managed company or a relatively hands-off operation for its members/owners with hired managers actually operating the company.

A final advantage is that limited liability companies are allowed more flexibility than corporations in how profits and losses are actually allocated to the members/owners. Thus, one member/owner may be allocated 50 percent of the profits (or losses) even though that member/owner only contributed 10 percent of the capital to start the company.

Warning!

The final decision of which business entity to choose depends upon many factors and should be carefully studied.

Chapter 2

Business Start-Up Checklists

Following are the first of many checklists that are provided in this book in order to help you organize your preparation for starting a business. These initial checklists provides an overview of the entire process of starting a business and, in many ways, is your blueprint for your personal business start-up. It incorporates references to many other forms, worksheets, and checklists from throughout this book. You will use the checklist that applies to the type of business entity that you decide to use in starting your business. Keep the list for your type of business handy as you proceed through the process of starting your own business whether you are starting a sole proprietorship, partnership, corporation, s-corporation or a limited liability company.

> ## ☼ Toolkit Tip!
>
> You will only use one of the following checklists for the type of business entity you will be using to start your business: a sole proprietorship, partnership, corporation, s-corporation or a limited liability company.

Sole Proprietorship Start-Up Checklist

- ☐ Read through this entire book to understand the process of starting a Sole Proprietorship
- ☐ Install the software and forms from the Forms-on-CD
- ☐ Complete the Business Plan Worksheet
- ☐ Prepare your written Business Plan
- ☐ Complete the Business Marketing Worksheet
- ☐ Prepare your written Marketing Plan
- ☐ Prepare the Business Financial Worksheet
- ☐ Prepare your written Financial Plan
- ☐ Prepare your written Executive Summary
- ☐ Compile your final Business Plan package
- ☐ Complete the Pre-Start-up Worksheet
- ☐ Review the Pre-Start-up and Document Filing Checklists
- ☐ Prepare your Sole Proprietorship Plan
- ☐ File and publish Intention to Conduct Business Under Fictitious or Assumed Name (with state or local authorities, if required. Please see Appendix on enclosed CD.)
- ☐ Prepare Employment Contracts for any employees of business
- ☐ Set up Business Accounting System
- ☐ Open Business Bank Account
- ☐ Set up business payroll (if you will have any employees)
- ☐ Set up company tax payment schedules

Partnership Start-Up Checklist

- ☐ Read through this entire book to understand the process of starting a Partnership
- ☐ Install the software and forms from the Forms-on-CD
- ☐ Complete the Business Plan Worksheet
- ☐ Prepare your written Business Plan
- ☐ Complete the Business Marketing Worksheet
- ☐ Prepare your written Marketing Plan
- ☐ Prepare the Business Financial Worksheet
- ☐ Prepare your written Financial Plan
- ☐ Prepare your written Executive Summary
- ☐ Compile your final Business Plan package
- ☐ Review the Partnership Paperwork Checklist
- ☐ Complete the Pre-partnership Worksheet
- ☐ Review the Pre-Partnership and Document filing Checklist
- ☐ Prepare a Partnership Agreement
- ☐ Register Partnership with state
- ☐ File and publish Intention to Conduct Business Under Fictitious or Assumed Name (with state or local authorities, if required. Please see Appendix on enclosed CD.)
- ☐ File and publish Statement of Partnership Authority (with state or local authorities, if required. Please see Appendix on enclosed CD.)
- ☐ Prepare Employment Contracts for any employees of business
- ☐ Set up Business Accounting System
- ☐ Open Partnership Business Bank Account
- ☐ Set up business payroll
- ☐ Set up Partnership tax payment schedules

Corporation Start-Up Checklist

- ☐ Read through this entire book to understand the process of starting a Corporation
- ☐ Install the software and forms from the Forms-on-CD
- ☐ Complete the Business Plan Worksheet
- ☐ Prepare your written Business Plan
- ☐ Complete the Business Marketing Worksheet
- ☐ Prepare your written Marketing Plan
- ☐ Prepare the Business Financial Worksheet
- ☐ Prepare your written Financial Plan
- ☐ Prepare your written Executive Summary
- ☐ Compile your final Business Plan package
- ☐ Review the Corporate Paperwork Checklist
- ☐ Complete the Pre-Incorporation Worksheet
- ☐ Review the Pre-Incorporation and Document filing Checklist
- ☐ Prepare and file your Application for Reservation of Corporate Name
- ☐ Prepare and file your Articles of Incorporation
- ☐ Prepare your Corporate Bylaws
- ☐ Hold first Directors meeting using First Board of Directors Meeting Checklist
- ☐ Hold first Shareholders meeting using First Shareholders Meeting Checklist
- ☐ Prepare any necessary Corporate Resolutions
- ☐ Prepare and issue any Corporate Stock
- ☐ Prepare Employment Contracts for any employees of business
- ☐ Set up Business Accounting System
- ☐ Open Corporate Business Bank Account
- ☐ Set up business payroll
- ☐ Set up corporate tax payment schedules

S-Corporation Start-Up Checklist

❑ Read through this entire book to understand the process of starting an S-Corporation

❑ Install the software and forms from the Forms-on-CD

❑ Complete the Business Plan Worksheet

❑ Prepare your written Business Plan

❑ Complete the Business Marketing Worksheet

❑ Prepare your written Marketing Plan

❑ Prepare the Business Financial Worksheet

❑ Prepare your written Financial Plan

❑ Prepare your written Executive Summary

❑ Compile your final Business Plan package

❑ Review the Corporate Paperwork Checklist

❑ Complete the Pre-Incorporation Worksheet

❑ Review the Pre-Incorporation and Document filing Checklist

❑ Prepare and file your Application for Reservation of Corporate Name

❑ Prepare and file your Articles of Incorporation

❑ Prepare your Corporate Bylaws

❑ Hold first Directors meeting using First Board of Directors Meeting Checklist

❑ Hold first Shareholders meeting using First Shareholders Meeting Checklist

❑ Prepare and file IRS Form 2553: Election by a small Business Corporation

❑ Prepare any necessary Corporate Resolutions

❑ Prepare and issue any Corporate Stock

❑ Prepare Employment Contracts for any employees of business

❑ Set up Business Accounting System

❑ Open corporate business bank account

❑ Set up business payroll

❑ Set up corporate tax payment schedules

Limited Liability Company Start-Up Checklist

❏ Read this entire book to understand the process of starting a Limited Liability Company

❏ Install the software and forms from the Forms-on-CD

❏ Complete the Business Plan Worksheet

❏ Prepare your written Business Plan

❏ Complete the Business Marketing Worksheet

❏ Prepare your written Marketing Plan

❏ Prepare the Business Financial Worksheet

❏ Prepare your written Financial Plan

❏ Prepare your written Executive Summary

❏ Compile your final Business Plan package

❏ Review the Limited Liability Company Paperwork Checklist

❏ Complete the Pre-organization Worksheet

❏ Review the Pre-organization and Document filing Checklist

❏ Prepare and file your Application of Reservation of Limited Liability Company Name

❏ Prepare and file Articles of Organization

❏ Prepare your Operating Agreement

❏ Hold first members meeting using First Members Meeting Checklist

❏ Prepare Employment Contracts for any employees of business

❏ Set up Business Accounting System

❏ Open company business bank account

❏ Set up business payroll

❏ Set up company tax payment schedules

Chapter 3

Developing a Business Plan

One of the most important and often overlooked aspects of starting a business is the process of preparing a Business Plan. It is through preparation of a formal business plan than you begin the process of refining what your business will actually be and, more importantly, how you can make it successful from the start. To develop a useful plan, you will need to research your business idea and determine how it can be developed into a feasible and successful business. You will use your business plan for many purposes: for your own use to continually fine-tune your actual business start-up; for obtaining financing, even if it is only from family members; and for presenting your business ideas to potential shareholders, employees, investors, suppliers, and anyone else with whom you may be doing business. Your plan needs to be dynamic and detailed. If you prepare your plan with care and attention, it will help guide you through the process of starting a successful business. If you take shortcuts in researching, thinking about, and preparing your plan, your path to business success will become an everyday struggle.

Toolkit Tip!

Your business plan will consist of three separate parts: a business plan, a marketing plan, and a financial plan.

This book has divided the preparation of your business plan into three separate parts. In this chapter, you will develop your overall plan. However, in the two following chapters, you will also develop plans that will become an integral part of your final business plan. Chapter 4 concentrates on the plans to market your business service or product. Chapter 5 provides a worksheet and instructions for preparing and implementing a strategy for financing your business. Together, the three plans that you create will comprise your total Business Plan package. Finally, after completing all three sections, you will prepare an Executive Summary. The instructions for preparing the summary are at the end of this chapter. With the information you will have gathered and set down in your plan, starting a successful business will be simplified and streamlined.

Each of these three chapters has a similar format. A worksheet is presented into which you will enter information that you have gathered or researched. Crucial business decisions will need to be made, even at this early stage, in order for you to honestly assess your chances for success. After completing the worksheet, you will use the compiled information to complete a written (printed) plan. This process will take some time to do correctly, but time spent at this stage of your business start-up will save you many times the effort and headaches later in the evolution of your business. All three of the Business Plan Worksheets are included on the Forms-on-CD. You may enter your answers to the questions directly on the forms which you can open in your own word-processing program. This will allow you to quickly and easily compile the answers that you have written out into the final Business Plan. Following this first worksheet are more detailed instructions for preparing your final Business Plan.

> ### ☼ Toolkit Tip!
> Take your time preparing your business plan. It will be the outline of how you will organize, market, and finance your business.

Business Plan Worksheet
Preliminary Business Concept Analysis

In one sentence, describe your business concept: _____
_____

What is your business service or product? _____
_____
_____

How long do you estimate that it will take to develop this service or product to the point of being ready for the public? _____
_____

What are the estimated costs of development of this product or service? _____
_____

Why do you think that this business concept will succeed? _____
_____
_____

Who is your target market? _____
_____

Is this market readily identifiable? _____
_____

What are the buying patterns of this market? _____
_____

Is there sufficient advance interest in this type of product or service? _____
_____

What are your expected annual sales/revenue volumes?
    Year one: $ _____
    Year two: $ _____
    Year three: $ _____
    Year four: $ _____
    Year five: $ _____

Company Description

What is your company's mission? _____
_____

What is the type of business entity of your company?_____
Who will be the directors of the company? _____
_____

Who will serve as the officers of the company? (not applicable to sole proprietorships or partnerships)

    President: _____

    Vice President: _____

    Treasurer: _____

    Secretary: _____

Where will the physical location of your company be? _____
_____

Where will be the company's main place of doing business? _____

Will there be any additional locations for the company? _____
_____

What geographic areas will your company serve? _____

What are the long-term plans for the business? (Expand, go public, sell to competitor, etc.)
_____
_____

Industry Analysis

In what industry will your company operate? _____

What is the overall size of the industry? _____

What is the growth rate of the industry? _____

What are any seasonal or business cycles in the industry? _____
_____

What have been the main technological advances in the past five years? _____
_____

What are projected technological advances in the industry for the next five years? _____
_____

Do any industry standards apply to your business? _____
_____

Are there any government regulatory approvals or requirements? _____
_____

Are there any local or state licenses necessary for the service or product? ____
_____

What are the main trade or business associations in your industry? _____
_____

To which associations do you currently belong? _____
_____

Product or Service Analysis

Description of product or service: _____
_____

What is the main purpose of the product or service? _____
_____

Is it a luxury item or a necessity? _____

What are the unique features of your product or service? (Cost, design, quality, capabilities, etc.) _____
_____
_____

What is the life of the product or service? _____
How does this product/service compare with the state-of-the-art for the industry?
_____

In what stage is the development of the product? (Idea, model, prototype, full production, etc.) _____

Describe the company's facilities: _____
_____

How will the product be produced or the service provided? _____
_____

Is it labor- or material-intensive to produce or supply? _____

What components or supplies are necessary to produce or supply this product?
_____

Has the service or product been the subject of any engineering or design tests?
_____

What types of quality control will be in place in the business? _____
_____

Are there any special technical considerations? _____
_____

What are the maintenance or updating requirements for the product/service? __
_____

Can the product be copyrighted, patented, or trade- or service-marked? _____
_____

Are there other products, services, or spin-offs that will be developed and marketed in future years? _____
_____

Are there any known dangers associated with the manufacture, supply, or use of the product/service? _____

What types of liabilities are posed by the product, service, or any other business operations?

    To employees: _____

    To customers: _____

    To suppliers: _____

    To distributors: _____

    To the public: _____

Are there any litigation threats posed by this business? _____

Are there any other problems or risks inherent in this type of business? _____

_____

What types of insurance coverage will be necessary for the business? _____

_____

What are the costs of the needed insurance coverage? _____

What steps will be taken to minimize any potential liabilities, dangers, or risks? _

_____

_____

Business Operations

Describe the type of facilities that your business will need to operate: _____

_____

_____

Estimate the cost of acquiring and maintaining the facilities for two years: _____

_____

Describe your production plan or service plan: _____

_____

_____

How will orders be filled and your product or service delivered?

_____

Will you work through any wholesalers or distributors? _____

_____

Who will be the main wholesalers/distributors? _____

_____
Describe the equipment or machinery that you will need for your business: ____

_____

Who will be the main suppliers of this equipment? _____

_____

What are the estimated costs of obtaining this equipment? _____

What type of inventory will you need? _____

Who will be the main suppliers of the inventory? _____

_____

Estimate the costs of obtaining sufficient inventory for the first two years of operation: _____

Management Analysis

What will be the organizational structure of the company? (Include an organizational chart) _____

_____

Who will manage the day-to-day affairs of the company? _____

Describe the management style of the central manager: _____

_____

What are the qualifications of the main management? _____

What type of workforce will be necessary for your business? _____

_____

How many employees will be needed?
Initially: _____
First year: _____
Second year: _____
Third year: _____
Fourth year: _____
Fifth year: _____

What are the job descriptions of the employees? _____

_____

What job skills will the employees need? _____

_____

Are employment and hiring/firing procedures and guidelines in place? _____

What will be the hourly wages or salaries of the employees?
    Salaried: _____
    Full-time: _____
    Part-time: _____

Will any fringe benefits be provided to employees?
    Sick pay: _____
    Vacation pay: _____
    Bonuses: _____
    Health insurance or benefits: _____
    Profit-sharing or stock options: _____
    Other benefits: _____

Estimate the annual cost for employee compensation for the first two years of operations:

_____

Will you need to contract with lawyers, accountants, consultants, designers, or specialists?

_____

Who will be the outside contractors you will use? _____

_____

Estimate the annual cost of outside contractors for the first two years of operations:

_____

Is the business bookkeeping system set up and working? _____

Are business bank accounts set up? _____

Are there administrative policies set up for billings, payments, accounts, etc.? __

_____

Supporting Documentation

Do you have any professional photos of the product, equipment, or facilities? __
_____

What contracts have already been signed? _____

Does the company hold any patents, trademarks, or copyrights? _____
_____

Have the company's registration papers been filed with the state and received?
_____

Do you have any samples of advertising or marketing materials? _____

Do you have references and resumés from each of the principals in the business? _____
_____

Do you have personal financial statements from each of the principals in the business?
_____

Have you prepared a time line chart for the company's development for the first five years?
_____

Have you prepared a list of the necessary equipment, with a description, supplier, and cost of each item noted? _____

Have you prepared current and projected balance sheets and profit/loss statements? _____

Preparing Your Business Plan

Once you have completed the previous worksheet and the worksheets in the next two chapters (relating to marketing and financial plans), you will need to prepare your final Business Plan and complete the Executive Summary. The Executive Summary is, perhaps, the most important document in the entire Business Plan, for it is in this short document that you will distill your entire vision of your company. Do not attempt to prepare the Executive Summary until you have completed all of the other worksheets and plans, for they will provide you with the insight that you will need to craft an honest and enthusiastic Executive Summary for your company.

To prepare your Business Plan, carefully read through the answers you have prepared for the Business Plan Worksheet to obtain a complete overview of your proposed business. Your task will be to carefully put the answers to the questions on the worksheet into a narrative format. If you have taken the time to fully answer the questions, this will not be a difficult task. If you have supplied the answers to the worksheet questions on the computer file version of the worksheet, you should be able to easily cut and paste your Business Plan sections together, adding only sentence and paragraph structure and connecting information. Keep the plan to the point but try to convey both a broad outline of the industry that you will be operating in and a clear picture of how your particular company will fit into that industry and succeed. Emphasize the uniqueness of your company, product, or service, but don't intentionally avoid the potential problems that your business will face. An honest appraisal of your company's risks and potential problems at this stage of the development of your company will convey to investors and bankers that you have thoroughly and carefully investigated the potential for your company to succeed.

For each subsection of the Business Plan Worksheet, use the answers to the questions to prepare your written plan. You may rearrange the answers within each section if you feel that it will present a clearer picture to those who will be reading your Business Plan. Try, however, to keep the information for each section in its own discreet portion of the Business Plan. You will use this same technique to prepare the written Marketing and Financial Plans in the following two chapters. Once you have prepared your written Business, Marketing, and Financial Plans, you are ready to prepare your Executive Summary.

Preparing Your Executive Summary

It is in the Executive Summary that you will need to convey your vision of the company and its potential for success. It is with this document that you will convince investors, suppliers, bankers, and others to take the risks necessary to back your dreams and help you to make them a reality. The Executive Summary portion of your Business Plan should be about one to three pages long. It should be concise, straightforward, and clearly written. Don't use any terms or technical jargon that the average person cannot understand. You may go into more detail in the body of the Business Plan itself, but keep the Executive Summary short and to the point. This document will be a distillation of the key points in your entire Business Plan. It is in the Executive Summary that you will need to infuse your potential backers with your enthusiasm and commitment to success. However, you will need to remain honest and forthright in the picture that you paint of your business and its competition. Use the following outline as a guide to assist you in preparing your Executive Summary. You will, of course, be using the information that you have included in your written Business, Marketing, and Financial Plans to prepare the Executive Summary. After completing your Executive Summary, there are some brief instructions to assist you in compiling your entire Business Plan package.

Executive Summary

Business Plan for _____

Executive Summary

In the year _____ , _____ was begun as a _____
in the State of _____ .

The purpose of the company is to: _____
_____

Our mission statement is as follows: This company is dedicated to providing the
highest quality _____ to a target market of _____ .

Our long-term goals are to: _____
_____
_____

Industry Analysis

The industry in which this company will operate is: _____
_____

The annual gross sales of the _____ industry are approximately
$ _____ .

Continue with a brief explanation of how your company will fit into this industry:
_____
_____
_____

Product or Service Analysis

The product/service that this company will provide is:_____

It is unique in its field because: _____

Continue with a brief explanation of product/service: _____

_____

_____

_____

Business Operations

Prepare a brief explanation of how the business will operate to obtain and deliver the product/service to the market. Include short explanations of strategies you will use to beat the competition: _____

_____

_____

Management of the Company

The company will be managed by: _____

_____

Include a brief summary of the management structure and the qualifications of the key management personnel and how their expertise will be the key to the success of the company: _____

_____

_____

_____

Market Strategy

The target market for this product/service is: _____

Prepare a brief analysis of your market research and marketing plans and why your product/service is better than any competitors: _____

_____

_____

_____

Financial Plans

In this section, briefly review the data on your Current Balance Sheet and Estimated Profit and Loss Statements and describe both the annual revenue projections and the company's immediate and long-term needs for financing: _____

_____

_____

_____

Compiling Your Business Plan

1. Prepare a Title page filling in the necessary information:

> Business Plan of (name of company),
> Begun in the State of (name of state)
> as a (type of entity) on (date of company organization)
> Address:
> Phone:
> Fax:
> Internet:
> E-mail:
> Date:
> Prepared by (name of preparer)

2. Include a Table of Contents listing the following items that you have:

- Executive Summary
- Business Plan
    Business Concept and Objectives
    Industry Analysis
    Product/Service Analysis
    Business Operations
    Management Analysis
- Marketing Plan
    Target Market Analysis
    Competitive Analysis
    Sales and Pricing Analysis
    Marketing Strategy
        Advertising and Promotion
        Publicity and Public Relations
- Financial Plan
    Financial Analysis
    Estimated Profit/Loss Statement
    Current Balance Sheet
- Appendix
    Photos of Product/Service/Facilities
    Contracts
    Incorporation Documents
    Bank Account Statements
    Personal Financial Statements of Principals

Proposed List of Equipment/Supplies/Inventory
Proposed Time Line for Corporate Growth

3. Neatly print out the necessary Business/Marketing/Financial Plans.

4. Compile all of the parts of your Plan and print multiple copies.

5. Assemble all of the parts into a neat and professional folder or notebook.

Congratulations! Your completed Business Plan will serve as an essential guide to understanding your business and will allow potential backers, investors, bankers, and others to quickly see the reality behind your business goals.

Chapter 4

Developing a Business Marketing Plan

An integral part of the process of starting a business is preparing a Marketing Plan. Whether the business will provide a service or sell a product, it will need customers in some form. Who those customers are, how they will be identified and located, and how they will be attracted to the business are crucial to the success of any small business. Unfortunately, it is also one part of a business start-up that is given less than its due in terms of time and effort spent to fully investigate the possibilities. In this chapter, a Business Marketing Worksheet is provided to assist you in thinking about your business in terms of who the customers may be and how to reach them. In many ways, looking honestly at who your customers may be and how to attract them may be the most crucial part of starting your business, for if your understanding of this issue is ill-defined or unclear, your business will have a difficult time succeeding.

☼ Toolkit Tip!

Your Marketing Plan is the key to your success as a business. It will provide you with insight into who your customers will be and how you plan to reach them.

In order to create your written Marketing Plan, simply follow the same process that you used in creating your Business Plan in Chapter 3. Take the answers that you have supplied on the following worksheet and edit them into a narrative for each of the four sections of the worksheet: Target Market Analysis; Competitive Analysis: Sales and Pricing Analysis; and Marketing Strategy.

Business Marketing Worksheet
Target Market Analysis

What is the target market for your product or service? _____

What types of market research have you conducted to understand your market?
_____
_____

What is the geographic market area you will serve? _____

Describe a typical customer:
   Sex: _____
   Marital status: _____
   Age: _____
   Income: _____
   Geographic location: _____
   Education: _____
   Employment: _____

Estimate the number of potential people in the market in your area of service: __
_____

What is the growth potential for this market? _____

How will you satisfy the customers' needs with your product/service? _____
_____

Will your product/service make your customers' life more comfortable? _____

Will your product/service save your customers' time or money or stress? _____

Competitive Analysis

Who are your main competitors? _____
_____

Are there competitors in the same geographic area as your proposed business?
_____

Are the competitors successful and what is their market share? _____

How long have they been in business? _____

Describe your research into your competitors' business operations: _____
_____

Are there any foreseeable new competitors? _____

What are the strengths and/or weaknesses of your competitor's product/service?
_____

Why is your product/service different or better than that of your competitors? ___
_____
_____

What is the main way that you will compete with your competitors (price, quality,
technology, advertising, etc.)? _____
_____

How will your customers know that your product/service is available? _____
_____

What is the main message that you want your potential customers to receive? _
_____

Why is your product/service unique? _____
_____

How will you be able to expand your customer base over time? _____
_____

Sales and Pricing Analysis

What are your competitors' prices for similar products/services? _____

Are your prices higher or lower, and why? _____

Will you offer any discounts for quantity or other factors? _____

Will you accept checks for payment? _____

Will you accept credit cards for payment? _____

Will you have a sales force? Describe: _____

What skills or education will the sales force need? _____

Will there be sales quotas? _____

Will the sales force be paid by salary, wages, or commission? _____

Are there any geographic areas or limitations on your sales or distribution? ____
_____

Will you sell through distributors or wholesalers? Describe: _____

Will there be dealer margins or wholesale discounts? _____

Do you have any plans to monitor customer feedback? Describe: _____
_____

Do you have warranty, guarantee, and customer return policies? Describe: ____
_____

Will any customer service be provided? Describe: _____
_____

What is your expected sales volume for the first five years?
    Year one: _____
    Year two: _____
    Year three: _____
    Year four: _____
    Year five: _____

Marketing Strategy

What is your annual projected marketing budget? _____

Have your company's logo, letterhead, and business cards already been designed? _____

Do you have a company slogan or descriptive phrase? _____

Has packaging for your product/service been designed? _____

Has signage for your facility been designed? _____

Describe your advertising plans:

Signs: _____
Brochures: _____
Catalogs: _____
Yellow Pages: _____
Magazines: _____
Trade journals: _____
Radio: _____
Television: _____
Newspapers: _____
Internet: _____
Trade shows: _____
Videos: _____
Billboards: _____
Newsletters: _____

Have advertisements already been designed? _____

Have you prepared a media kit for publicity? _____

Describe your plans to receive free publicity in the media via news releases or new product/service releases:

Radio: _____
Television: _____
Newspapers: _____
Magazines: _____
Internet: _____

Have you requested inclusion in any directories, catalogs, or other marketing vehicles for your industry? _____

Describe any planned direct mail campaigns: _____

Describe any planned telemarketing campaigns: _____

Describe any internet-based marketing plans:_____

_____

E-mail account: _____

Website: _____

Blog: _____

Will there be any special or seasonal promotions of your product/service? _____

_____

How will your customers actually receive the product/service? _____

_____

Chapter 5

Developing a Business Financial Plan

The third crucial part of your initial Business Plan entails how your business will obtain enough money to actually survive until it is successful. The failure of many small businesses relates directly to underestimating the amount of money needed to start and continue the business. Most business owners can, with relative ease, estimate the amount of money needed to start a business. The problem comes with arriving at a clear estimate of how much money will be necessary to keep the business operating until it is able to realistically support itself. If you can honestly determine how much is actually necessary to allow the business time to thrive before you can take out profits or pay, the next challenge is to figure out where to get that amount of money. To assist you, a Business Financial Worksheet follows. Following the worksheet are instructions on preparing both a Estimated Profit and Loss Statement and a Current Balance Sheet. Both of these financial forms will help you put some real numbers into your plans. When you have completed the Worksheet and your two financial forms, use the same technique that you used in Chapters 3 and 4 to convert your answers to a narrative. After your written Financial Plan is completed, you will need to return to the instructions at the end of Chapter 3, complete your Executive Summary, and compile your completed parts into your entire final Business Plan package.

Business Financial Worksheet

Describe the current financial status of your company: _____

_____

Income and Expenses

Estimate the annual expenses for the first year in the following categories:

Advertising expenses: _____

Auto expenses: _____

Cleaning and maintenance expenses: _____

Charitable contributions: _____

Dues and publications: _____

Office equipment expenses: _____

Freight and shipping expenses: _____

Business insurance expenses: _____

Business interest expenses: _____

Legal and accounting expenses: _____

Business meals and lodging: _____

Miscellaneous expenses: _____

Postage expenses: _____

Office rent/mortgage expenses: _____

Repair expenses: _____

Office supplies: _____

Sales taxes: _____

Federal unemployment taxes: _____

State unemployment taxes: _____

Telephone/internet expenses: _____

Utility expenses: _____

Wages and commissions: _____

Estimate the first year's annual income from the following sources:

Sales income: _____

Service income: _____

Miscellaneous income: _____

Estimate the amount of inventory necessary for the first year: _____
_____

Estimate the amount of inventory that will be sold during the first year: _____
_____

Estimate the Cost of Goods Sold for the first year: _____

Using the above information, complete the Estimated Profit and Loss Statement as explained later.

Assets and Liabilities

What forms of credit have already been used by the business? _____

How much cash is available to the business? _____

What are the sources of the cash? _____

What types of bank accounts are in place for the business and what are the balances?
_____
_____

What types of assets are currently owned by the business?
Current assets:	_____
Inventory:	_____
Cash in bank:	_____
Cash on hand:	_____
Accounts receivable:	_____
Fixed and depreciable:	_____
Autos/trucks:	_____
Buildings:	_____
Equipment:	_____
Amount of depreciation taken on any of above:	_____
Fixed non-depreciable:	_____
Land:	_____
Miscellaneous:	_____
Stocks/bonds:	_____

What types of debts does the business currently have?
- Current liabilities: _____
  - Taxes due: _____
  - Accounts payable: _____
  - Short-term loans/notes payable: _____
  - Payroll accrued: _____
  - Miscellaneous: _____
- Long-term liabilities: _____
  - Mortgage: _____
  - Other loans/notes payable: _____

Financial Needs

Based on the estimated profits and losses of the business, how much credit will be necessary for the business?
- Initially: _____
- First year: _____
- Second year: _____
- Third year: _____
- Fourth year: _____
- Fifth year: _____

Estimate the cash flow for the business for the first five years:
- First year: _____
- Second year: _____
- Third year: _____
- Fourth year: _____
- Fifth year: _____

From what sources are the necessary funds expected to be raised?
- Cash on hand: _____
- Personal funds: _____
- Family: _____
- Friends: _____
- Conventional bank financing: _____
- Finance companies: _____
- Equipment manufacturers: _____
- Leasing companies: _____
- Venture capital: _____
- U.S. Small Business Administration: _____
- Equity financing _____

(Check with current Securities and Exchange rules on sales of shares)

Preparing a Profit and Loss Statement

A Profit and Loss Statement is the key financial statement for presenting how your business is performing over a period of time. The Profit and Loss Statement illuminates both the amounts of money that your business has spent on expenses and the amounts of money that your business has taken in over a specific period of time. Along with the Balance Sheet, which is discussed later in this chapter, the Profit and Loss Statement should become an integral part of both your short- and long-range business planning.

This section will explain how to prepare an Estimated Profit and Loss Statement for use in your Business Plan. The Estimated Profit and Loss Statement can serve a valuable business planning service by allowing you to project estimated changes in your business over various time periods and examine what the results may be. Projections of various business plans can be examined in detail and decisions can then be made on the basis of clear pictures of future scenarios. Your estimates of your business profits and losses can take into account industry changes, economic factors, and personal business decisions. Your estimates are primarily for internal business planning purposes, although it may be useful to use an Estimated Profit and Loss Statement to convey your future Business Plans to others. As a trial exercise, you should prepare an Estimated Profit and Loss Statement using your best estimates before you even begin business. You may wish to prepare such pre-business statements for monthly, quarterly, and annual time periods. You may also desire to prepare Estimated Profit and Loss Statements for the first several years of your business's existence.

The Estimated Profit and Loss Statement differs from other types of Profit and Loss Statements in that the figures that you will use are projections based on expected business income and expenses for a time period in the future. The value of this type of financial planning tool is to allow you to see how various scenarios will affect your business. You may prepare this form as either a monthly, quarterly, or annual projection. To prepare this form, use the data that you have collected for your Business Financial Worksheet.

1. The first figure that you will need will be your Estimated Gross Sales Income. If your business is a pure service business, put your estimated income on the *Estimated Service Income Total* line. If your business income comes from part sales and part service, place the appropriate figures on the correct lines.

2. If your business will sell items from inventory, you will need to calculate your Estimated Cost of Goods Sold. In order to have the necessary figures to make

this computation, you will need to prepare a projection of your inventory costs and how many items you expect to sell. Fill in the Estimated Cost of Goods Sold figure on the Estimated Profit and Loss Statement. If your business is a pure service business, skip this line. Determine your Estimated Net Sales Income Total by subtracting your Estimated Cost of Goods Sold from your Estimated Gross Sales Income.

3. Calculate your Estimated Total Income for the period by adding your Estimated Net Sales Income Total and your Estimated Service Income Total and any Estimated Miscellaneous Income (for example: interest earned on a checking account).

4. Fill in the appropriate Estimated Expense account categories on the Estimated Profit and Loss Statement. If you have a large number of categories, you may need to prepare a second sheet. Based on your future projections, fill in the totals for each of your separate expense accounts. Add in any Estimated Miscellaneous Expenses.

5. Total all of your expenses and subtract your Estimated Total Expenses figure from your Estimated Total Income figure to determine your Estimated Pre-Tax Profit for the time period.

Estimated Profit and Loss Statement

For the period of:

	ESTIMATED INCOME		
Income	Estimated Gross Sales Income		
	Less Estimated Cost of Goods Sold		
	Estimated Net Sales Income Total		
	Estimated Service Income Total		
	Estimated Miscellaneous Income Total		
	Estimated Total Income		
	ESTIMATED EXPENSES		
Expenses	Advertising expenses		
	Auto expenses		
	Cleaning and maintenance expenses		
	Charitable contributions		
	Dues and publications		
	Office equipment expenses		
	Freight and shipping expenses		
	Business insurance expenses		
	Business interest expenses		
	Legal and accounting expenses		
	Business meals and lodging		
	Miscellaneous expenses		
	Postage expenses		
	Office rent/mortgage expenses		
	Repair expenses		
	Office supplies		
	Sales taxes		
	Federal unemployment taxes		

State unemployment taxes	
Telephone/Internet expenses	
Utility expenses	
Wages and commissions	
Estimated General Expenses Total	
Estimated Miscellaneous Expenses	
Estimated Total Expenses	

Estimated Pre-Tax Profit (Income less Expenses)	

Preparing a Balance Sheet

A Profit and Loss Statement provides a view of business operations over a particular period of time. It allows a look at the income and expenses and profits or losses of the business during the time period. In contrast, a Balance Sheet is designed to be a look at the financial position of a company on a specific date. It shows what the business owns and owes on a fixed date. Its purpose is to depict the financial strength of a company as shown by its assets and liabilities. It is merely a visual representation of the basic business financial equation: assets − liabilities = equity (or *net worth*). Essentially, the Balance Sheet shows what the company would be worth if all of the assets were sold and all the liabilities were paid off. A value is placed on each asset and on each liability. These figures are then balanced by adjusting the value of the owner's equity figure in the equation. Your Balance Sheet will total your current and fixed assets and your current and long-term liabilities. Even if your business is very new, you will need to prepare a Balance Sheet of where the business currently stands financially. Use the figures that you have gathered for the previous Business Financial Worksheet to complete your Current Balance Sheet. Please follow the instructions below to prepare your Current Balance Sheet for your Business Financial Plan:

1. Your Current Assets consist of the following items:

    - Cash in Bank (from your business bank account balance)
    - Cash on Hand
    - Accounts Receivable (if you have any yet)
    - Inventory (if you have any yet)
    - Prepaid Expenses (these may be rent, insurance, prepaid supplies, or similar items that have been paid for prior to their actual use)

2. Total all of your Current Assets on your Current Balance Sheet.

3. Your Fixed Assets consist of the following items, which should be valued at your actual cost:

    - Equipment
    - Autos and Trucks
    - Buildings

4. Total your Fixed Assets (except land) on your Current Balance Sheet. Total all of the depreciation that you have previously deducted for all of your fixed assets (except land). Include in this figure any business deductions that you have taken

for Section 179 write-offs on business equipment. *Note*: If you are just starting a business, you will not have any depreciation or Section 179 deductions as yet. Enter this total depreciation figure under "Less Depreciation" and subtract this figure from the figure for Total Fixed Assets (except land).

5. Enter the value for any land that your business owns. Land may not be depreciated. Add Total Fixed Assets (except land) amount, minus the (less depreciation) figure, and the value of the land. This is your Total Fixed Assets value.

6. Add any Miscellaneous Assets not yet included. These may consist of stocks, bonds, or other business investments. Total your Current, Fixed, and Miscellaneous Assets to arrive at your Total Assets figure.

7. Your Current Liabilities consist of the following items:

   • Accounts Payable (if you have any yet)
   • Miscellaneous Payable (include here the principal due on any short-term notes payable. Also include any interest on credit purchases, notes, or loans that has accrued but not been paid. Also list the current amounts due on any long-term liabilities. Finally, list any payroll or taxes that have accrued but not yet been paid)

8. Your Fixed Liabilities consist of Loans Payable (the principal of any long-term note, loan, or mortgage due). Any current amounts due should be listed as "Current Liabilities."

9. Total your Current and Fixed Liabilities to arrive at Total Liabilities.

10. Subtract your Total Liabilities from your Total Assets to arrive at your Owner's Equity. For a corporation, this figure represents the total of contributions by the owners or stockholders plus earnings after paying any dividends. Total Liabilities and Owner's Equity will always equal Total Assets.

Current Balance Sheet

As of:

ASSETS			
Current Assets	Cash in Bank		
	Cash on Hand		
	Accounts Receivable		
	Inventory		
	Prepaid Expenses		
	Total Current Assets		
Fixed Assets	Equipment (actual cost)		
	Autos and Trucks (actual cost)		
	Buildings (actual cost)		
	Total Fixed Assets (except land)		
	(less depreciation)		
	Net Total		
	Add Land (actual cost)		
	Total Fixed Assets		
	Total Miscellaneous Assets		
	Total Assets		
LIABILITIES			
Current Liabilities	Accounts Payable		
	Miscellaneous Payable		
	Total Current Liabilities		
Fixed Liabilities	Loans Payable (long-term)		
	Total Fixed Liabilities		
	Total Liabilities		
Owner's Equity	Net Worth or Capital Surplus + Stock Value		

Chapter 6

Business Paperwork

The business arena in America operates on a daily assortment of legal forms. There are more legal forms in use in American business than are used in the operations and government of many foreign countries. While large corporations are able to obtain and pay expensive lawyers to deal with their legal problems and paperwork, most small businesses cannot afford such a course of action. Unfortunately, many businesspeople who are confronted with such forms do not understand the legal ramifications of the use of them. They simply sign the forms with the expectation that it is a fairly standard document, without any unusual legal provisions. They trust that the details of the particular document will fall within what is generally accepted within the industry or trade. In most cases, this may be true. In many situations, however, it is not. Our court system is clogged with cases in which two businesses are battling over what was really intended by the incomprehensible legal language in a certain legal document.

Much of the confusion over business paperwork comes from two areas: First, there is a general lack of understanding among many in business regarding the framework of law; and second, many business documents are written in antiquated legal jargon that is difficult for even most lawyers to understand and nearly impossible for a lay person to comprehend. The various legal documents that are used in this book are, however, written in plain English. Standard legal jargon, as used in most lawyer-prepared documents, is totally incomprehensible for most people. Despite the lofty arguments by attorneys regarding the need for such strained and difficult language, the vast majority of legalese is absolutely unnecessary. As with any form of communication, clarity, simplicity, and readability should be the goal in legal documents.

Unfortunately, in some specific instances, certain obscure legal terms are the only words that accurately and precisely describe some things in certain legal contexts. In those few cases, the unfamiliar legal term will be defined when first used. Generally, however, simple terms are used throughout this book. In most cases, masculine and feminine terms have been eliminated and the generic "it" or "them" used instead. In the few situations in which this leads to awkward sentence construction, "his or her" or "he or she" may be used instead.

All of the legal documents contained in this book have been prepared in essentially the same manner by which attorneys create legal forms. Many people believe that lawyers compose each legal document that they prepare entirely from scratch. Nothing could be further from the truth. Invariably, lawyers begin their preparation of a legal document with a standardized legal form book. Every law library has multi-volume sets of these encyclopedic texts which contain blank forms for virtually every conceivable legal situation. Armed with these pre-prepared legal forms, lawyers, in many cases, simply fill in the blanks and have their secretaries retype the form for the client. Of course, the client is generally unaware of this process. As the lawyers begin to specialize in a certain area of legal expertise, they compile their own files containing such blank forms.

This book provides a set of legal forms that has been prepared with the problems and normal legal requirements of the small business in mind. These forms are intended to be used in those situations that are clearly described by the specific language of each particular form. Of course, while most business document use will fall within the bounds of standard business practices, some legal circumstances will present non-standard situations. The forms in this book are designed to be readily adaptable to most usual business situations. They may be carefully altered to conform to the particular transaction that confronts your business. However,

> **♀ Toolkit Tip!**
>
> If you are unclear about the definition of any term or word used in this book, please check the Glossary at the end of this book.

if you are faced with a complex or tangled business situation, the advice of a competent lawyer is highly recommended.

The proper and cautious use of the forms provided in this book will allow the typical business to save considerable money on legal costs over the course of the life of the business, while enabling the business to comply with legal and governmental regulations. Perhaps more importantly, these forms will provide a method by which the businessperson can avoid costly misunderstandings about what exactly was intended in a particular situation. By using the forms provided to clearly document the proceedings of everyday business operations, disputes over what was really meant can be avoided. This protection will allow the business to avoid many potential lawsuits and operate more efficiently in compliance with the law.

The Importance of Business Recordkeeping

The amount of paperwork and recordkeeping required by business may often seem overwhelming. Sometimes, it may even seem senseless. However, there are some very important reasons why detailed records of business operations are necessary.

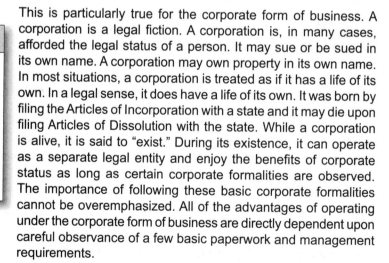

Toolkit Tip!

Careful and complete recordkeeping is particularly important for those using the corporate form of business.

This is particularly true for the corporate form of business. A corporation is a legal fiction. A corporation is, in many cases, afforded the legal status of a person. It may sue or be sued in its own name. A corporation may own property in its own name. In most situations, a corporation is treated as if it has a life of its own. In a legal sense, it does have a life of its own. It was born by filing the Articles of Incorporation with a state and it may die upon filing Articles of Dissolution with the state. While a corporation is alive, it is said to "exist." During its existence, it can operate as a separate legal entity and enjoy the benefits of corporate status as long as certain corporate formalities are observed. The importance of following these basic corporate formalities cannot be overemphasized. All of the advantages of operating under the corporate form of business are directly dependent upon careful observance of a few basic paperwork and management requirements.

Each major action that a corporation undertakes must be carefully documented. Even if there are only a few, or even a single shareholder, complete records of corporate activities must be recorded. There must be *minutes*, which are records of shareholders meetings that outline the election of directors of the corporation. Directors meetings must also be documented and the actions of directors recorded in the form of resolutions. Stock certificates must be issued and the ownership of them must be carefully tracked. This is true regardless of the size of the corporation. In fact, as the size of the corporation decreases, the importance of careful recordkeeping actually increases.

Corporate existence can be challenged in court. This will most likely happen in circumstances where a creditor of the corporation or victim of some corporate disaster is left without compensation, due to the limited liability of the corporation. Despite the fact that the corporation has been accepted by the state as a legal entity, if the formalities of corporate existence have not been carefully followed, the owners of a corporation are at risk. The court may decide that a single shareholder corporation merely used the corporation as a shell to avoid liability. The court is then empowered to *pierce the corporate veil*, or declare that the corporation was actually merely the alter ego of the owner. In either outcome, the court can disregard the existence of the corporation and the creditors or victims can reach the personal assets of the owner. This most often will occur when a corporation is formed without sufficient capitalization to reasonably cover normal business affairs; when the corporation has not maintained sufficient insurance to cover standard contingencies; when the owner has mingled corporate funds with his or her own; and when there are no records to indicate that the corporation was actually operated as a separate entity. The results of such a lawsuit can be devastating. The loss of personal assets and the loss of corporate legal status for tax purposes can often lead to impoverishment and bankruptcy.

This difficulty is not a rarity. Each year, many corporations are found to be shams that were not operated as separate business entities. In a lawsuit against a small corporation, an attack on the use of corporate formalities is often the single most powerful weapon of the opposition. The best defense against an attack on the use of a corporate business form is to always have treated the corporation as a separate entity. This requires documenting

> ### ⌵ Toolkit Tip!
> *Piercing the corporate veil* is the term used to describe a legal action that may ultimately result in corporate owners losing their lack of personal liability for the debts and liabilities of the corporation.

☀️Toolkit Tip!

Every business should set up a clear system of filing so that all required paperwork can be easily accessed when necessary.

each and every major business activity in minutes, records, and resolutions. When it is desired that the corporation undertake a particular activity, the directors should meet and adopt a resolution that clearly identifies the action and the reasons for the action. If major actions are undertaken, the shareholders may also need to meet and document their assent. This is true even if there is only one shareholder who is also the single director. With such records, it is an easy task to establish that the actions taken were done for the benefit of the corporation and not for the personal betterment of the individual owner or owners. As long as it can be clearly shown that the owners respected the corporate separateness, the corporate existence cannot be disregarded by the courts, even if there is only one shareholder who is also the sole director and only officer of the corporation. It is not the size of the corporation, but rather the existence of complete corporate records, that provides the protection from liability for the owners of the corporation. It is crucial to recognize this vital element in operating a corporation. Careful, detailed recordkeeping is the key to enjoying the tax benefits and limited liability of the corporate business structure.

All businesses, even non-corporation forms, need to be certain that their paperwork and recordkeeping practices are clear and consistent. Paperwork may be necessary to present to a bank loan officer, your own tax preparer, an IRS auditor, or an investor. Establishing an organized filing system that will allow you to find and use any paperwork when needed will go a long way towards keeping your business running as smoothly as possible. The following checklists provide a simple list of the major paperwork requirements for each type of business entity. The paperwork listed for each type of business should be kept on file for the life of the business.

Sole Proprietorship Paperwork Checklist

☐ Sole Proprietorship Checklist

☐ Statement of Intention to Conduct Business Under an Assumed Name (filed with state and county if required or desired. Check Appendix on the enclosed CD)

☐ Business insurance or health benefit plans

☐ Sole proprietorship accounting books

☐ Annual financial reports

☐ Sole proprietorship tax records (filed with state and federal tax authorities)

Partnership Paperwork Checklist

☐ Pre-partnership Checklist

☐ Partnership Agreement

☐ Statement of Partnership Authority (filed with state and county if required or desired. Check Appendix on the enclosed CD)

☐ Amendment to Partnership Agreement

☐ Amendment to or Cancellation of Statement of Partnership Authority (filed with state and county if required or desired. Check Appendix on the enclosed CD)

☐ Statement of Intention to Conduct Business Under an Assumed Name (filed with state and county if required or desired. Check Appendix on the enclosed CD)

☐ Partnership loans to partners (in the partnership record book)

☐ Partnership pension plans (in the partnership record book)

☐ Partnership insurance or health benefit plans (in the partnership record book)

☐ Partnership accounting books

☐ Annual financial reports (in the partnership record book)
☐ Termination of Partnership Agreement
☐ Partnership tax records (filed with state and federal tax authorities)

Corporation Paperwork Checklist

☐ Pre-Incorporation Checklist
☐ Reservation of Corporate Name (filed with state)
☐ Articles of Incorporation (filed with state)
☐ Amendments to Articles of Incorporation (filed with state)
☐ Certificate of Good Standing (requested from state)
☐ Bylaws of the corporation (in corporate record book)
☐ Amendments to the bylaws of the corporation (in corporate record book)
☐ Minutes of first meeting of the board of directors (in corporate record book)
☐ Minutes of the first meeting of the shareholders (in corporate record book)
☐ Minutes of the annual board of directors meetings (in corporate record book)
☐ Minutes of the annual meetings of the shareholders (in corporate record book)
☐ Minutes of any special board of directors meetings (in corporate record book)
☐ Minutes of any special shareholders meetings (in corporate record book)
☐ Shareholder proxies (in corporate record book)
☐ Shareholder voting agreements (in corporate record book)
☐ Resolutions of the board of directors (in corporate record book)
☐ Resolutions of the shareholders (in corporate record book)
☐ Corporate loans to officers or directors (in corporate record book)
☐ Corporate pension or profit-sharing plans (in corporate record book)

- ☐ Corporate insurance or health benefit plans (in corporate record book)
- ☐ Form and content of stock certificates (in corporate record book)
- ☐ Stock transfer book (in corporate record book)
- ☐ Corporate accounting books
- ☐ Annual financial reports (in corporate record book)
- ☐ Annual reports (filed with state)
- ☐ Articles of Merger (filed with state)
- ☐ Articles of Dissolution (filed with state)
- ☐ Corporate tax records (filed with state and federal tax authorities)
- ☐ Applications to qualify as foreign corporation (filed with other states in which the corporation desires to conduct active business)

S-Corporation Paperwork Checklist

- ☐ Pre-Incorporation Checklist
- ☐ Reservation of Corporate Name (filed with state)
- ☐ Articles of Incorporation (filed with state)
- ☐ Amendments to Articles of Incorporation (filed with state)
- ☐ Certificate of Good Standing (requested from state)
- ☐ Bylaws of the corporation (in corporate record book)
- ☐ Minutes of first meeting of the board of directors (in corporate record book)
- ☐ Minutes of the first meeting of the shareholders (in corporate record book)
- ☐ Minutes of the annual board of directors meetings (in corporate record book)
- ☐ Amendments to the bylaws of the corporation (in corporate record book)
- ☐ Minutes of the annual meetings of the shareholders (in corporate record book)
- ☐ Minutes of any special board of directors meetings (in corporate record book)

- ☐ Minutes of any special shareholders meetings (in corporate record book)
- ☐ Stock transfer book (in corporate record book)
- ☐ Corporate accounting books
- ☐ Annual financial reports (in corporate record book)
- ☐ Annual reports (filed with state)
- ☐ Articles of Merger (filed with state)
- ☐ Articles of Dissolution (filed with state)
- ☐ Corporate tax records (filed with state and federal tax authorities)
- ☐ Applications to qualify as foreign corporation (filed with other states in which the corporation desires to conduct active business)
- ☐ Corporate insurance or health benefit plans (in corporate record book)
- ☐ Form and content of stock certificates (in corporate record book)
- ☐ Shareholder proxies (in corporate record book)
- ☐ Shareholder voting agreements (in corporate record book)
- ☐ Resolutions of the board of directors (in corporate record book)
- ☐ Resolutions of the shareholders (in corporate record book)
- ☐ Corporate loans to officers or directors (in corporate record book)
- ☐ Corporate pension or profit-sharing plans (in corporate record book)
- ☐ IRS Form 2553: Election by a Small Business Corporation (filed with IRS)

Limited Liability Company Paperwork Checklist

- ☐ Pre-Organization Checklist
- ☐ Application for Reservation of Limited Liability Company Name (filed with state)
- ☐ Articles of Organization (filed with state)
- ☐ Amendment to Articles of Organization (filed with state)

☐ Operating Agreement of the limited liability company (in company record book)

☐ Amendments to the Operating Agreement of the limited liability company (in company record book)

☐ Minutes of the first meeting of the members (in company record book)

☐ Minutes of the annual meetings of the members (in company record book)

☐ Member proxies (in company record book)

☐ Limited liability company loans to members (in company record book)

☐ Limited liability company pension or profit-sharing plans (in company record book)

☐ Limited liability company insurance or health benefit plans (in company record book)

☐ Limited liability company accounting books

☐ Annual financial reports (in company record book)

☐ Articles of Dissolution (filed with the state)

☐ Limited liability company tax records (filed with state and Federal tax authorities)

☐ Applications to qualify as foreign limited liability company (filed with other states in which the limited liability company desires to conduct active business)

Chapter 7

Starting Business as a Sole Proprietorship

Having completed your Business Plan, including the Marketing and Financial Plans, you are ready to begin to understand, in detail, the type of business entity that you have chosen: the sole proprietorship. As noted earlier, there are numerous advantages to operating a business as a sole proprietorship, but there are also pitfalls. By understanding the actual operation of a sole proprietorship and the framework of laws within which sole proprietorships operate, it is easier to avoid the difficulties that come with the sole proprietorship form of business.

Sole proprietorships are the most common form of business operation. This is due, primarily, to the simplicity of this form of business. They are the easiest to set up. They are flexible. The taxation of sole proprietorships is relatively easy to understand. They allow the business to be under the complete control of the owner, and, unlike corporations or limited liability companies, they have very few paperwork requirements for compliance with state regulations.

Formation of a Sole Proprietorship

The formation of a sole proprietorship requires no special registration requirements in any state, beyond the registration of the use of a fictitious name for the business. There may, of course, be particular registration requirements that apply to the particular business that the sole proprietorship may be engaged in, for example, the sale of firearms or the packaging of food products. Thus, the formation of a sole proprietorship is a relatively simple matter and is accomplished by the act of beginning to engage in a business. Each year thousands of individuals begin their sole proprietorship businesses with little or no preparation or planning. Although this type of business is simple to begin, it is also prone to failure for the same reason. Starting a business as a corporation, a limited liability company, or even a partnership requires more paperwork and planning, and thus allows the business owners a greater opportunity to make careful, well thought out decisions at the planning stages of the business. The step-by-step planning process in this book for starting a sole proprietorship will take you through a similar planning process and provide opportunities to foresee and avoid some of the potential problems that you may encounter as a sole proprietor.

Sole Proprietorship Property

There are a few general rules that govern sole proprietorship property. Property acquired by a sole proprietorship is the property of the owner of the sole proprietorship. Unlike a corporation, limited liability company, or partnership, the sole proprietorship is not, itself, a legal entity for the purpose of holding property. This means that the sole proprietorship is ignored for property purposes and the general laws relating to the ownership of property will apply. Thus, if a sole proprietor is married, the particular state laws that apply to the acquisition of property by a married person will apply. In many ways, this simplifies the issue of property ownership for the sole-owner business. It allows for easy transfer or sale of any business property by the sole owner. However, it also means that in order to obtain financing, the sole proprietor must be personally liable for any mortgages or debts incurred for the purchase of business property.

> **⚡ Warning!**
>
> A sole proprietorship is not a separate legal entity and you will be liable for all debts and liabilities of the company.

Sole Proprietorship Liability

In general, the owner of a sole proprietorship is personally liable for any loss or injury caused to any person in the course of the business. The owner of a sole proprietorship is also personally liable for any debts and obligations of the sole proprietorship. This issue is the major difference between operating a business as a sole proprietorship and operating as a corporation or limited liability company. In both corporations and limited liability companies, most states now allow one person to own and operate the company as a sole owner. However, as long as they comply with the extensive paperwork requirements of operating the corporation or limited liability company, the sole owners of those types of businesses do not place their personal assets at risk in the company's business. What this means is that if the sole owner of a corporation defaults on a loan that was made in the name of the corporation, only the assets of the corporation itself may be reached by the creditor in a court proceeding and judgement. If a sole proprietor defaults on a business loan, all of the personal assets (including the sole proprietor's own home) are at risk to collection and enforcement of a claim by a creditor.

This seemingly great disparity in liability is, in fact, not so great in the real world of business. Unless a corporation or limited liability company has sufficient other assets to offer as collateral for a business loan, virtually all financial institutions will require that the owners of a corporation or limited liability company personally obligate themselves to pay back the loan, thus putting their personal assets at risk in the same way as a sole proprietor. Regarding liability for injuries sustained by customers or employees, business liability insurance can provide security from the loss of personal assets for a sole proprietor. The actual day-to-day difference for a business caused by the personal liability of a sole proprietor is, in fact, minimal.

Sole Proprietorship Books And Records

Unlike corporations, partnerships, and limited liability companies, the owners of sole proprietorships are not required by state law to keep books and records. Although there are no state regulations relating to record-keeping, every sole proprietorship is required to keep sufficient records to comply with Federal tax requirements regarding business records. Taxation of sole proprietorships will be discussed in Chapter 15.

In general, the laws that relate to the affairs and conduct of an individual apply equally to the affairs and conduct of the owner of a sole proprietorship. Because the sole proprietorship form of business is not a legal entity itself, there is no effect from this type of business structure on the operation of laws relating to liability, property, taxation, or any other laws.

Pre-Start-up Activities

The planning stage is vital to the success of any sole proprietorship. The structure of a new sole proprietorship must be carefully tailored to the specific needs of the business. By filling out a Pre-Start-up Worksheet, potential business owners will be able to have before them all of the basic data to use in preparing the necessary sole proprietorship paperwork. The process of preparing this worksheet will also help uncover any potential problems that the business may face.

> **⚙ Toolkit Tip!**
>
> The selection of your business name is often crucial to the success of a sole proprietorship. Choose a name that will continue to work as your business grows.

Please take the time to carefully and completely fill in all of the spaces. Following the worksheet, there is a Pre-Start-up checklist that provides a clear listing of all of the required actions necessary to begin a sole proprietorship business. Follow this checklist carefully as the sole proprietorship start-up process proceeds. Unfamiliar terms relating to business are explained in the glossary of this book. As the worksheet is filled in, please refer to the following explanations:

Sole proprietorship name: The selection of a name is often crucial to the success of a sole proprietorship. The name must not conflict with any existing company names, nor must it be deceptively similar to other names. Many states require or allow the registration of the use of a fictitious sole proprietorship name. Please refer to the Appendix on the enclosed CD to see if your state offers a form specifically for this registration.

Owner: This listing should provide the name, address, and phone number of the proposed owner of the sole proprietorship.

Principal place of business: This must be the address of the actual physical location of the main business. It may not be a post office box. If the sole proprietorship is home-based, this address should be the home address.

Purpose of the sole proprietorship: Here you may note the specific business purpose of the sole proprietorship. In your Sole Proprietorship Plan, you will also note that your sole proprietorship has a general purpose of engaging in any and all lawful businesses in the state in which you operate.

> **☞ Toolkit Tip!**
>
> Your sole proprietorship can have employees. You will need to obtain a federal employer identification number if you choose to do so.

State/local licenses required: Here you should note any specific requirements for licenses to operate your type of business. Most states require obtaining a tax ID number and a retail, wholesale, or sales tax license. A Federal tax ID number must be obtained by all sole proprietorships that will be employing any additional persons. Additionally, certain types of businesses will require health department approvals, state board licensing, or other forms of licenses: If necessary, check with a competent local attorney for details regarding the types of licenses required for your locality and business type.

Patents/copyrights/trademarks: If patents, copyrights, or trademarks will be part of the business of the sole proprietorship, they should be noted here.

State of sole proprietorship: In general, the sole proprietorship should be begun in the state in which it will conduct business.

Proposed date to begin sole proprietorship business: This should be the date on which you expect the sole proprietorship to begin its legal existence.

Initial investment: This figure is the total amount of money that will be invested in the business by the sole owner.

Initial indebtedness: If there is to be any initial indebtedness for the sole proprietorship, please list it here.

Proposed bank for sole proprietorship bank account: In advance of conducting sole proprietorship business, you should determine the bank that will handle the sole proprietorship accounts. Obtain from the bank the necessary bank paperwork, which will be signed by the owner.

Cost of setting up sole proprietorship: This cost should reflect the cost of obtaining professional assistance (legal or accounting); the cost of procuring the necessary supplies; and any other direct costs of the sole proprietorship process.

Fiscal year and accounting type: For accounting purposes, the fiscal year and accounting type (cash or accrual) of the sole proprietorship should be chosen in advance. Please consult with a competent accounting professional.

Insurance: Under this heading, consider the types of insurance that you will need, ranging from general casualty to various business liability policies. Also consider the need for the owner of the sole proprietorship to secure life and/or disability insurance.

> **Toolkit Tip!**
>
> Prior to conducting sole proprietorship business, you should determine the bank that will handle the sole proprietorship accounts.

The Business Start-up Toolkit

Pre-Start-up Worksheet

Name, address and phone of owner

Name_____
Address_____
_____
Phone_____

Proposed name of the company

First choice: _____
_____

Alternate choices: _____
_____
_____

Location of Business

Address of principal place of business: _____
_____

Description of principal place of business: _____
_____
_____
_____

Ownership of principal place of business (own or lease?): _____
_____

Other places of business: _____
_____
_____
_____

Type of Business

Purpose of company: _____

_____

State/local licenses required: _____

_____

Patents/copyrights/trademarks: _____

_____

State of formation: _____

Proposed date to begin company business: _____

Initial investment total: $ _____
        Date when due: _____

Initial indebtedness: $ _____

Proposed bank for company bank account: _____

_____

Cost of setting up company: _____

Fiscal year: _____

Accounting type (cash or accrual?): _____

Insurance needs: _____

_____

Sole Proprietorship Pre-Start-up Checklist

☐ Check your state's website for information regarding registration of business name (see Appendix on the enclosed CD)

☐ Complete Pre-Start-up Worksheet

☐ Prepare and file Statement of Intention to Conduct Business Under an Assumed or Fictitious Name (if required-check Appendix on the enclosed CD)

☐ Prepare Sole Proprietorship Plan

☐ Open company business bank account

☐ Prepare annual financial reports (in company record book)

☐ Maintain company tax records (filed with state and Federal authorities)

☐ Check state tax, employment, licensing, unemployment, and workers' compensation requirements

☐ Check insurance requirements

☐ Prepare company accounting ledgers

☐ Prepare company record book (looseleaf binder)

Registration of a Sole Proprietorship

The choice of a name for a business is an important aspect in the success of the business. Many business owners choose business names that contain their own names, for example: Mary and Bill's Restaurant or Smith and Jones Furniture Refinishing Company. As long as the owners' own names are the main designation of the business name, no registration of the name is generally required. If, however, the owner of a sole proprietorship chooses a name that is fictitious, many states require some type of registration of the assumed name. Examples of fictitious names might be The Landing Restaurant or Imperial Furniture Refinishing Company: names that do not identify the owners of the businesses. The main rationale for such fictitious name registration is to provide a public record of who owns businesses; owners that cannot be identified solely by the business name. This allows for a central registry of some kind, should a third party need to file a lawsuit or claim of some kind against the unidentified owner.

> **⏀ Definition:**
>
> **Fictitious Name:**
> Any business name—other than one using your own given name—is considered a fictitious name and must be registered as such with either state or local authorities.

Some states do not require registration but simply allow business owners to register their business names as a method to prevent infringement of others upon the use of a particular name, in the manner of registering the trademark or tradename of a business. The Appendix of this book on the enclosed CD provides a listing of each state's business name registration requirements. Note that some states require registration with state authorities, often the Secretary of State, while other states provide for registration in the county in which the business intends to do business.

In all states, there are either statutory rules or judge-decided case law that prevent a business from adopting a name that is deceptive to the public. Thus, for example, a business cannot imply that it is owned or operated by a licensed practitioner in a state-regulated profession if such is not, in fact, the case. Nor may a business adopt a name that is deceptively similar to the name of another business.

In many states, there is a method by which to check a registry of business names that are in use. This allows potential conflicts with other business names to be resolved prior to the adoption of a name. In addition, some states provide for the reservation of a business name even before the actual operation of the business has commenced.

Finally, some states require the publication of a statement in local newspapers that provides a notice to the public that a certain business will be operating in a community under an assumed or fictitious name. This allows the public to be notified of the names and addresses of the actual owners of the business. Please carefully check the listing for your state in the Appendix on the enclosed CD for the requirements that you will need to follow in the registration of your business name. Following is a standard form for registering a business name. Although this form should suffice in most locales, your own state or local authorities may proscribe a mandatory form for such registration. Please check with your particular registration authorities.

Sole Proprietorship Plan

Toolkit Tip!

A simple sole proprietorship plan is for your own benefit in understanding how you are setting up your small business.

Next, you will prepare your Sole Proprietorship Plan. The Sole Proprietorship Plan provides the framework for the operation of the sole proprietorship business. Although not required by any state or local law, this plan will provide you with a record of your intentions and plans for your business. It mirrors documents that are prepared by partnerships, corporations, and limited liability companies. The purpose of this plan is different from the Business Plan that you prepared in Chapters 3-5. That plan was for the purpose of presenting your business plans to others for financing or other reasons. The plan in this chapter is to provide you, the owner of the sole proprietorship, with the details of how your business will be operated. Although the preparation of this plan may seem overly formal for a simple business, it will provide you with a written plan for how to set up your business in the most beneficial manner for its success. Have your completed Pre-Start-up Worksheet before you as you prepare your plan. If you are using a computer and word-processing program, simply select those clauses from the Forms-on-CD that you wish to use in your Sole Proprietorship Plan and print out a completed plan.

Statement of Intention to Conduct Business Under an Assumed or Fictitious Name

The undersigned party does hereby state his/her intention to carry on the business of _____ , at the business location of _____ , in the City of _____ , in the State of _____ , under the assumed or fictitious name of:

_____

The owner's name, home address, and percentage of ownership of the above-named business are as follows:

Name

_____

Address

_____

Percentage of Ownership : 100 percent

Signed on _____ , 20 _____

_____
Business Owner Signature

_____
Business Owner Printed Name

Sole Proprietorship Plan Checklist

- ☐ The name and address of the sole proprietor
- ☐ The main office of the sole proprietorship
- ☐ The purpose of the sole proprietorship
- ☐ Amount of initial capital and contributions to the sole proprietorship
- ☐ Cash or accrual accounting
- ☐ Life insurance
- ☐ Disability insurance
- ☐ Accounting matters
- ☐ Calendar or other accounting periods
- ☐ Insurance
- ☐ Bank account
- ☐ Business liability insurance
- ☐ Additional provisions

Sole Proprietorship Plan

This Sole Proprietorship Plan is made on _____ , 20 ___ , by
_____ , of _____ , City of _____ ,
State of _____ .

Sole Proprietorship Name

The sole proprietorship shall be known as: _____

This name shall be property of the sole proprietorship.

Sole Proprietorship Office

The sole proprietorship's principal place of business shall be:
_____

Purpose of the Sole Proprietorship

The purpose of this sole proprietorship is to:_____
_____

In addition, the sole proprietorship may also engage in any lawful business
under the laws of the State of _____ .

Start-up Capital

The start-up capital will be a total of $ _____ . The owner of the company
agrees to dedicate the following property, services, or cash to the use of the
company:

Property/Services/Cash

_____

Accounting Matters

The company will maintain accounting records on the (cash or accrual) basis
and on a calendar year basis.

Bank Account

The business will maintain a business checking bank account at: _____
_____

Insurance

The owner shall buy and maintain life insurance on his or her life in the amount of $ _____ .

The owner shall buy and maintain disability insurance in the amount of $ _____ .

The owner shall buy and maintain business liability insurance on the operations of the business in the amount of $ _____ .

Additional Provisions

The following additional provisions are part of this Plan:

Dated _____

_____
Owner Signature

_____
Printed Name of Owner

Chapter 8

Starting Business as a Partnership

Having completed your Business Plan, including the Marketing and Financial Plans, you are ready to begin to understand, in detail, the type of business entity that you have chosen: the partnership. As noted in Chapter 1, there are numerous advantages to operating a business as a partnership, but there are also pitfalls. By understanding the actual operation of a partnership and the framework of laws in which partnerships operate, it is easier to avoid the difficulties that come with the partnership form of business.

Partnerships are one of the most common forms of business operation in which two or more people wish to work together. They are fairly simple to set up. They are flexible. The pass-through taxation of partnerships is relatively easy to understand. And partnerships allow two or more persons to work together to succeed at a common business goal. In every state, partnerships and the relationships between partners are governed by statute. A majority of states have adopted a set of partnership rules called the Uniform Partnership Act. It outlines how a partnership is formed, how partnership property is handled, the legal liability and responsibilities of partners and partnerships, and various other situations. A newer version of this law, entitled the Revised Uniform Partnership Act, has been enacted by many

Toolkit Tip!

Check in the Appendix on the enclosed CD to see which set of partnership rules your state operates under, either the Uniform Partnership Act or the Revised Uniform Partnership Act (Louisiana and Texas have their own versions.)

other states. Only the states of Louisiana and Texas have chosen to adopt their own versions of partnership law, although they are relatively similar to the laws of the other 49 states. The Appendix of this book on the enclosed CD includes information from each of these acts. All of these acts outline the relationships between partners and between the partnership and third parties. Let's look at what these acts govern.

Formation of a Partnership

> **☼ Toolkit Tip!**
>
> To be certain that your business will be recognized as a partnership, all partners should complete and sign a partnership agreement.

The association of two or more persons to carry on a business for profit as co-owners constitutes a partnership, whether or not the persons intend to form a partnership. An "association" that has been formed under specific state laws relating to associations is not a partnership. In determining whether a partnership has been formed, the following rules apply:

- Joint tenancy, tenancy-in-common, tenancy-by-the-entireties, joint property, common property, or part ownership does not, by itself, establish a partnership, even if the co-owners share profits made by the use of the property

- The sharing of gross returns does not, by itself, establish a partnership, even if the persons sharing them have a joint or common right or interest in property from which the returns are derived

- A person who receives a share of the profits of a business is presumed to be a partner in the business, unless the profits were received in payment:
  - of a debt, by installments or otherwise
  - for services as an independent contractor
  - of wages or other compensation of an employee
  - of rent
  - of an annuity or other retirement benefit of a deceased or retired partner
  - of interest or other charge on a loan, even if the payment amount varies with the business's profit
  - for the sale of the goodwill of a business
  - for the sale of other property

Partnership Property

There are a number of general rules that govern partnership property. Property acquired by a partnership is property of the partnership and not of the partners individually. In general, property is considered to be partnership property if it is acquired in the name of the partnership and with partnership funds. All property that is originally brought into the partnership or subsequently acquired by purchase or otherwise on account of the partnership is considered to be partnership property.

Property is also partnership property if it is acquired by one or more partners, and in the title or deed to the property there is an indication of the person's capacity as a partner or of the existence of a partnership, even when there is no indication of the name of the partnership. Property is acquired in the name of the partnership by acquisition of one or more partners in their capacity as partners in the partnership, if the name of the partnership is specifically indicated in the instrument transferring title to the property. Property is presumed to be partnership property if it is purchased with partnership assets, even if not acquired in the name of the partnership or one or more partners. Property acquired in the name of one or more of the partners, without an indication in the instrument transferring title to the property of the person's capacity as a partner or of the existence of a partnership and without use of partnership assets, is presumed to be separate (non-partnership) property, even if used for partnership purposes.

Under the Revised Uniform Partnership Act, all partnership property is owned by the partnership as an entity, not by the partners as co-owners. Under the Uniform Partnership Act, a partner is co-owner with his or her partners of specific partnership property, holding the property as a tenant-in-partnership. Each individual partner has no interest that can be transferred, either voluntarily or involuntarily, in specific partnership property. The only transferable interest of a partner in the partnership is the partner's share of the profits and losses of the partnership and the partner's right to receive distributions. A partner's interest in the partnership is personal property, not real estate, even if the partnership itself holds title to real estate.

☼ Toolkit Tip!

You may wish to read through the actual provisions of your state's partnership act. See the Appendix on the enclosed CD for information on how to locate these laws.

The property rights of a partner under the Uniform Partnership Act, unless altered by the partnership agreement, are that a partner has an equal right with his or her partners to possess specific partnership property for partnership purposes; but he or she has no right to possess the property for any other purpose without the consent of his or her partners. A partner's right in specific partnership property is not assignable except in connection with the assignment of rights of all the partners in the same property.

In the event of the death of a partner, the deceased partner's right in specific partnership property vests in the surviving partner or partners. This is true in all cases except where the deceased was the last surviving partner, in which case his or her right in the property vests in his or her legal representative. The surviving partner or partners or the legal representative of the last surviving partner has no right to possess partnership property except for a partnership purpose. A partner's right in specific partnership property is not subject to allowances to a surviving spouse, heirs, or next of kin.

Partner Acting As an Agent of the Partnership

⚡ Warning!

Any partner can bind the entire partnership, unless the partner specifically had no authority to do so and the person dealing with the partner knew this fact.

Each partner is an agent of the partnership for the purpose of its business. This means that any act of a partner, including the signing of any document in the partnership's name, binds the partnership. This is true unless the partner had no authority to act for the partnership in the particular matter *and* the person with whom the partner was dealing knew or had received notification that the partner lacked authority. For such an act to be binding on the partnership it also must be an act apparently in the ordinary course of partnership business, and in the general geographic area in which the partnership operates. An act of a partner that is not apparently for carrying on the ordinary course of partnership business binds the partnership only if the act was authorized by all of the other partners.

Under the Uniform Partnership Act, unless authorized by the other partners or unless they have abandoned the business, only all of the partners, together and unanimously, have the authority to do the following:

102

- Assign the partnership's property in trust for creditors or on the assignee's promise to pay the debts of the partnership

- Dispose of the goodwill of the business

- Do anything that would make it impossible to carry on the ordinary business of the partnership

- Confess a judgment (admit the liability of the partnership in a lawsuit)

- Submit a partnership claim or liability to arbitration or reference

Partnership Liability

In, general, a partnership is liable for any loss or injury caused to any person. The partnership is also liable for any penalty incurred, as the result of a wrongful act or omission of a partner acting in the ordinary course of business of the partnership or with authority of the partnership. If, in the course of the partnership's business or while acting with authority of the partnership, a partner receives or causes the partnership to receive money or property of a person who is not a partner, and the money or property is misapplied by the partner, the partnership is also liable for the loss. In addition, under the Uniform Partnership Act, an admission or representation made by any partner concerning partnership affairs within the scope of his or her authority is evidence against the partnership. Giving notice to any partner of a matter concerning partnership affairs operates as notice to or knowledge of the partnership, except in the case of fraud committed by or with the consent of that partner.

> **꙯ Toolkit Tip!**
>
> If a partnership is liable to a third party, that liability is generally shared by all partners.

Partner's Liability

All partners are liable jointly and severally for all debts and obligations of the partnership unless otherwise agreed to by the person bringing the claim against the partnership. Under the Revised

Uniform Partnership Act, a major exception to this rule is that a person admitted as a partner into an existing partnership is not personally liable for any partnership obligation incurred before the person's admission as a partner. Under the older Uniform Partnership Act, such a later partner is liable for obligations that arose before he or she became a partner, but the obligation may only be paid out of partnership property, not the personal assets of the new partner.

Partner's Rights And Duties

:💡:Toolkit Tip!

Each partner has a right to share in the profits and a responsibility to share the losses of the partnership. The proportion of profits or losses should be spelled out in the partnership agreement.

With regard to how partnerships are actually operated, each partner is deemed to have an account that is credited with an amount equal to the money plus the net value of any of the property that the partner contributes to the partnership. The partner's account is also credited with the partner's share of the partnership profits. This account is also debited or charged with an amount equal to the money plus the net value of any other property and any liabilities distributed by the partnership to the partner and the partner's share of the partnership's losses.

Each partner is entitled to an equal share of the partnership's profits and is chargeable with a share of the partnership's losses in proportion to the partner's share of the profits. A partnership must also reimburse a partner for any payments made and indemnify a partner for liabilities incurred by the partner in the ordinary course of the business of the partnership or for the preservation of its business or property. In addition, a partnership is required to reimburse a partner for an advance to the partnership beyond the amount of money or property that the partner agreed to contribute to the partnership. A payment or advance made by a partner for partnership business constitutes a loan to the partnership that accrues interest from the date of the payment or advance.

There are a number of important rules regarding management of a partnership. One of the most central is that each partner has equal rights in the management and conduct of the partnership's business. In addition, a partner may use or possess partnership property only on behalf of the partnership. A partner is not entitled to payment for services performed for the partnership, except for reasonable compensation for services rendered in winding up the business of the partnership. The partners only share in the profits of the partnership. A person may become a partner only with the consent of all of the partners. A difference arising in the ordinary course of business of a partnership may be decided by a majority of the partners. An act outside the ordinary course of business of a partnership and an amendment to the Partnership Agreement may be undertaken only with the consent of all of the partners. A partner has no right to receive, and may not be required to accept, a distribution in kind.

Partnership Books And Records

Every partnership is required to keep its books and records, if any, at the chief executive office of the partnership. The partnership is also required to provide partners and their attorneys access to the books and records of the partnership. This rule also applies to former partners for the records of the period during which they were partners. The right of access provides the opportunity to inspect and copy books and records during ordinary business hours. A partnership may impose a reasonable charge, covering the costs of labor and material, for copies of documents furnished.

> **Toolkit Tip!**
> Each partner has a right to examine the books and records of the partnership during normal business hours.

Partnership Agreement

A Partnership Agreement may change certain portions of these rules. In general, relations among partners and between partners and a partnership are governed by the Partnership Agreement, except that the Partnership Agreement may not do the following:

- Vary the rights and duties relating to filing a registration statement in those states that require such statements (generally, states that have adopted the Revised Uniform Partnership Act—please see Appendix on the CD)

- Unreasonably restrict the right of access to books and records, or eliminate the duty of loyalty

- Unreasonably reduce the duty of care

- Eliminate the obligation of good faith and fair dealing

- Vary the power to dissociate as a partner

- Vary the right of a court to expel a partner

- Vary the requirement to wind up partnership business

- Restrict rights of third parties who are not partners

Partnership Registration

Toolkit Tip!

If your state has adopted the Revised Uniform Partnership Act, you will need to file a partnership registration statement with either county or state officials.

In those states that have adopted the Revised Uniform Partnership Act (see Appendix on the enclosed CD), a partnership registration statement may be filed in the county where the partnership has its chief executive office or often with the Secretary of State or its equivalent. Such a statement filed by a partnership must be signed by at least two partners. All such statements may be amended or canceled by filing an amendment or cancellation that names the partnership, identifies the statement, and states the substance of the amendment or cancellation. A copy of any statement filed should also be sent to every non-filing partner and to any other person named as a partner in the statement. However, failure to send a copy of a statement to a partner or other person does not limit the effectiveness of the statement as to a person who is not a partner. Such a Statement of Partnership Authority must include the name of the partnership, the street address of its chief executive office, the names and mailing addresses of all of the partners (or the name and address of an agent appointed and maintained by the partnership to maintain a list of the names and mailing addresses of all of the partners), and the names of the partners authorized to execute an instrument transferring real property held in the name of the partnership.

These Statements of Partnership Authority may also state or include the authority, or limitations on the authority, of some or all of the partners to enter into other transactions on behalf of the partnership, and any other matters.

A filed Statement of Partnership Authority supplements or limits the authority of a partner to enter into transactions on behalf of the partnership with respect to others. A person who is not a partner is deemed to know of a limitation on the authority of a partner to transfer real property held in the name of the partnership if a certified copy of the filed statement containing the limitation on authority is on record in the office for recording transfers of such real property. In addition, a person who is not a partner is not deemed to know of a limitation on the authority of a partner merely because the limitation is contained in a filed statement.

A Statement of Partnership Authority form, an Amendment of Statement of Partnership Authority form, and a Cancellation of Statement of Partnership Authority form are included this chapter.

General Standards of a Partner's Conduct

For those states following the Revised Uniform Partnership Act, there are some additional standards of conduct laid out. The central rule is that the only fiduciary duties a partner owes to the partnership and the other partners are the duty of loyalty and the duty of care.

> **Toolkit Tip!**
> If your state has adopted the Revised Uniform Partnership Act, general standards of partnership conduct are provided by law.

A partner's duty of loyalty to the partnership and the other partners includes the following:

- To account to the partnership and hold as trustee for the partnership any property, profit, or benefit derived by the partner in the conduct and winding up of the partnership's business or derived from a use by the partner of partnership property, including the appropriation of a partnership opportunity

- To refrain from dealing with the partnership in the conduct or winding up of the partnership's business as or on behalf of a party having an interest adverse to the partnership

- To refrain from competing with the partnership before the dissolution of the partnership

A partner's duty of care to the partnership and the other partners in the conduct and winding up of the partnership's business is limited to refraining from engaging in grossly negligent or reckless conduct, intentional misconduct, or a knowing violation of the law. In addition, a partner is required to discharge the duties to the partnership and the other partners consistent with the obligation of good faith and fair dealing. A partner does not violate a duty or obligation merely because the partner's conduct furthers the partner's own interest. A partner may lend money to and transact other business with the partnership, and as to each loan or transaction, the rights and obligations of the partner are the same as those of a person who is not a partner.

In addition, there are numerous complex provisions under both the Uniform Partnership and the Revised Uniform Partnership Acts regarding the dissociation of a partner and the dissolution of a partnership. The details of these sections are beyond the scope of this book.

Pre-Partnership Activities

Toolkit Tip!

All partners should be involved in the completion of your pre-partnership worksheet.

The planning stage is vital to the success of any partnership. The structure of a new partnership must be carefully tailored to the specific needs of the business. Attorneys typically use a Pre-Partnership Worksheet to assemble all of the necessary information from which to plan the partnership process.

By filling out a Pre-Partnership Worksheet, potential business owners will be able to have before them all of the basic data to use in preparing the necessary partnership paperwork. The process of preparing this worksheet will also help uncover any potential differences of opinion among the persons who are desiring to form the partnership. Often, conflicts and demands are not known until the actual process of determining the partnership structure begins. Frank discussions regarding the questions of voting rights, division of profits and losses, and other management decisions often will enable potential associates to resolve many of the difficult problems of partnership operation in advance. The use of a written worksheet will also provide all persons involved with a clear and permanent record of the information. This may provide the principals of the partnership with vital support for later decisions that may be required.

All persons involved in the planned partnership should participate in the preparation of the following worksheet. Please take time to carefully and completely fill in all of the spaces. Following the worksheet, there is a Pre-Partnership Checklist, that provides a clear listing of all of the required actions necessary to begin a partnership business. Follow this checklist carefully as the partnership process proceeds.

Unfamiliar terms relating to partnerships are explained in the glossary of this book. As the Pre-Partnership Worksheet is filled in, please refer to the following explanations:

> ⚡ **Warning!**
> You should be careful that your choice of a partnership name is not deceptively similar to that of another business.

Partnership name: The selection of a name is often crucial to the success of a partnership. The name must not conflict with any existing company names, nor can it be deceptively similar to other names. It is often wise to clearly explain the business of the partnership through the choice of name. Many states require or allow the registration of the use of a fictitious partnership name. Check the Appendix on the enclosed CD for the listing for your state on partnership name registration.

Parties involved: Provide the names, addresses, and phone numbers of all of the people who are involved in the planning stages of the partnership.

Principal place of business: This must be the address of the actual physical location of the main business. It may not be a post office box. If the partnership is home-based, this address should be the home address.

Purpose of the partnership: Here you may note the specific business purpose of the partnership. In your Partnership Agreement you will also note that your partnership has a general purpose of engaging in any and all lawful business in your state.

All partner-ships must obtain a fed-eral employer tax identifica-tion number, using IRS Form SS-4.

State/local licenses required: Here you should note any specific requirements for licenses to operate your type of business. Most states require obtaining a tax ID number and a retail, wholesale, or sales tax license. A Federal tax ID number must be obtained by all partnerships. Additionally, certain types of businesses will require health department approvals, state board licensing, or other forms of licensing. If necessary, check with a competent local attorney for details regarding the types of licenses required for your locality and business type.

Patents/copyrights/trademarks: If patents, copyrights, or trademarks will need to be transferred into the partnership, they should be noted here.

State of partnership: In general, the partnership should be begun in the state in which it will conduct business.

Proposed date to begin partnership business: This should be the date on which you expect the partnership to begin its legal existence.

Duration of partnership: Decide if the partnership is to be for a certain term, to end on a certain date, or to continue until the partners' death.

Initial investment: This figure is the total amount of money or property that will be transferred, or services that will be rendered to the partnership by each partner upon the beginning of part-nership business. List also the dates on which the contributions must be made.

Additional contributions by partners: If there are to be planned additional partner contributions of money, services, or property, list them here.

Share of Profits and Losses: Under this heading, list the proportionate share of the profits and losses of the partnership for each partner. The shares can be equal, or related to the proportionate contributions of each partner.

Distribution of Profits and Losses: Here decide how the partnership will distribute its profits and cover its losses. If the partnership will retain a portion of the profits for reinvestment, note that here.

Initial indebtedness: If there is to be any initial indebtedness for the partnership, please list here.

Management of the partnership: If the business will be managed equally or in differing proportions by the partners, note that here. If one or more partners will be appointed as managing partners, also make note of that decision.

Date of first partnership meeting: This will be the date proposed for holding the first meeting of the partnership.

Proposed bank for partnership bank account: In advance of partnership, you should determine the bank that will handle the partnership account. Obtain from the bank the necessary bank paperwork, that will be signed by partners at the first partners meeting.

> ### ᐁ Toolkit Tip!
> Deciding on the proportions of partnership management and voting can be the most critical part of setting up your partnership.

Cost of setting up partnership: This cost should reflect the cost of obtaining professional assistance (legal and accounting); the cost of procuring the necessary supplies; and any other direct costs of the partnership process.

Required quorum for a partnership meeting: This is the percentage of partners who must be represented at a partnership meeting in order to officially transact any partnership business. This is normally a "majority" (over 50 percent), although this figure can be set higher.

Annual partnership meeting: The date, time, and place of the annual partnership meeting should be specified.

Required vote for partnership action: Once it is determined that a quorum of partners is present at a meeting, this is the percentage of partners that must vote in the affirmative in order to officially pass any partnership business. This is normally a "majority" (more than 50 percent), although this figure can be set higher and can be made to be unanimous for certain items or even for all partnership decisions. Note any such provisions here.

🔆 Toolkit Tip!

In general, all partners should be treated similarly under the terms of the partnership agreement.

Fiscal year and accounting type: For accounting purposes, the fiscal year and accounting type (cash or accrual) of the partnership should be chosen in advance. Please consult with a competent accounting professional.

Financial authority: Here list the authority of each proposed partner to sign checks, borrow money in the partnership's name, or sign documents in the name of the partnership.

Loans to partners: In this item, decide if you wish the partnership to have the ability to make loans directly to the partners.

Salaries of partners: Here you should decide if the partners will earn a salary for their work on behalf of the partnership.

Draws of partners: In this listing, make note of the ability of partners to obtain draws against their individual shares of the annual profits of the partnership. These draws can be monthly, quarterly, annual, or on some other basis.

Partner expense accounts: Here note if partners are allowed expense accounts for the normal expenses of the business. If so, note the maximum monthly amount of the expense account.

Transfer of partnership interests: Under this listing, a decision should be made as to whether and how partners are allowed to transfer their ownership interest in the partnership. This may range from "not at all" to "freely" or may be by unanimous or majority consent of the other partners.

Expulsion of partners: Here you should consider the terms and conditions for removing a partner.

Insurance: Under this heading, consider the types of insurance that you will need, ranging from general casualty to various business liability policies. Also consider the need for the partners or the partnership to provide the partners with life and/or disability insurance.

New partners: Will new partners be allowed into the partnership? Here note the terms and conditions for their entry.

Termination of partnership: How will the partnership end? Here list any considerations relating to the dissolution of the partnership that you may wish to be considered.

Amendments to partnership agreement: Here should be the determination of how to amend the Partnership Agreement. The forms in this book are designed to allow the Partnership Agreement to be amended either by unanimous or majority vote of the partners.

Following the Pre-Partnership Worksheet is a Pre-Partnership Checklist. Please use this checklist to be certain that you have completed all of the necessary steps for beginning a partnership. Once all of the persons involved in the partnership have completed the Pre-Partnership Worksheet, agreed on all of the details, and reviewed the Pre-Partnership Checklist, the actual process of drafting the Partnership Agreement may begin. Have the completed Pre-Partnership Worksheet before you as you prepare the agreement in the next chapter.

Toolkit Tip!

Although it is possible to amend, your completed partnership agreement should include all relevant points from the outset.

Pre-Partnership Worksheet

Proposed Name of the Partnership

First choice: _____

Alternate choices: _____
_____
_____

Parties Involved in Forming the Partnership

Name   Address/Phone
_____
_____
_____
_____
_____

Location of Business

Address of principal place of business: _____
_____

Description of principal place of business: _____
_____

Ownership of principal place of business (own or lease): _____
_____

Other places of business: _____
_____

Type of Business

Purpose of business: _____

_____

State/local licenses required: _____

Patents/copyrights/trademarks: _____

Partnership Matters

State of partnership: _____

Proposed date to begin partnership business: _____

Duration of partnership: _____

Initial investment total: $ _____
Date when due: _____

Name	Cash/Property/Service	Value

Additional contributions: $ _____
Date when due: _____

Name	Cash/Property/Service	Value

Partners' shares of profits and losses:

Name   Proportionate Share of Profits and Losses

_____

_____

_____

_____

_____

Distribution and retention of profits and losses:

Initial indebtedness: _____

Management of the partnership:

Name   Proportionate Share of Management

_____

_____

_____

_____

_____

_____

_____

Managing partner (if any): _____

Proposed date of first partnership meeting: _____

Proposed bank for partnership bank account: _____

Cost of setting up partnership: _____

Required quorum for partnership meetings: _____

Annual partnership meeting:
Place   Date   Time

_____

_____

Required vote for partnership actions (majority/%/unanimous?): _____

Fiscal year: _____

Accounting type (cash or accrual): _____

Financial authority:
Name   Authority to Do

_____
_____
_____
_____

Loans to partners: _____

Salaries of partners:
Name   Salary

_____
_____
_____
_____
_____
_____
_____

Draws of partners: _____

Partner expense accounts: _____

Transfer of partnership interests: _____

Expulsion of partners: _____

Insurance needs: _____

New partners: _____

Termination of partnership: _____

Amendments to Partnership Agreement: _____
_____
_____
_____

Pre-Partnership Checklist

☐ Complete Pre-Partnership Worksheet

☐ Check annual fees and filing requirements, if any (see Appendix on the enclosed CD)

☐ Prepare Partnership Agreement. If desired, have attorney review Agreement, prior to signing

☐ Review tax impact of partnership with an accountant

☐ Check state tax, employment, licensing, unemployment, and workers' compensation requirements

☐ Open partnership bank account

☐ Check insurance requirements

☐ Prepare partnership accounting ledgers

☐ Prepare partnership record book (loose-leaf binder)

Partnership Agreement

The central legal document for any partnership is the Partnership Agreement. The Partnership Agreement provides the framework for the management of the partnership business. Along with state law, the Partnership Agreement provides a clear outline of the rights and responsibilities of all parties to a partnership. In particular, the Partnership Agreement provides the actual details of the operational framework for the business. The Partnership Agreement is the internal document that will contain the basic rules for how the partnership is to be run. Every partnership should have a written Partnership Agreement. Many of the provisions cover relatively standard procedural questions, relating to quorums and voting. Other provisions may need to be specifically tailored to the type of business for which the Partnership Agreement is intended. The Partnership Agreement provided in this book specifies that the vote to amend the Partnership must be unanimous.

The Partnership Agreement can contain very specific or very general provisions for the internal management of the company. Typically, the Partnership Agreement covers five general areas:

- The rights and responsibilities of partners

- The distribution of profits and losses

- Methods for amending the Partnership Agreement

- Financial matters

- Methods for changing or ending the partnership

> **☼ Toolkit Tip!**
>
> The partnership agreement in this chapter is meant to be an outline for the completion of your final agreement.

This chapter contains a Partnership Agreement with a choice of clauses in some cases. Put a checkmark by those clauses that you wish to include in your agreement (only one per paragraph). Then using the text form Partnership Agreement on the CD, simply retain those clauses from you wish to use and delete the clauses that you do not want. When you have a completed agreement, print it out for signatures and save a copy for your records..

Partnership Agreement Checklist

Use this checklist in preparing your Partnership Agreement

- ☐ Designation and authority of managing partner(s)
- ☐ The name and address of each partner
- ☐ The name of the partnership
- ☐ The main office of the partnership
- ☐ The purpose of the partnership
- ☐ Term (duration) of the partnership
- ☐ Management of the partnership
- ☐ Amount of initial capital and contributions to the partnership
- ☐ Any additional planned contributions to the partnership
- ☐ Penalties on failure to make contributions
- ☐ Interest on contributions
- ☐ Loans to the partnership
- ☐ Each partner's share in the profits and losses of the partnership
- ☐ Distribution of the profits and losses of the partnership
- ☐ Date and time of the annual partnership meetings
- ☐ Place of partnership meetings
- ☐ Partners quorum
- ☐ Partners proxies
- ☐ Partners voting
- ☐ Partners consent agreements
- ☐ Powers of the partners
- ☐ Fiduciary duties of the partners
- ☐ Accounting matters
- ☐ Cash or accrual basis accounting
- ☐ Calendar year or other fiscal period

- ❏ Financial matters
- ❏ Signature for checking
- ❏ Authorization to borrow money
- ❏ Authorization to sign documents
- ❏ Bank account
- ❏ Loans to partners
- ❏ Draws to partners
- ❏ Salaries to partners
- ❏ Partner expense accounts
- ❏ Transfers of partnership interests
- ❏ Expulsion of partners
- ❏ Automatic expulsion of partners
- ❏ Limits on remedies of expelled partners
- ❏ Insurance
- ❏ Life insurance
- ❏ Disability insurance
- ❏ Mediation or arbitration
- ❏ Admission of new partners
- ❏ Responsibility of new partners
- ❏ Withdrawal from partnership
- ❏ Agreement not to compete
- ❏ Termination of the partnership
- ❏ Amendments to the Partnership Agreement
- ❏ Additional provisions
- ❏ General provisions

Partnership Agreement

This Partnership Agreement is made on _____ , 20 _____ , by and between the partners whose signatures are on this agreement.

Agreement.

The parties to this Agreement agree to carry on a partnership operating under the laws of the State of _____ under the following terms and conditions:

Partnership Name.

The partnership shall be known as: _____
This name shall be property of the partnership.

Partnership Office.

The partnership's principal place of business shall be: _____

Purpose of the Partnership.

The purpose of this partnership is to: _____

In addition, the partners agree that the partnership may also engage in any lawful business under the laws of the State of _____ as the partners may agree to, from time to time.

Term of the Partnership.

☐   The partnership will begin on _____ , 20 ____, and end on _____ , 20 _____ .

☐   The partnership will begin on _____ , 20 ____, and end when terminated by agreement of all of the partners.

☐   The partnership will begin on _____ , 20 ____, and end on the death or withdrawal of any partner.

Contributions and Start-up Capital.

The start-up capital will be a total of $ _____ . Each partner of the partnership agrees to contribute the following property, services, or cash to this total amount:

Name   Cash/Services/Property   Value

_____

_____

_____

If the partner's contribution is cash, the contribution shall be delivered to the partnership on or before _____ , 20 _____ .

If the partner's contribution is property, the contribution shall be delivered to the partnership on or before _____ , 20 _____ .

If the partner's contribution is in the form of services, the services which are to be performed are as follows: _____ .

and shall be performed according to the following schedule: _____

Additional Contributions.

☐ If additional capital is required by the partnership and is determined by a majority vote of the partners, then each partner shall be required to contribute to such additional capital in proportion to each partner's interest in the partnership as set forth in this Agreement.

☐ If additional capital is required by the partnership and is determined by a unanimous vote of the partners, then each partner shall be required to contribute to such additional capital in proportion to each partner's interest in the partnership as set forth in this Agreement.

☐ Each partner shall be required to contribute a _____ percent share of his or her profits to the partnership on an annual basis.

☐ Each partner shall contribute the following property, cash, or services to the partnership on an annual basis:

Name	Cash/services/property	Value

☐ If the partner's contribution is cash, the contribution shall be delivered to the partnership on or before _____ , 20 _____ .

☐ Additional Contributions. If the partner's contribution is property, the contribution shall be delivered to the partnership on or before _____ , 20 _____ .

☐ If the partner's contribution is in the form of services, the services which are to be performed are as follows: _____ , and shall be performed according to the following schedule: _____

☐ Each partner shall be required to work in the partnership business as follows: _____

Failure to Make Contributions.

☐ If any partner shall fail to make their initial or additional contributions as indicated by this Agreement, any Amendment to this Agreement, or any additional Agreement between the partners, whether such contributions were to be cash, services, or property, then this partnership shall be immediately terminated and each partner who has made a contribution shall be entitled to an immediate return of any property or cash contributed or for reimbursement from the partnership for any services provided.

☐ If any partner shall fail to make their initial or additional contributions as indicated by this Agreement, any Amendment to this Agreement, or any additional Agreement between the partners, then this partnership shall continue as a partnership of only those partners who have satisfied their contribution requirements. Any partner who has failed to satisfy their contribution requirements will not be a partner of this partnership. Each partner who has made a contribution shall then be entitled to a share of partnership profits and losses in proportion to the amount of their contribution to the total contributions. If any additional partnership contributions are necessary, such additional contributions shall be determined by the remaining partners as specified under the terms of this Agreement regarding Additional Contributions.

Interest on Contributions.

❏ No interest shall be paid to any partner for any capital contributions.

❏ Interest at the rate of _____ percent per annum shall be paid on each partner's capital contributions that were paid in cash. The interest shall be an expense of the partnership and paid to the partner who is entitled to it on an annual basis.

Loans to Partnership.

In addition to capital contributions, the following cash or property will be loaned to the partnership under the terms specified:

Name of Partner   Cash/Property Loaned   Terms of Loan

_____

_____

_____

Share of the Partnership.

❏ Each partner's proportional share of the profits and losses of the partnership shall be as follows:

Name   Percent of Ownership of Partnership

_____

_____

_____

_____

❏ Each partner's share of the profits and losses of the partnership shall be equal.

❏ Each partner's proportional share of the profits of the partnership shall be as follows: _____

And each partner's proportional share of the losses of the partnership shall be as follows: _____

Distribution of Profits and Losses.

☐ Any profits or losses of the partnership shall be determined and distributed to the partners on a monthly basis according to their proportionate share of the profits and losses of the partnership.

☐ Any profits or losses of the partnership shall be determined and distributed to the partners on a quarterly basis according to their proportionate share of the profits and losses of the partnership.

☐ Any profits or losses of the partnership shall be determined and distributed to the partners on an annual basis according to their proportionate share of the profits and losses of the partnership.

☐ Any profits or losses of the partnership shall be determined and distributed to the partners on a monthly basis according to their proportionate share of the profits and losses of the partnership. However, the first $ _____ of the profits each month shall be retained by the partnership for reinvestment in the partnership.

☐ Any profits or losses of the partnership shall be determined and distributed to the partners on a quarterly basis according to their proportionate share of the profits and losses of the partnership. However, the first $ _____ of the profits each quarter shall be retained by the partnership for reinvestment in the partnership.

☐ Any profits or losses of the partnership shall be determined and distributed to the partners on an annual basis according to their proportionate share of the profits and losses of the partnership. However, the first $ _____ of the profits each year shall be retained by the partnership for reinvestment in the partnership.

☐ Any profits or losses of the partnership shall be determined and distributed to the partners on a monthly basis according to their proportionate share of the profits and losses of the partnership. However, _____ percent of the profits each month shall be retained by the partnership for reinvestment in the partnership.

☐ Any profits or losses of the partnership shall be determined and distributed to the partners on a quarterly basis according to their proportionate share of the profits and losses of the partnership. However,

_____ percent of the profits each quarter shall be retained by the partnership for reinvestment in the partnership.

❑ Any profits or losses of the partnership shall be determined and distributed to the partners on an annual basis according to their proportionate share of the profits and losses of the partnership. However, _____ percent of the profits each year shall be retained by the partnership for reinvestment in the partnership.

Management of the Partnership.

❑ Each partner shall have an equal right to manage and control the partnership. All partnership decisions will be made by majority vote, except the following major decisions, which must be decided by unanimous vote:

The partners can select, by unanimous vote, one or more of the partners to act as managing partners of the partnership.

❑ Each partner shall have an equal right to manage and control the partnership. All partnership decisions will be made by majority vote. The partners can select, by majority vote, one or more of the partners to act as managing partners of the partnership.

❑ Each partner shall have an equal right to manage and control the partnership. Partnership decisions will be made by unanimous vote. The partners can select by unanimous vote, one or more of the partners to act as managing partners of the partnership.

❑ Each partner shall have a right to manage and control the partnership in the following proportions: _____

All partnership decisions will be made by majority vote, except the following major decisions, which must be decided by unanimous vote:

The partners can select, by unanimous vote, one or more of the partners to act as managing partners of the partnership.

❑ Each partner shall have a right to manage and control the partnership in the following proportions: _____

All partnership decisions will be made by majority vote.

The partners can select, by majority vote, one or more of the partners to act as managing partners of the partnership.

☐ Each partner shall have a right to manage and control the partnership in the following proportions: _____

Partnership decisions will be made by unanimous vote.

The partners can select, by unanimous vote, one or more of the partners to act as managing partners of the partnership.

Managing Partner(s).

☐ One or more managing partners may be selected under the terms of this Agreement. The salary of the managing partner(s) shall be $ _____ . The managing partner(s) shall have the authority to conduct the day-to-day business of the partnership, without consultation with the other partners. This shall include hiring and firing employees, signing partnership checks, withdrawing funds from partnership accounts, borrowing money up to the amount of $ _____, and maintaining the books and records of the partnership. The managing partner(s) shall not have the authority to make major decisions for the partnership without the majority approval of the other partners. Major decisions are defined as follows: _____

☐ One or more managing partners may be selected under the terms of this Agreement. The salary of the managing partner(s) shall be $ _____ . The managing partner(s) shall have the authority to conduct the day-to-day business of the partnership, without consultation with the other partners. This shall include hiring and firing employees, signing partnership checks, withdrawing funds from partnership accounts, borrowing money up to the amount of $ _____ , and maintaining the books and records of the partnership. The managing partner(s) shall not have the authority to make major decisions for the partnership without the unanimous approval of the other partners. Major decisions are defined as follows: _____ .

Date and Time of Annual Partnership Meeting.

The annual partnership meeting will be held on the _____ of every year at _____ __. m. This meeting is for the purpose of assessing the current status of the partnership and transacting any necessary business. If this day is a legal holiday, the meeting will be held on the next day.

Place of Partnership Meetings.

The place for the meeting will be the principal office of the partnership.

Partners Quorum.

A quorum for a partners meeting will be a majority of the partners. Once a quorum is present, business may be conducted at the meeting, even if partners leave prior to adjournment.

Partners Proxies.

At all meetings of partners, a partner may vote by signed proxy or by power of attorney. To be valid, a proxy must be filed with the partnership prior to the stated time of the meeting. No proxy may be valid for more than 11 months, unless the proxy specifically states otherwise. Proxies may always be revoked prior to the meeting for which it is intended. Attendance at the meeting for which a proxy has been authorized always revokes the proxy.

Partners Voting.

The vote of the holders of a majority of partnership interests entitled to vote will be sufficient to decide any matter, unless a greater number is required by the Partnership Agreement or by state law. Adjournment shall be by majority vote of those entitled to vote.

Partners Consent Agreements.

Any action that may be taken at a Partnership meeting may be taken instead without a meeting if an agreement is consented to, in writing, by all of the partners who would be entitled to vote.

Powers of the Partners.

The partners will have all powers available under state law, including the power to appoint and remove managers and employees; the power to change the offices; the power to borrow money on behalf of the partnership, including the power to execute any evidence of indebtedness on behalf of the partnership; and the power to enter into contracts on behalf of the partnership.

Fiduciary Duty of the Partners.

Each director owes a fiduciary duty of good faith and reasonable care with regard to all actions taken on behalf of the partnership. Each partner must perform her/his duties in good faith in a manner which she/he reasonably believes to be in the best interest of the partnership, using ordinary care and prudence.

Accounting Matters.

The partnership will maintain accounting records which will be open to any partner for inspection at any reasonable time. These records will include separate income and capital accounts for each partner. The accounting will be on the accrual basis and on a calendar year basis. The capital account of each partner will consist of no less than the value of the property, cash, or services that the partner shall have contributed with their initial or additional contributions to the partnership.

Financial Matters.

☐   The partners will determine the accounting methods and fiscal year of the partnership. All checks, drafts, or other methods of payment shall be signed by all of the partners. All notes, mortgages, or other evidence of indebtedness shall be signed by all of the partners. No money will be borrowed or lent by the partnership unless authorized by a unanimous vote of the partners. No contracts will be entered into on behalf of the partnership unless authorized by a unanimous vote of the partners. No documents may be executed on behalf of the partnership unless authorized by a unanimous vote of the partners.

☐   The partners will determine the accounting methods and fiscal year of the partnership. All checks, drafts, or other methods of payment shall be signed by all of the Partners or by a partner selected as manager to carry on the day-to-day business of the partnership. All notes, mortgages, or other evidence of indebtedness shall be signed by all of the partners. No money will be borrowed or lent by the partnership unless authorized by a majority vote of the partners. No contracts will be entered into on behalf of the partnership unless authorized by a majority vote of the partners. No documents may be executed on behalf of the partnership unless authorized by a majority vote of the partners.

Bank Account.

The partnership will maintain a business checking bank account at: _____

Loans to Partners.

☐ The partnership may not lend any money to any partner unless the loan has been approved by a unanimous vote of all partners of the partnership.

☐ The partnership may not lend any money to any partner unless the loan has been approved by a majority vote of all partners of the partnership.

Draws to Partners.

☐ All partners are entitled to monthly draws from the expected profits of the partnership. The draws will be debited against the income account of the partner. The amount of the draws shall be determined by a majority vote of the partners.

☐ All partners are entitled to monthly draws from the expected profits of the partnership. The draws will be debited against the income account of the partner. The amount of the draws shall be determined by unanimous vote of the partners.

☐ All partners are entitled to quarterly draws from the expected profits of the partnership. The draws will be debited against the income account of the partner. The amount of the draws shall be determined by a majority vote of the partners.

☐ All partners are entitled to quarterly draws from the expected profits of the partnership. The draws will be debited against the income account of the partner. The amount of the draws shall be determined by unanimous vote of the partners.

☐ No partners are entitled to draws against the expected profits of the partnership.

Salaries to Partners.

☐ All partners are eligible to be paid reasonable salaries for work or services they perform in the partnership business.

☐ No partners are eligible to be paid salaries for any work or services they perform in the partnership business. Such work or services shall be considered contributions to the partnership.

Partnership Expense Accounts.

☐ No partner shall have an expense account. Reimbursement for business expenses may be made by majority vote of the partners.

☐ No partner shall have an expense account. Reimbursement for business expenses may be made by unanimous vote of the partners.

☐ Each partner shall receive an expense account of up to $ _____ per month for the payment of reasonable and necessary business expenses in the regular course of partnership business. Each partner shall provide the partnership with a written record of such expenses in order to obtain reimbursement.

Transfers of Partnership Interests.

☐ A partner may transfer all or part of his or her interest in the partnership to any other party without the consent of the other partners.

☐ A partner may transfer all or part of his or her interest in the partnership to any other party without the consent of the other partners. However, the partnership has the right of first refusal to purchase the partner's interest on the same terms and conditions as the partner's offer from the third party. This option to buy must be exercised by the partnership within 30 days from notice of the offer to buy by a third party.

☐ A partner may transfer all or part of his or her interest in the partnership to any other party only with the unanimous consent of the other partners.

❑ A partner may transfer all or part of his or her interest in the partnership to any other party only with the majority consent of the other partners.

❑ A partner may not transfer any or all of his or her interest in the partnership.

Expulsion of Partners.

A partner may be expelled from the partnership at any time by the unanimous consent of the other partners. Upon expulsion, the expelled partner shall cease to be a partner and shall have no interest, rights, authority, power, or ownership in the partnership or any partnership property. The expelled partner shall be entitled to receive value for his or her interest in the partnership as determined by the terms of this Agreement. The partnership shall continue in business without interruption without the expelled partner.

Automatic Expulsion of Partners. A partner is automatically expelled from the partnership at any time upon the occurrence of any of the following:

a. A partner files a petition for or becomes subject to an order for relief under the Federal Bankruptcy Code.
b. A partner files for or becomes subject to any order for insolvency under any state law.
c. A partner makes an assignment for the benefit of creditors.
d. A partner consents to or becomes subject to the appointment of a receiver over a substantial portion of his or her assets.
e. A partner consents to or becomes subject to an attachment or execution of a substantial portion of his or her assets.

On the date of any of the above events, the expelled partner shall cease to be a partner and shall have no interest, rights, authority, power, or ownership in the partnership or any partnership property. The expelled partner shall be entitled to receive value for his or her interest in the partnership as determined by the terms of this Agreement. The partnership shall continue in business without interruption without the expelled partner.

Limit on Remedies of Expelled Partners.

The expulsion of a partner shall be final and shall not be subject to mediation, arbitration, or review by any court of any jurisdiction.

Insurance.

❑ Each partner shall buy and maintain life insurance on the life of each other partner in the amount of $ _____ .

❑ Each partner shall buy and maintain disability insurance on the life of each other partner in the amount of $ _____ .

❑ The partnership shall buy and maintain life insurance on the life of each partner in the amount of $ _____ and such insurance shall be considered assets of the partnership.

❑ The partnership shall buy and maintain disability insurance on the life of each partner in the amount of $ _____ and such insurance shall be considered assets of the partnership.

❑ On the withdrawal, termination, or expulsion of any partner for any reason other than their death or disability, any insurance policies on the partner's life or health on which the partnership paid premiums shall become the personal property of the departing partner and the cash value (if any) of such policy shall be considered as a draw against the departing partner's income account.

Mediation or Arbitration.

❑ Except as otherwise provided by this Agreement, the partners agree that any dispute arising related to this Agreement will be settled by voluntary mediation, if possible. The mediator shall be chosen by a majority vote of the partners. All costs of mediation will be shared equally by all partners involved in the dispute.

❑ Except as otherwise provided by this Agreement, the partners agree that any dispute arising related to this Agreement will be settled by voluntary mediation, if possible. The mediator shall be chosen by a unanimous vote of the partners. All costs of mediation will be shared equally by all partners involved in the dispute.

❑ Except as otherwise provided by this Agreement, the partners agree that any dispute arising related to this Agreement will be settled by binding arbitration, if possible. The arbitrator shall be chosen by a majority vote of the partners. All costs of arbitration will be borne by all partners involved in the dispute as directed by the arbitrator.

❏ Except as otherwise provided by this Agreement, the partners agree that any dispute arising related to this Agreement will be settled by binding arbitration, if possible. The arbitrator shall be chosen by a unanimous vote of the partners. All costs of arbitration will be borne by all partners involved in the dispute as directed by the arbitrator.

Admission of New Partners.

❏ A new partner may be admitted to the partnership only by unanimous consent of the partners. Admission of a new partner shall not cause the termination of the original partnership entity, but it shall continue with the additional partner.

❏ A new partner may be admitted to the partnership by majority consent of the partners. Admission of a new partner shall not cause the termination of the original partnership entity, but it shall continue with the additional partner.

Responsibility of New Partners.

Any new partner to the partnership shall be responsible for and assume full personal liability equal to all other partners for all partnership debts, liabilities, and obligations whenever incurred.

❏ Any new partner to the partnership shall be responsible for and assume full personal liability for all partnership debts, liabilities, and obligations whenever incurred only up to the amount of the value of the initial and any additional contributions of the new partner.

❏ Any new partner to the partnership shall be responsible for and assume full personal liability only for those partnership debts, liabilities, and obligations incurred after the date of their acceptance as a new partner.

Withdrawal from the Partnership.

❏ If any partner withdraws from the partnership for any reason (including the death or disability of the partner), the partnership shall continue and be operated by the remaining partners. The withdrawing partner or his or her personal representative will be obligated to sell his or her interest to the remaining partners, and the remaining partners will be obligated to buy that interest. The value of the withdrawing partner's interest will be his or her proportionate share of the total value of the partnership. If necessary, the total value of the partnership will be made by an independent appraisal made within 90 days of the partner's withdrawal. The costs of the appraisal will be shared equally by all partners, including the withdrawing partner.

❏ If any partner withdraws from the partnership for any reason (including the death or disability of the partner), the partnership shall cease to exist. All partnership assets and liabilities will be divided by the partners as provided by the terms of this Agreement relating to the termination of the partnership.

Outside Activities of Partnership.

❏ No partner, during or after the partnership, shall engage in any business that is in competition with the partnership in any manner. The prohibition against competition shall continue for a period of _____ years after the partner leaves the partnership and for any business within _____ miles of the partnership's principal place of business. This non-competition agreement shall end with the termination of the partnership.

❏ During or after the partnership, each partner may engage in any other business activities, even if such activities compete with the partnership.

Termination of the Partnership.

❏ The partnership may be terminated at any time by unanimous consent of the partners. Upon termination, the partners agree to apply the assets and money of the partnership in the following order:

a. To pay all the debts and obligations of the partnership
b. To distribute the partners' income accounts to the partners in their proportional share
c. To distribute the partners' capital accounts to the partners in their proportional share
d. To distribute any remaining assets to the partners in their proportional share

❏ The partnership may be terminated at any time by majority vote of the partners. Upon termination, the partners agree to apply the assets and money of the partnership in the following order:

a. To pay all the debts and obligations of the partnership
b. To distribute the partners' income accounts to the partners in their proportional share
c. To distribute the partners' capital accounts to the partners in their proportional share
d. To distribute any remaining assets to the partners in their proportional share.

Amendments to the Partnership Agreement.

☐   This Partnership Agreement may be amended in any manner by unanimous vote of the partners.

☐   This Partnership Agreement may be amended in any manner by majority vote of the partners.

Additional Provisions.

The following additional provisions are part of this Agreement: _____

Modification of Agreement.

☐ No modification of this Agreement shall be effective unless it is in writing and signed by all partners.

☐ No modification of this Agreement shall be effective unless it is in writing and signed by a majority of the partners.

This Agreement binds and benefits all partners and any successors, inheritors, assigns, or representatives of the partners. Time is of the essence of this Agreement. This document is the entire Agreement between the partners. Any attached papers that are referred to in this Agreement are part of this Agreement. Any alleged oral agreements shall have no force or effect. This Agreement is governed by the laws of the State of _____ . If any portion of this Agreement is held to be invalid, void, or unenforceable by any court of law of competent jurisdiction, the rest of the Agreement shall remain in full force and effect.

Dated_____

Partner Signature

Printed Name of Partner

Partner Signature

Printed Name of Partner

Partner Signature

Printed Name of Partner

Partner Signature

Printed Name of Partner

Partner Signature

Printed Name of Partner

Partner Signature

Printed Name of Partner

Amendments to Partnership Agreement

Sometime in the course of your partnership, changed conditions may require that you amend or change certain portions of your partnership agreement. In the initial partnership agreement that you prepared you should have included a clause that allows for the amendment of the agreement either by majority or unanimous vote. Most portions of the agreement may be changed by amendment. However, state law in all states restricts the right to change certain general conditions and rules of partnership law and partners liability. The things that you can not alter by amending your partnership agreement, even if you and your partners are in unanimous agreement are as follows:

> ⚡ **Warning!**
>
> Even by unanimous agreement of the partners, you can not change any provisions of your state's rules for registration.

- Vary the rights and duties relating to filing a registration statement (in those states which require such statements, generally, states which have adopted the Revised Uniform Partnership Act—please see Appendix on the enclosed CD)

- Unreasonably restrict the right of access to books and records, or eliminate the duty of loyalty

- Unreasonably reduce the duty of care

- Eliminate the obligation of good faith and fair dealing

- Vary the power to dissociate as a partner

- Vary the right of a court to expel a partner

- Vary the requirement to wind up partnership business

- Restrict rights of third parties who are not partners

Besides these general statutory restrictions, partners may agree to alter or amend their agreement in any manner. To make amendments to your original Partnership Agreement, use the following Amendment to Partnership Agreement form.

Amendment to Partnership Agreement

This Amendment to Partnership Agreement is made on _____ , 20 ____ by and between _____ , of _____ , City of _____ , State of _____ and _____ , of _____ , City of _____ , State of _____ . It is intended to permanently amend the Partnership Agreement between the above parties which was dated _____ , 20 ____ .

The above noted Partnership Agreement is hereby amended to read as follows:

All other portions of the original Partnership Agreement dated_____ , 20 ____ , not changed by this Amendment to Partnership Agreement remain in full force and effect and are ratified and confirmed.

_____
Signature of Partner

_____
Printed Name of Partner

_____
Signature of Partner

_____
Printed Name of Partner

Termination of a Partnership

In all virtually partnerships, there will come a time when the partners will desire that the partnership cease to exist. In order for the dissolution of the partnership to proceed as amicably as possible, it is wise to carefully consider all aspects of the impending end of the partnership and to draft a comprehensive Termination of Partnership Agreement that will cover each aspect of dissolution of the business to each partner's satisfaction. The termination of a business partnership is, perhaps, one of the most difficult business situations to confront. The following worksheet is designed to assist you in understanding the factors that will be important as you proceed to terminate your business partnership. Following the worksheet is a Termination of Partnership Agreement that you may use as an outline to prepare your own custom-tailored agreement.

⚡ **Warning!**

Be sure that all of your partnership debts and liabilities are provided for before you terminate the partnership.

Partnership Termination Worksheet

Date proposed for termination: _____

Reason for termination: _____

Valuation of partnership business: $ _____

Appraisal of partnership property: $ _____

Who will appraise the partnership property? _____

Does anyone hold a right of first refusal or option to purchase the business? ____
_____

Is an outside purchase or lease of the business involved? _____

If so, what are the proposed terms of the outside purchaser's offer to buy or lease the business? _____

Are these terms unanimously acceptable to the partners? _____

Is the business to be sold or leased to an existing partner? _____

If so, what are the proposed terms of the existing purchaser's offer to buy or lease the business? _____

Are these terms unanimously acceptable to the partners? _____

Will the partnership business be discontinued with no purchase of partnership assets? _____

What disposition will be made of the partnership name? _____

What date is set for the sale/lease/liquidation of the partnership? _____

What are the proportionate shares of profits and losses of each partner? _____
_____

What is the liquidation or sale value of all of the partnership assets? _____
_____

What is the value of all of the partnership liabilities, other than to the partners?

_____

_____

What will be the remaining partnership assets after all partnership liabilities have been met? _____

How much will be distributed to each partner's income account? _____

How much will be distributed to each partner's capital account? _____

How much additional partnership funds will be distributed to each partner? _____

_____

Who will wind up the partnership business? _____

What is the estimated date for the distribution of the final partnership assets?

_____

_____

Termination of Partnership Agreement

This Termination of Partnership Agreement is made on _____ , 20 ___ by and between _____ , of _____ , City of _____ , State of _____ and _____ , of _____ , City of _____ , State of _____ . It is intended to permanently Terminate the Partnership which was created by the Partnership Agreement between the above parties which was dated _____ , 20 ___ .

The above noted Partners agree to terminate their Partnership under the following terms and conditions:

1. After _____ , 20 ___ , no partner shall engage in any further partnership business nor incur any further partnership obligations, other than to liquidate the assets of the partnership and, in general, wind up the partnership's affairs.

2, The partners agree that each asset of the partnership has a present fair market value equal to the assets value as shown on the financial records of the partnership. However, if an asset is sold, the partners agree that such asset shall be deemed to have a fair market value equal to its sale price.

3. The partner's agree that their proportionate shares of the assets and liabilities of the partnership are as follows:

4. The partnership shall proceed to have an accounting made of all of the assets and liabilities of the partnership. The equities of the partnership creditors and partners shall be determined on the date of the accounting, which shall be no later than _____ , 20 ___ . Any liabilities incurred or funds received by the partnership after this date shall be distributed to the partners according to their proportionate shares.

5. Any partnership assets shall be sold. Any partner shall have the right to purchase any partnership asset before any sale to an outside purchaser. The proceeds from the sale of the partnership assets, along with any partnership funds shall be applied to the partnership liabilities in the following order:

a. To pay all the debts and obligations of the partnership
b. To the partner's income accounts to the partners in their proportional share
c. To the partner's capital accounts to the partners in their proportional share
d. To any remaining assets to the partners in their proportional share.

6. Every partner hereby represents that he or she has not obligated the partnership in any way that does not appear on the records of the partnership, nor has he or she received any funds or assets that do not appear on the records of the partnership.

7. The partnership name shall be disposed of as follows:

8. No modification of this Agreement shall be effective unless it is in writing and signed by a majority of the partners. This Agreement binds and benefits all partners and any successors, inheritors, assigns, or representatives of the partners. Time is of the essence of this Agreement. This document is the entire Termination of Partnership Agreement between the partners. Any attached papers which are referred to in this Agreement are part of this Agreement. Any alleged oral agreements shall have no force or effect. This Agreement is governed by the laws of the State of _____ . If any portion of this Agreement is held to be invalid, void, or unenforceable by any court of law of competent jurisdiction, the rest of the Agreement shall remain in full force and effect.

Dated _____

_____
Signature of Partner

_____
Printed Name of Partner

_____
Signature of Partner

_____
Printed Name of Partner

Registration of Partnerships

With the recent adoption of the Revised Uniform Partnership Act by some 20 states, registration of partnerships is now regulated at the state level in those states. Please check the Appendix to see if your state is one of those governed by this Revised Act. The Revised Act affords the partnership the opportunity to register an official Statement of Partnership Authority with officials in the jurisdiction in which the partnership holds real estate. The purpose of such a Statement is to afford a public record and public notice of those individual partners who have the authority to bind the partnership in contractual affairs, particularly those relating to real property. The registration is a simple matter of completing a statement noting who has authority to do what within the partnership. It is also possible to amend or cancel any such Statement of Partnership Authority in those states that have adopted the Revised Uniform Partnership Act. These statements are most often initially filed with the Secretary of State. In order to act as an effective and legal notice to third parties, a certified copy of the Statement must then be recorded in the records of the county in which the partnership does business or holds real estate.

Following are three sample forms for complying with the provisions of the Revised Act: Statement of Partnership Authority, Amendment to Statement of Partnership Authority, and Cancellation of Partnership Authority. Please check the Appendix on the enclosed CD and with your state and local authorities for any additional information on registration of partnerships.

Statement of Partnership Authority

Under the terms of the laws of the State of _____ , this Statement of
Partnership Authority is filed in the County of _____ , State of ____
_____ by the _____ Partnership, formed by virtue of the
Partnership Agreement dated _____ , 20 ___ , by and between
_____ , of _____ , City of _____ , State
of _____ and _____ , of _____ , City of
_____ , State of _____ .

The principal office of the partnership is at:

The names and current addresses of all partners are as follows:

Name/Address

_____
_____
_____
_____

The following partners are authorized to execute instruments transferring
real property which is held in the name of the partnership:

Name

_____
_____
_____
_____

The following partners are authorized to enter into contracts on behalf of
the partnership:

Name

_____
_____
_____
_____

Other than the above mentioned persons and authority, no other persons
shall have the ability to bind the partnership in any manner.

It is intended that this Statement of Partnership Authority serve as full and complete notice to any person or entity who intends to have any dealings with the above named Partnership.

Dated _____ , 20 ___ .

_____
Partner Signature

_____
Printed Name of Partner

_____
Partner Signature

_____
Printed Name of Partner

Amendment to Statement of Partnership Authority

Under the terms of the laws of the State of _____ , this Amendment to Statement of Partnership Authority is filed in the County of _____ , State of _____ by the _____ Partnership, formed by virtue of the Partnership Agreement dated _____ , 20 ____ , by and between _____ , of _____ , City of _____ , State of _____ and _____ , of _____ , City of _____ , State of _____ .

This Amendment alters the Statement of Partnership Authority which was dated _____ , 20 ____ , and filed with the _____ office on _____ , 20 ____ .

The above mentioned Statement of Partnership Authority is amended as follows:

Other than the above mentioned amendments, the original Statement of Partnership Authority which was dated _____ , 20 ____ , and filed with the _____ office on _____ , 20 ____ , remains in full force and effect and is ratified and confirmed.

It is intended that this Amendment and the original Statement of Partnership Authority serve as full and complete notice to any person or entity who intends to have any dealings with the above named Partnership.

Dated _____ , 20 ____ .

_____
Partner Signature

_____
Printed Name of Partner

_____
Partner Signature

_____
Printed Name of Partner

Cancellation of Statement of Partnership Authority

Under the terms of the laws of the State of _____ , the Cancellation of Statement of Partnership Authority is filed in the County of_____ , State of _____ by the _____ Partnership, formed by virtue of the Partnership Agreement dated_____ , 20 _____ , by and between _____ , of _____ , City of _____ , State of _____ and _____ , of _____ , City of _____ , State of _____ .

This Cancellation fully and completely revokes and cancels the Statement of Partnership Authority which was dated _____ , 20 _____ , and filed with the _____ office on _____ , 20 ____ , and any Amendments thereto.

It is intended that this Cancellation serve as full and complete notice to any person or entity who intends to have any dealings with the above named Partnership.

Dated _____ , 20 ____ .

_____
Partner Signature

_____
Printed Name of Partner

_____
Partner Signature

_____
Printed Name of Partner

Registration of Partnership Name

The choice of a name for a business is an important aspect in the success of the business. Many business owners choose business names which contain their own names, for example: Mary and Bill's Restaurant or Smith and Jones Furniture Refinishing Company. As long as the owners' own names are the main designation of the business name, no registration of the name is generally required. If, however, the owners of the partnership chooses a name which is fictitious, many states require some type of registration of the assumed name. Examples of a fictitious name might be The Landing Restaurant or Imperial Furniture Company: names which do not identify the owners of the businesses. The main rationale for such fictitious name registration is to provide a record of who owns business; owners that can not be identified solely by the business name. This allows for a central registry of some kind, should a third party need to file a lawsuit or claim of some kind against the unidentified owner.

Some states do not require registration, but simply allow business owners to register their business names as a method to prevent infringement of others upon the use of a particular name, in the manner of registering the trademark or trade name of a business. The Appendix of this book on the enclosed CD provides a listing of each state's business name registration requirements. Note that some states require registration with state authorities, often the Secretary of State, while other states provide for registration in the county in which the business intends to do business.

In all states, there are either statutory rules or judge-decided case law that prevent a business from adopting a name which is deceptive to the public. Thus, for example, a business can not imply that it is owned or operated by a licensed practitioner in a state-regulated profession if such is not, in fact, the case. Nor may a business adopt a name which is deceptively similar to the name of another business. In many states, there is a method by which to check a registry of business names that are in use. This allows potential conflicts with another business name to be resolved prior to the adoption of the name. In addition, some states provide for the reservation of a business name even before the actual operation of the business has commenced.

The Business Start-Up Toolkit

> **Toolkit Tip!**
>
> Check the Appendix on the enclosed CD to see if your state requires the publication of a notice of operating a business under an assumed or fictitious name.

Finally, some states require the publication of a statement in local newspapers that provide a notice to the public that a certain business will be operating in a community under an assumed or fictitious name. This allows the public to be notified of the names and addresses of the actual owners of the business. Please carefully check the listing for your state in the Appendix on the enclosed CD for the requirements that you will need to follow in the registration of your business name. Following is a standard form for registering a business name. Although this form should suffice in most locales, your own state or local authorities may proscribe a mandatory form for such registrations. Please check with your particular registration authorities.

Statement of Intention to Conduct Business Under an Assumed or Fictitious Name

The undersigned parties do hereby state their intention to carry on the business of _____ , at the business location of _____ _____ , in the City of _____ , in the State of _____ , under the assumed or fictitious name of:_____
_____

The owners' names, home addresses, and percentages of ownership of the above-named business are as follows:

Name   *Address*   *Percentage of Ownership*
_____
_____
_____
_____
_____
_____

Signed on _____ , 20 _____ .

_____
Signature of Business Owner

_____
Signature of Business Owner

_____
Signature of Business Owner

Chapter 9

Starting Business as a Corporation

Pre-Incorporation Activities

The planning stage of incorporation is vital to the success of any corporation. The structure of a new corporation, including the number of directors, number of shares of stock, and other matters, must be carefully tailored to the specific needs of the business. Attorneys typically use a pre-incorporation worksheet to assemble all of the necessary information needed to plan the incorporation process.

By filling out a Pre-Incorporation Worksheet, potential business owners will be able to have before them all of the basic data to use in preparing the necessary incorporation paperwork. The process of preparing this worksheet will also help uncover any potential differences of opinion among the persons who are desiring to form the corporation. Often, conflicts and demands are not known until the actual process of determining the corporate structure begins. Frank discussions regarding the questions of voting rights, number of directors, and other management decisions often will enable potential associates to resolve many of the difficult problems of corporate management in advance. The use of a written worksheet will also provide all persons involved with a clear and permanent record of the information. This may provide the principals of the corporation with vital support for later decisions that may be required.

All persons involved in the planned corporation should participate in the preparation of the following worksheet. Please take the time to carefully and completely fill in all the spaces. Following the worksheet, there is a Pre-Incorporation Checklist which provides a clear listing of all of the required actions necessary to incorporate a business. Follow this checklist carefully as the incorporation process proceeds. After the Pre-Incorporation Checklist, there is a Document Filing Checklist that provides a listing of the corporate documents that are normally required to be filed with the state corporation office. Finally, there is a discussion and form for reserving the corporate name with the state corporation department. If required, the name reservation form will be the first form filed with the state corporation department.

Unfamiliar terms relating to corporations are explained in the glossary of this book. As the Pre-Incorporation Worksheet is filled in, please refer to the following explanations:

Name/address of state corporation department: The appendix of this book on the enclosed CD provides this name and address. You should contact this department immediately, requesting all available information on incorporation of a for-profit business corporation in your state. Although the forms on the enclosed CD are state-specific and the appendix provides up-to-date information on state requirements, state laws and fees charged for incorporation are subject to change. Having the latest available information will save you time and trouble.

Proposed name of the corporation: The selection of a corporate name is often crucial to the success of a corporation. The name must not conflict with any existing company names, nor must it be deceptively similar to other names. It is often wise to clearly explain the business of the corporation through the choice of name. In addition, most states require that some part of the company name identify the fact that the business is a corporation. All states allow for a reservation of the corporate name in advance of actual incorporation and state-specific forms are provided on the CD for this purpose. Check the Appendix on the enclosed CD for the listing for your state.

Toolkit Tip!

Check the Appendix on the enclosed CD for the website address of your state's incorporation department and contact them for the latest available information on incorporation in your state.

Toolkit Tip!

The enclosed CD provides state-specific forms for filing Articles of Incorporation and for reserving a corporate name.

Parties involved: This listing should provide the names, addresses, and phone numbers of all of the people who are involved in the planning stages of the corporation.

Principal place of business: This must be the address of the actual physical location of the main business. It may not be a post office box. If the corporation is home-based, this address should be the home address.

Purpose of corporation: Many states allow the use of an "all-purpose" business purpose clause in describing the main activity of the business; for example, "to conduct any lawful business." However, a few states require a specific business purpose to be identified in the Articles of Incorporation. Please check in the Appendix on the enclosed CD to see if this is a requirement in your state. If you must specify a purpose, be concise and specific, but broad enough to allow for flexibility in operating your business.

> ### ⚡ Warning!
> If your corporation will be selling any products or services, you will need to register your corporation with your state tax authorities.

State/local licenses required: Here you should note any specific requirements for licenses to operate your type of business. Most states require obtaining a tax ID number and a retail, wholesale, or sales tax license. A federal tax ID (FEIN) number must be obtained by all corporations. Additionally, certain types of businesses will require health department approvals, state board licensing, or other forms of licenses. If necessary, check with a competent local attorney for details regarding the types of licenses required for your locality and business type.

Patents/copyrights/trademarks: If patents, copyrights, or trademarks will need to be transferred into the corporation, they should be noted here.

> ### ☀ Toolkit Tip!
> It is advisable to incorporate your business in the state where you will be doing business.

State of incorporation: In general, the corporation should be incorporated in the state in which it will conduct business. In the past, the state of Delaware was regarded as the best state in which to incorporate. This was due to the fact that Delaware was the first state to modernize its corporation laws to reflect the realities of present-day corporate business. This is no longer the case. Virtually all states have now enacted corporate laws very similar to those in Delaware. In the vast majority of situations, it is preferable to be incorporated in your home state.

Corporate existence: The choices here are perpetual (forever) or limited to a certain length. In virtually all cases, you should choose perpetual.

Proposed date to begin corporate business: This should be the date on which you expect the corporation to begin its legal existence. Until this date (actually, until the state formally accepts the Articles of Incorporation), the incorporators of your corporation will continue to be legally liable for any business conducted on behalf of the proposed corporation.

Incorporators: This should be the person (or persons) who will prepare and file the Articles of Incorporation. Most states allow for one incorporator. However, a few require more than one. Please check the Appendix on the enclosed CD for the requirements in your particular state.

⊘ Definition:

Incorporators: These are the persons who will be filing the Articles of Incorporation. They need not be involved in the actual operation of the corporation after it has begun business.

Proposed date of first directors meeting: This will be the date proposed for holding the first meeting of the board of directors, at which the corporate bylaws will be officially adopted.

Proposed bank for corporate bank account: In advance of incorporation, you should determine the bank which will handle the corporate accounts. Obtain from the bank the necessary bank resolution, which will be signed by the board of directors at the first directors meeting.

Cost of incorporation: The state fees for incorporation are listed in the Appendix on the enclosed CD. This cost should also reflect the cost of obtaining professional assistance (legal or accounting); the cost of procuring the necessary supplies; and any other direct costs of the incorporation process.

Proposed number of directors: Most states allow a corporation to have a single director. A number of states require three directors unless there are fewer than three shareholders, in which case the state allows for the number of directors to equal the number of shareholders. Please check the Appendix on the enclosed CD for the requirements in your particular state.

Proposed first board of directors: You should list the names and addresses of the proposed members of the first board of directors. Although not a requirement in every state, the Articles of Incorporation used in this book provide that these persons be listed. It is not possible to keep the names of the directors of a corporation secret.

Corporation's registered agent and office address: You should list the name and actual street address of the person who will act as the registered agent of the corporation. All states (except New York) require that a specific person be available as the agent of the corporation for the service of process (i.e., to accept subpoenas or summonses on behalf of the corporation). The person need not be a shareholder, director, or officer of the corporation. The registered agent need not be a lawyer. Normally, the main owner, chairperson of the board of directors, or president of the corporation is selected as the registered agent.

Proposed first officers: This information is not provided in the Articles of Incorporation and need not be made public. You should list here the persons who are proposed as the first officers of the business.

Qualification in other states: If the corporation desires to actively conduct business in a state other that the main state of incorporation, it is necessary to "qualify" the corporation in that state. This generally requires obtaining a Certificate of Authority to Transact Business from the other state. In this context, a corporation from another state is referred to as a "foreign" corporation. If you desire that your corporation qualify for activities in another state, you are advised to consult a competent business attorney.

Required quorum for shareholders meeting: This is the percentage of ownership of shares of issued stock in the corporation that must be represented at a shareholders meeting in order to officially transact any shareholder business. This is normally set at a "majority" (over 50 percent), although this figure can be set higher.

Annual shareholders meeting: The place, date, and time of the annual shareholders meeting should be specified.

Required vote for shareholders action: Once it is determined that a quorum of shareholders is present at a meeting, this is the percentage of ownership of shares of issued stock in the corporation that must vote in the affirmative in order to officially pass any shareholder business. This is normally set at a "majority" (over 50 percent), although this figure can be set higher and can be made to be unanimous.

Fiscal year and accounting type: For accounting purposes, the fiscal year and accounting type (cash or accrual) of the corporation should be chosen in advance. Please consult with a competent accounting professional.

Amendments to Articles of Incorporation: Under this item should be the determination of which bodies of the corporation will have the authority to amend the Articles of Incorporation. The forms in this book are designed to allow the Articles of the corporation to be amended by the board of directors only upon approval by the shareholders.

Amendments to Bylaws: The determination of which bodies of the corporation will have the authority to amend the bylaws should be decided. The forms in this book are designed to allow the bylaws of the corporation to be amended by the board of directors only upon approval by the shareholders.

> **☼ Toolkit Tip!**
>
> Prior to incorporating, you should understand how your company's bookkeeping and account-ing systems will operate. You may need to consult an accounting professional.

Annual directors meeting: The place, date, and time of the annual board of directors meeting should be specified.

Required quorum for directors meeting: This is the percentage of directors that must be present at a board of directors meeting in order to officially transact any directors business. This is normally set at a "majority" (over 50 percent), although this figure can be set higher.

Required vote for directors action: Once it is determined that a quorum of directors is present at a meeting, this is the percentage of directors who must vote in the affirmative in order to officially pass any board of directors business. This is normally set at a "majority" (over 50 percent), although this figure can be set higher and can be made to be unanimous.

Initial total investment: This figure is the total amount of money or property that will be transferred to the corporation upon its beginning business. This transfer will be in exchange for the issuance of shares of stock in the corporation. This is also referred to as "paid-in capital." A few states require a minimum amount of "paid-in-capital" before beginning corporate business. Please check your state's listing in the Appendix on the enclosed CD.

Initial indebtedness: If there is to be any initial indebtedness for the corporation, please list here.

Initial authorized number of shares: This figure is required to be listed in the Articles of Incorporation. The number of shares of stock to be authorized should be listed. For small corporations, this number may be influenced by the incorporation fee structure of the state of incorporation. For example, some states allow for a minimum incorporation fee when only a certain minimum number of stock shares are authorized. Please see the Appendix on the enclosed CD for the requirements in your state and check with your state corporation department.

> **Toolkit Tip!**
>
> Most corporations today do not specify a 'par' value for their stock, but rather designate that their shares should be 'no-par' value, allowing the shares to be issued at the actual price paid per share.

Par value or no-par value: This refers to an arbitrary indication as to the value of the stock. The designation of stock as having a certain "par" value is not an indication of the actual value of the shares of stock. Shares must be sold for a price at or above par value. If no-par value is assigned, the shares are issued for the actual price paid per share. The choice of par or no-par value stock may affect the issuance of dividends and should be referred to the corporate accountant.

Proposed sales of shares of stock: Here should be listed the names, cash or property, and value of potential sales of shares of stock which may be approved by the board of directors once the corporation is officially authorized to issue stock.

Following the Pre-Incorporation Worksheet are a Pre-Incorporation Checklist and a Document Filing Checklist. Please use these checklists to be certain that you have completed all the necessary steps for incorporation. Once all the persons involved have completed the Pre-Incorporation Worksheet, agreed on all of the details, and reviewed the Pre-Incorporation and Document Filing Checklists, the actual process of incorporation may begin.

If the choice for a corporate name may be similar to another business, or if the incorporators wish to insure that the name will be available, an Application for Reservation of Corporate Name may be filed. This is a simple form requesting that the state corporation department hold a chosen corporate name until the actual Articles of Incorporation are filed, at which time the name will become the official registered name of the corporation. There will be a fee required for the filing of this form and some states prefer that preprinted state forms be used. Please check in the Appendix on the enclosed CD and with the specific state corporation department for information. In any event, the information required will be the same as is necessary for this sample form.

Toolkit Tip!

Each state has differing requirements for corporations. Please check your state's listing in the Appendix on the enclosed CD.

Pre-Incorporation Worksheet
Name/Address of State Corporation Department (from Appendix)

_____
_____
_____
_____
_____

Proposed Name of the Corporation

First choice: _____

Alternate choices: _____

_____

Parties Involved in Forming the Corporation

Name/Address/Phone Number

_____
_____
_____
_____
_____

Location of Business

Address of principal place of business: _____

_____

Description of principal place of business: _____

_____

Ownership of principal place of business (own or lease?): _____

_____

Other places of business: _____

_____

Type of Business

Purpose of corporation: _____

State/local licenses required: _____

Patents/copyrights/trademarks: _____

Incorporation Matters

State of incorporation: _____

Corporate existence (limited or perpetual?): _____

Proposed date to begin corporate business: _____

Names and addresses of those who will act as incorporators:

Name/Address

_____

_____

_____

_____

_____

Proposed date of first directors meeting: _____

Proposed bank for corporate bank account: _____

Cost of incorporation: _____

Corporate Management

Proposed number of directors: _____

Proposed first board of directors:

Name/Address

_____

_____

_____

_____

_____

_____

_____

_____

Corporation's registered agent and office address:

_____

_____

Proposed first officers:

	Name	Address
President:	_____	_____
Vice President:	_____	_____
Secretary:	_____	_____
Treasurer:	_____	_____

Is qualification in other states necessary? _____

Corporate Bylaws

Required quorum for shareholders meeting: _____

Annual shareholders meeting:

Place/Date/Time

_____

_____

Required vote for shareholders actions (majority/%/unanimous?): _____

Fiscal year: _____

Accounting type (cash or accrual?): _____

Authority to amend the following corporate documents:

Articles of Incorporation:_____ directors_____ shareholders_____ either

Bylaws: _____ directors_____ shareholders_____ either

Annual Directors Meeting:

Place/Date/Time

_____

_____

Required quorum for directors meetings: _____

Required vote for directors actions (majority/%/unanimous?): _____

Corporate Stock

Initial total investment: $ _____

Initial indebtedness: $ _____

Initial authorized number of shares: _____

Par value or no-par value: _____

Proposed sales of shares of stock:

Name	Cash/Property	Amount

Pre-Incorporation Checklist

☐ Write state corporation office for information (see Appendix on enclosed CD)

☐ Complete Pre-Incorporation Worksheet

☐ Check annual fees and filing requirements

☐ Prepare Articles of Incorporation (see Appendix on the enclosed CD for state-specific name for "Articles ") If desired, have attorney review Articles of Incorporation prior to filing

☐ Review tax impact of incorporation with an accountant

☐ Check state tax, employment, licensing, unemployment, and workers compensation requirements

☐ Check insurance requirements

☐ Procure corporate seal (if desired)

☐ Prepare stock certificates

☐ Prepare corporate accounting ledgers

☐ Prepare corporate record book (looseleaf binder)

Document Filing Checklist

☐ Application for Reservation of Corporate Name (if desired)

☐ Articles of Incorporation (mandatory, see Appendix on the enclosed CD for state-specific name for "Articles ")

☐ Amendments to Articles of Incorporation (mandatory, if applicable)

☐ Annual Corporate Reports (mandatory)

☐ Change of Address of Registered Agent (mandatory)

☐ Articles of Merger (mandatory, if applicable)

☐ Articles of Dissolution (mandatory, if applicable)

☐ Any other required state forms (see Appendix on the enclosed CD)

Articles of Incorporation

Ø Definition:

Articles of Incorporation: This document contains the formal rules that govern the operation of a corporation. Their acceptance by the state marks the beginning of the corporation's existence.

The central legal document for any corporation is the Articles of Incorporation. In some states, this document may be called a Certificate of Incorporation, Charter of Incorporation, or Articles of Organization. Please check the Appendix on the enclosed CD for the requirements in your particular state. This form outlines the basic structure of the corporation and details those matters that are relevant to the public registration of the corporation. The name, purpose, owners, registered agent, address, and other vital facts relating to the existence of the corporation are filed with the state by using this form. Upon filing of the Articles of Incorporation, payment of the proper fee, and acceptance by the state corporation department, the corporation officially begins its legal existence. Until the state has accepted the articles, the incorporators are not shielded from liability by the corporate form. Some states have chosen to confuse matters slightly by referring to another form that may be issued by the state as a Certificate of Incorporation. Please check the Appendix on the enclosed CD for the state requirements for the state of your potential incorporation. For clarity, however, this book will refer to the incorporator-prepared document as the Articles of Incorporation.

There are a number of items that are required to be noted in all Articles of Incorporation. The articles may also include many other details of the corporation's existence. Please check in the Appendix on the enclosed CD and with your state incorporation department for specific details. Following is a checklist of items which are mandatory or optional for Articles of Incorporation.

Articles of Incorporation Checklist

The mandatory details for Articles of Incorporation for most states are:

☐ Title and introduction

☐ The name of the corporation

☐ The purpose and powers of the corporation

☐ The duration of the corporation

☐ The amount of initial capital of corporation (optional in some states)

☐ The number of shares of stock that the corporation is authorized to issue to shareholders

☐ Par value or no-par value for shares of stock (optional in some states)

☐ The name of the registered agent of the corporation

☐ The address of the office of the registered agent of the corporation

☐ The name, address, and age of each incorporator

☐ The number of directors (optional in some states)

☐ The names and addresses of the initial director or directors

☐ The signatures of the incorporators

☐ The signature of the registered agent

In addition, the following items may also be included at your option:

☐ The terms and qualifications for board members

☐ Provisions relating to the powers of the directors, officers, or shareholders

☐ Designation of different classes of stock

☐ Preemptive or cumulative voting rights

☐ Voting and other rights or restrictions on stock

☐ Additional articles

☐ Election to be a close corporation under state law

☐ Provisions indemnifying corporate officers and directors

The Articles of Incorporation for your corporation should include all of the required information. Since the articles are a public record, all of the information in them will be available for inspection. However, since the names of the directors will usually be required to be revealed in the annual reports that are filed with the state, there is no purpose in attempting to conceal identities of actual management of the corporation. Much of the information that is not required in the articles may instead be put into the bylaws of the corporation. In this manner, the actual management structure and details will remain unavailable for public inspection.

🔆Toolkit Tip!

State-specific Articles of Incorporation are on the enclosed CD. The information required, however, will be the same as is noted in this chapter.

This chapter contains explanation of typical clauses for preparing Articles of Incorporation. A few states may require additional articles. Most of the information required for preparing the clauses for this form will be on your Pre-Incorporation Worksheet, which you prepared previously. Optional clauses may be added to state-supplied forms where necessary. Articles of Incorporation can be amended at any time. However, this generally requires a formal filing with the state and the issuance of a Certificate of Amendment of Articles of Incorporation. It also normally requires the payment of a fee. For these reasons, it is often a good idea to put only those items in the original articles that are unlikely to require changes in the near future.

The articles must be properly signed. Although not required by all states, they may need to be notarized. A few states require that the articles be published as legal notices in newspapers. Please check the Appendix on the enclosed CD for the requirements in your particular state. The signed Articles of Incorporation and the proper fee should be sent to the proper state office. Upon receipt, the state corporation department will check for duplication or confusing conflicts with the names of any other registered corporations. They will also check to be certain that all the statutory requirements have been fulfilled and that the proper fee has been paid. If everything is in order, the business will officially be incorporated and will be able to begin to conduct business as a corporate entity. Some states have different procedures for indicating the beginning existence of a corporation. For example, you may need to request an official Certificate of Filing, Certificate of Good Standing, or other type of certificate and pay a fee for this record. Check with your state corporation department.

Name of the Corporation (Mandatory)

The name of the corporation should be unique. It should not be confusingly similar to any other business name in use within your state. In addition, it should not contain any terms which might lead people to believe that it is a governmental or financial institution. Finally, it must generally contain an indication that the business is a corporation, such as "Inc.," "Incorporated," "Corporation," or "Limited." Some states allow the use of the word "Company" in the name of corporations. Others do not. If you wish to use a term of corporate designation other than "Corporation" or "Incorporated" (or abbreviations of these), please check in the appendix and with your state corporation department.

Purpose and Powers of the Corporation (Mandatory)

Many states allow a general statement of purpose: "to transact any and all lawful business for which corporations may be incorporated under the Business Corporation Act of the State of _____ ." Others may require that you specifically state the purpose of your corporation, such as: "to operate a retail dry-cleaning business." Please check the Appendix on the enclosed CD for the requirements in your particular state. If you are required to state a specific purpose, try to be broad enough to allow your business flexibility without the necessity of later amending the Articles of Incorporation to reflect a change in direction of your business. (Please note that Kentucky and Massachusetts are referred to as "Commonwealths," rather than "States.")

Duration of the Corporation (Mandatory)

All states allow for a *perpetual duration* for corporations, meaning that the corporation can continue in existence forever. Unless there is a specific business reason to indicate otherwise, this is generally the safest choice. A limited duration statement is not an acceptable method to dissolve a corporation.

Minimum Capitalization (Usually mandatory)

This clause refers to the amount of capital which will form the initial basis for operating the corporation. Several states have specific dollar amounts of minimum capital that are required for a corporation to be incorporated, ranging from $500.00 to $1,000.00. All other states have no minimum and you may delete this clause. Please check in the Appendix on the enclosed CD and check with your state corporation department.

Authorization to Issue Stock (Mandatory)

The number of shares of stock that will be issued is a business determination. There is no specific reason that the number of shares should be large. In fact, in some states the amount of fees charged for incorporation is based upon the number of shares that are authorized to be issued. Please check in the Appendix on the enclosed CD for the requirements in your particular state.

Par or No-Par Value (Generally, mandatory; may be optional)

This refers to the arbitrary value that has been assigned to your shares of stock. It does not refer to the actual purchase price required for the shares of stock. Please consult with the corporation's accountant if you have questions regarding this.

Name of the Registered Agent (Mandatory)

The registered agent for a corporation is the person upon whom *service of process* (summons, subpoena, etc.) can be served. This person must be an adult who is a resident of the state of incorporation. The usual choice is the main owner of the corporation. Residents of New York are required to have the Secretary of State be the authorized agent for service of process. Please see the Appendix on the enclosed CD and check with your state corporation department.

Address of the Registered Agent (Mandatory)

This address must be an actual place, usually the offices of the corporation. It may not be a post office box or other unmanned location.

Name[s], Address[es], and Age[s] of Incorporator[s] (Mandatory)

This is the name and address of the person or persons who are filing for incorporation. The minimum age requirement for incorporating a business is generally 18. A few states allow corporations or partnerships to act as incorporators. Please check in the Appendix on the enclosed CD or with your state corporation department.

Number of Directors (Usually mandatory)

The minimum number of directors allowed is generally one. However, a few states require three directors if there are more than two shareholders. Thus, in those states, if there is only one shareholder, there may be one director. If there are two shareholders, there must be two directors. But if there are three shareholders or more, there must be three directors. Please check the Appendix on the enclosed CD.

Name[s] and Address[es] of Initial Director[s] (Usually mandatory)

If required, this would be the name and address of the initial director or directors of the corporation until the first meeting of the shareholders of the corporation either elect or replace these directors.

Preemptive Rights (Optional)

You may include any preemptive stock rights in the articles, if desired. Preemptive rights are like a right of first refusal. If a corporation proposes to authorize new shares of stock, preemptive rights allow current shareholders the right to acquire an equivalent percentage of the new shares based on their current percentage of ownership. This prevents their ownership percentage from being watered down by the authorization and issuance of new shares of stock. Under the laws of some states, preemptive rights exist unless the Articles of Incorporation specifically state that they do not. In other states, preemptive rights *do not* exist unless the Articles of Incorporation specifically state that they do. The best method of dealing with this issue is to include one of the following clauses into your Articles as a optional clause.

This corporation shall have preemptive rights for all shareholders.

Or:

This corporation shall have no preemptive rights for any shareholders.

Preferences and Limitations on Stock (Optional)

Any voting preferences or limitations on transfers or other rights or restrictions on stock can be listed or it may be listed in the bylaws of the corporation, if preferred.

Additional Articles

Most states allow you to add additional articles to the state-provided forms.

Corporate Bylaws

The bylaws of a corporation are the third part of the triangle that provides the framework for the management of the corporate business. Along with state law and the Articles of Incorporation, the bylaws provide a clear outline of the rights and responsibilities of all parties to a corporation. In particular, the bylaws provide the actual details of the operational framework for the business. The bylaws are the internal document that will contain the basic rules on how the corporation is to be run. Every corporation must have a set of bylaws. Many of the provisions cover relatively standard procedural questions, relating to quorums, voting, and stock. Other provisions may need to be specifically tailored to the type of business for which the bylaws are intended. They are generally able to be amended by vote of the board of directors, unless the Articles of Incorporation or the bylaws themselves have transferred that authority to the shareholders. The bylaws provided in this book specify that the power to amend them is vested in the board of directors, but that the shareholders have the power to approve or reject any amendment.

The bylaws can contain very specific or very general provisions for the internal management of the company. Typically, the bylaws cover five general areas:

- The rights and responsibilities of the shareholders
- The rights and responsibilities of the directors
- The rights and responsibilities of the officers
- Financial matters
- Methods for amending the bylaws

This chapter contains sample clauses for preparing your corporate bylaws. Once you have chosen which of the clauses you will use and have filled in any required information, use the forms on the enclosed CD to complete your bylaws. Your completed bylaws should be both formally adopted at the first board of directors meeting and approved at the first shareholders meeting. The following is a checklist for use in preparing your bylaws:

Corporate Bylaws Checklist

- ☐ Power to designate the location of principal office of the corporation
- ☐ Power to designate the registered office and agent of the corporation
- ☐ Date, time, and place of annual shareholders meeting
- ☐ Procedures for special shareholders meetings
- ☐ Notice and waivers for shareholders meetings
- ☐ Voting eligibility requirements for shareholders
- ☐ Quorum and votes required for actions of shareholders
- ☐ Shareholders proxy requirements
- ☐ Shareholders consent resolutions
- ☐ Shareholders cumulative voting rights
- ☐ Powers of board of directors
- ☐ Number of directors and term of office
- ☐ Directors election procedures
- ☐ Date, time, and place of annual board of directors meeting
- ☐ Procedures for special board of directors meetings
- ☐ Notice and waivers for board of directors meetings
- ☐ Quorum and votes required for actions by board of directors
- ☐ Board of directors consent resolutions
- ☐ Removing and filling vacancies of directors
- ☐ Salaries of directors
- ☐ Fiduciary duty of directors
- ☐ Number of officers and appointment and terms of officers
- ☐ Removing and filling vacancies of officers
- ☐ Duties of officers
- ☐ Salaries of officers

- ☐ How stock certificates are to be handled
- ☐ Restrictions on the rights to transfer shares of stock (if any)
- ☐ How corporate financial matters are to be handled
- ☐ Whether officers or directors can borrow money from the corporation
- ☐ Bylaw amendment procedures
- ☐ Signatures of Secretary of Corporation and Chairperson of Board

Corporate Bylaws

Corporate Bylaws of

_____,

a corporation incorporated under the laws of the State of _____.

Corporate Office and Registered Agent. The board of directors has the power to determine the location of the corporation's principal place of business and registered office, that need not be the same location. The board of directors also has the power to designate the corporation's registered agent, who may be an officer or director.

Date, Time, and Place of Shareholders Annual Meeting. The annual shareholders meeting will be held on _____,20 _____,at _____o'clock ____.m., at the offices of the corporation located at ___ _____.

This meeting is for the purpose of electing directors and for transacting any other necessary business. If this day is a legal holiday, the meeting will be held on the next day.

Shareholders Special Meetings. Special meetings of the shareholders may be called at any time and for any purpose. These meetings may be called by either the president or the board of directors or upon request of 25 percent of the shareholders of the corporation. The request for a special meeting must be made in writing that states the time, place, and purpose of the meeting. The request should be given to the secretary of the corporation who will prepare and send written notice to all shareholders of record who are entitled to vote at the meeting.

Place of Shareholders Meetings. The board of directors has the power to designate the place for shareholders meetings, unless a waiver of notice of the meeting signed by all shareholders designates the place for the meeting. If no place is designated, either by the board of directors or all of the shareholders, then the place for the meeting will be the principal office of the corporation.

Notice and Waivers of Shareholders Meetings. Written notice of shareholders meetings must be sent to each shareholder of record entitled to vote at the meeting. The notice must be sent no less than _____ days nor more than _____days before the date of the meeting. The notice should be sent to the shareholder's address as shown in the corporate stock transfer book. The notice will include the place, date, and time of the meeting. Notices for special meetings must also include the purpose of the meeting. When notices are sent, the secretary of the corporation must prepare an Affidavit of Mailing of Notices. Shareholders may waive notice of meetings if done in writing, except that attendance at a meeting is considered a waiver of notice of the meeting.

Shareholders Entitled to Notice, to Vote, or to Dividends. For the purpose of determining which shareholders are entitled to notice, to vote at meetings, or to receive dividends ,the board of directors may order that the corporate stock transfer book be closed for _____ days prior to a meeting or the issuance of a dividend. The shareholders entitled to receive notice, vote at meetings, or receive dividends are those who are recorded in the stock transfer book upon the closing of the book. Instead of closing the book, the board of directors may also set a Record Date. The shareholders recorded in the stock transfer book at the close of business on the Record Date will be entitled to receive notice, vote at meetings, or receive dividends. A list of shareholders entitled to receive notice, vote at meetings, or receive dividends will be prepared by the secretary when necessary and provided to the officers of the corporation. Every shareholder who is entitled to receive notice, vote, or receive dividends is also entitled to examine this list and the corporate stock transfer book.

Shareholders Quorum. A quorum for a shareholders meeting will be a majority of the outstanding shares that are entitled to vote at the meeting, whether in person or represented by proxy. Once a quorum is present, business may be conducted at the meeting, even if shareholders leave prior to adjournment.

Shareholders Voting. Each outstanding share of the corporation that is entitled to vote as shown on the stock transfer book will have one (1) vote. The vote of the holders of a majority of the shares entitled to vote will be sufficient to decide any matter, unless a greater number is required by the Articles of Incorporation or by state law. Adjournment shall be by majority vote of those shares entitled to vote.

Shareholders Proxies. At all meetings of shareholders, a shareholder may vote by signed proxy or by power of attorney. To be valid, a proxy must be filed with the secretary of the corporation prior to the stated time of the meeting. No proxy may be valid for over 11 months, unless the proxy specifically states otherwise. Proxies may always be revokable prior to the meeting for which they are intended. Attendance at the meeting by a shareholder for which a proxy has been authorized always revokes the proxy.

Shareholders Consent Resolutions. Any action that may be taken at a shareholders meeting may be taken instead without a meeting if a resolution is consented to, in writing, by all shareholders who would be entitled to vote on the matter.

Shareholders Cumulative Voting Rights. For the election of directors, each shareholder may vote in a cumulative manner, if desired. Cumulative voting will mean that if each shareholder has one (1) vote per director to be elected, the shareholder may vote all votes for a single director or spread the votes among directors in any manner.

Powers of the Board of Directors. The affairs of the corporation will be managed by the board of directors. The board of directors will have all powers available under state law, including, but not limited to: the power to appoint and remove officers, agents, and employees; the power to change the offices, registered agent, and registered office of the corporation; the power to issue shares of stock; the power to borrow money on behalf of the corporation, including the power to execute any evidence of indebtedness on behalf of the corporation; and the power to enter into contracts on behalf of the corporation.

Number of Directors and Term of Office. The number of directors will be as shown in the Articles of Incorporation and may be amended. The number is currently _____. Each director will hold office for _____ year(s) and will be elected at the annual meeting of the shareholders.

Date and Time of Annual Meeting of the Board of Directors. The annual board of directors meeting will be held on _____, 20 _____, at _____ o 'clock ____.m., at the offices of the corporation located at _____ _____.

This meeting is for the purpose of appointing officers and for transacting any other necessary business. If this day is a legal holiday, the meeting will be held on the next day.

Place of Board of Directors Meetings. The board of directors has the power to designate the place for directors meetings. If no place is designated, then the place for the meeting will be the principal office of the corporation.

Special Meetings of the Board of Directors. Special meetings of the board of directors may be called at any time and for any purpose. These meetings may be called by either the president or the board of directors. The request for a special meeting must be made in writing that states the time, place, and purpose of the meeting. The request should be given to the secretary of the corporation who will prepare and send written notice to all directors.

Notice and Waivers of Board of Directors Meetings. Written notice of board of directors meetings must be sent to each director. The notice must be sent no less than _____ days nor more than _____ before the date of the meeting. The notice should be sent to the director's address as shown in the corporate records. The notice will include the place, date, and time of the meeting, and for special meetings, the purpose of the meeting. When notices are sent, the secretary of the corporation must prepare an Affidavit of Mailing of Notices. Directors may waive notice of meetings if done in writing, except that attendance at a meeting is considered a waiver of notice of the meeting.

Board of Directors Quorum. A quorum for directors meetings will be a majority of the directors. Once a quorum is present, business may be conducted at the meeting, even if directors leave prior to adjournment.

Board of Directors Voting. Each director will have one (1) vote. The vote of a majority of the directors will be sufficient to decide any matter, unless a greater number is required by the Articles of Incorporation or state law. Adjournment shall be by majority vote.

Board of Directors Consent Resolutions. Any action that may be taken at a directors meeting may be taken instead without a meeting if a resolution is consented to, in writing, by all directors.

Removal of Directors. A director may be removed from office, with or without cause, at a special meeting of the shareholders called for that purpose.

Filling Directors Vacancies. A vacancy on the board of directors may be filled by majority vote of the remaining directors, even if technically less than a quorum. A director elected to fill a remaining term will hold office until the next annual shareholders meeting.

Salaries of Directors. The salaries of the directors will be fixed by the board of directors and may be altered at any time by the board. A director may receive a salary even if he or she receives a salary as an officer.

Fiduciary Duty of Directors. Each director owes a fiduciary duty of good faith and reasonable care with regard to all actions taken on behalf of the corporation. Each director must perform his or her duties in good faith in a manner that he or she reasonably believes to be in the best interests of the corporation, using ordinary care and prudence.

Number of Officers. The officers of the corporation will include a president, vice-president, treasurer, and secretary. Any two (2) or more offices may be held by the same person.

Appointment and Terms of Officers. The officers of the corporation will be appointed by the directors at the first meeting of the board of directors. Each officer will hold office until death, resignation, or removal by the board of directors.

Removal of Officers. Any officer may be removed by the board of directors, with or without cause. Appointment of an officer does not create any contract rights for the officer.

Filling Vacancies of Officers. A vacancy in any office for any reason may be filled by the board of directors for the unexpired term.

Duties of the President. The president is the principal executive officer of the corporation and is subject to control by the board of directors. The president will supervise and control all of the business and activities of the corporation. The president will preside at all shareholders and directors meetings, and perform any other duties as prescribed by the board of directors.

Duties of the Vice-President. If the president is absent, dies, or is incapacitated, the vice-president will perform the duties of the president. When acting for the president, the vice-president will have all of the powers and authority of the president. The vice-president will also perform any other duties as prescribed by the board of directors.

Duties of the Secretary. The secretary will keep the minutes of all shareholders and directors meetings. The secretary will provide notices of all meetings as required by the bylaws. The secretary will be the custodian of the corporate records, corporate stock transfer book, and corporate seal. The secretary will keep a list of the addresses of all shareholders, directors, and officers. The secretary will sign, along with other officers, the corporation's stock certificates. The secretary will also perform any other duties as prescribed by the board of directors.

Duties of the Treasurer. The treasurer will be custodian of all corporate funds and securities. The treasurer will receive and pay out funds that are receivable or payable to the corporation from any source. The treasurer will deposit all corporate funds received into the corporate bank accounts as designated by the board of directors. The treasurer will also perform any other duties as prescribed by the board of directors.

Salaries of Officers. The salaries of the officers will be fixed by the board of directors and may be altered at any time by the board. An officer may receive a salary even if he or she receives a salary as a director.

Stock Certificates. Certificates that represent shares of ownership in the corporation will be in the form designated by the board of directors. Certificates will be signed by all officers of the corporation. Certificates will be consecutively numbered. The name and address of the person receiving the issued shares, the certificate number, the number of shares, and the date of issue will be recorded by the secretary of the corporation in the corporate stock transfer book. Shares of the corporation's stock may only be transferred on the stock transfer book of the corporation by the holder of the shares in whose name they were issued as shown on the stock transfer book, or by his or her legal representative.

Financial Matters. The board of directors will determine the accounting methods and fiscal year of the corporation. All checks, drafts, or other methods for payment shall be signed by an officer determined by resolution of the board of directors. All notes, mortgages, or other evidence of indebtedness shall be signed by an officer determined by resolution of the board of directors. No money will be borrowed or loaned by the corporation unless authorized by a resolution of the board of directors. No contracts will be entered into on behalf of the corporation unless authorized by a resolution of the board of directors. No documents may be executed on behalf of the corporation unless authorized by a resolution of the board of directors. A board of directors resolution may be for specific instances or a general authorization.

Loans to Officers or Directors. The corporation may not lend any money to an officer or director of the corporation unless the loan has been approved by a majority of the shares of all stock of the corporation, including those shares that do not have voting rights.

Amendments to the Bylaws. These bylaws may be amended in any manner by majority vote of the board of directors at any annual or special meeting. Any amendments by the board of directors are subject to approval by majority vote of the shareholders at any annual or special meeting.

Dated: _____, 20 _____

_____
Signature of Secretary of Corporation

_____
Printed Name of Secretary of Corporation

Approved by the Board of Directors on _____, 20 _____

Approved by the Shareholders on _____, 20 _____

Corporate Directors Meetings

The board of directors of a corporation transacts business as a group. Each individual director has no authority to bind the corporation (unless the board of directors as a group has previously authorized him or her to exercise that power). Even in a corporation with a single director, there must be formal records of meetings and of the resolutions adopted by the board.

Corporate boards of directors must, at a minimum, hold an annual meeting to appoint the officers of the corporation for the coming year, decide if dividends will be declared for the year, and make any other annual decisions regarding the financial matters of the business. Typically, boards will hold special meetings for specific topics much more frequently.

> **⚡ Warning!**
>
> You must hold at least an annual corporate directors meeting and keep accurate minutes of the meetings. Failure to do so could subject you to personal liability for corporate actions or debt.

Whenever official corporate matters are discussed as a group, the board of directors should hold a meeting, keep minutes, and record the decisions made as corporate resolutions. This is not a difficult task and it will provide a clear record of the agreements made by the board for future reference. Prior to any annual or special meetings of the board, notice must be given to each board member according to the time limits set in the bylaws. If all board members are in agreement, an easier method to fulfill the notice requirement is to have the board sign waivers of notice. This document and all of the other documents necessary to conduct and record board meetings are contained in this chapter. Before each type of board meeting is a checklist of the information necessary to fill in the minutes and other forms. Follow the appropriate checklist for each meeting.

First Board of Directors Meeting Checklist

☐ Name of corporation

☐ Date of meeting

☐ Location of meeting

☐ Officers present at meeting

☐ Others present at meeting

☐ Name of temporary chairperson presiding over meeting

☐ Name of temporary secretary acting at meeting

☐ Calling of meeting to order and quorum present

☐ Proper notification of meeting

☐ Notices sent and affidavit filed /or waivers filed

☐ Articles of Incorporation filed with state

☐ Date of filing

☐ Effective date of incorporation

☐ Approve and ratify any acts of incorporators taken on behalf of corporation prior to effective date of incorporation

☐ Elect officers of corporation

☐ Decide on annual salaries of officers

☐ Direct that any organizational expenses be reimbursed to incorporators

☐ Authorize opening of corporate bank account

☐ Approve corporate seal, stock certificate, and stock transfer book

☐ Approve corporate bylaws

☐ Approve issuance of stock in exchange for transfers of property or money

☐ Designate fiscal-year dates

☐ Designate accounting basis (cash or accrual basis)

☐ Document any other necessary business

☐ Adjournment of meeting

☐ Date and secretary signature on minutes

Notice of First Board of Directors Meeting of _____

TO:

In accordance with the bylaws of this corporation, the first organizational meeting of the board of directors will be held on _____ , 20 _____ , at _____ o'clock ____ . m. , at the offices of the corporation located at _____ .

Dated: _____ , 20 _____

_____
Signature of Incorporator

_____
Printed Name of Incorporator

_____
Signature of Incorporator

_____
Printed Name of Incorporator

_____
Signature of Incorporator

_____
Printed Name of Incorporator

Waiver of Notice of First Board of Directors Meeting

of _____

We, the undersigned incorporators of this corporation, waive any required notice and consent to the holding of the first meeting of the board of directors of this corporation on _____ , 20 _____ , at _____ o'clock ____ . m., at the offices of the corporation, located at _____ _____.

Dated: _____ , 20 _____

Signature of Incorporator/Printed Name of Incorporator

_____, _____
_____, _____
_____, _____
_____, _____
_____, _____
_____, _____
_____, _____

Minutes of the First Board of Directors Meeting of _____

The first meeting of the board of directors of this corporation was held on
_____ , 20 _____ , at _____ o'clock ___ . m., at the offices of the corporation, located at _____
_____ .

Present at the meeting were the following people:
_____
_____
_____
_____

all of whom are designated as directors of this corporation in the Articles of Incorporation.

The following other persons were also present:
_____
_____
_____
_____

1. _____
   was elected as the temporary chairperson of the board.

   _____
   was elected as the temporary secretary of the board.

2. The chairperson announced that the meeting had been duly called by the incorporators of the corporation, called the meeting to order, and determined that a quorum was present.

3. The secretary then presented an Affidavit of Mailing of Notice or a Waiver of Notice of the meeting which was signed by all directors. Upon motion made and carried, the secretary was ordered to attach the Affidavit of Notice or the Waiver of Notice to the minutes of this meeting.

4. The chairperson reported that the Articles of Incorporation had been duly filed with the State of _____ on _____ , 20 _____ , and that the incorporation was effective as of _____ , 20 _____ .

Upon motion made and carried, a copy of the Articles of Incorporation was ordered to be attached to the minutes of this meeting.

5. Upon motion made and carried, the board of directors RESOLVED that:

The joint and individual acts of _____ and _____ , the incorporators of this corporation, which were taken on behalf of the corporation, are approved, ratified, and adopted as acts of the corporation.

6. The following persons were elected as officers of the corporation to serve until the first annual board of directors meeting:

_____ , President
_____ , Vice-President
_____ , Treasurer
_____ , Secretary

7. Upon motion made and carried, the annual salaries of the officers were fixed at the following rates until the next annual meeting of the board of directors:

President $ _____
Vice-President $ _____
Secretary $ _____
Treasurer $ _____

8. Upon motion made and carried, the board of directors RESOLVED that:

The officers of this corporation are authorized and directed to pay all fees and expenses necessary for the organization of this corporation. The officers are also directed to procure and prepare the necessary books for corporate accounting.

9. Upon motion made and carried, the board of directors
RESOLVED that:
The officers of this corporation be authorized and directed to open a bank account with _____ , located at _____ _____ , and to deposit all funds of the corporation into this account, with checks payable upon the corporate signature of _____ _____ only.

And further RESOLVED that:

The officers of this corporation are authorized to execute any formal Bank Resolutions and documents which may be necessary to open such an account. A copy of the formal Bank Resolution for opening this account is hereby adopted and ordered to be attached to the minutes of this meeting.

10. A proposed Corporate Seal, Corporate Stock Certificate, and Corporate Stock Transfer Book were presented.

Upon motion made and carried, the board of directors
RESOLVED that:

The Seal, Stock Certificates, and Stock Transfer Book presented at this meeting are adopted and approved as the Seal, Stock Certificates, and Stock Transfer Book of this corporation. A specimen copy of the Stock Certificate is ordered to be attached to the minutes of this meeting.

11. A copy of the proposed bylaws of the corporation was presented at the meeting and read by each director.

Upon motion made and carried, the board of directors
RESOLVED that:

The proposed bylaws of this corporation are approved and adopted. A copy of these bylaws are ordered to be attached to the minutes of this meeting.

12. The following persons have offered to transfer the property or money listed below to the corporation in exchange for the following number of shares of common capital stock in the corporation:

Name/Property or Money/Number of Shares

_____

_____

_____

_____

Upon motion made and carried, the board of directors
RESOLVED that:

The assets proposed for transfer are good and sufficient consideration and
the officers are directed to accept the assets on behalf of the corporation
and to issue and deliver the appropriate number of shares of stock in this
corporation to the respective persons. The shares of stock issued shall be
fully paid and non-assessable common capital stock of this corporation.

13. Upon motion made and carried, the board of directors
RESOLVED that:

The fiscal year of this corporation shall begin on _____ ,
20 _____ , and end on _____ , 20 _____ .
This corporation shall report its income and expenses on a(n) _____
basis.

14. The following other business was conducted:

There being no further business, upon motion made and carried, the meeting
was adjourned.

Dated: _____ , 20 _____

Corporate Seal

_____
Signature of Secretary of Corporation

_____
Printed Name of Secretary of Corporation

Annual Board of Directors Meeting Checklist

The following information should be covered and documented in the minutes of the annual board of directors meeting:

- ☐ Review current employment agreements
- ☐ Review current insurance coverage
- ☐ Name of corporation
- ☐ Date and time of meeting
- ☐ Location of meeting
- ☐ Notification of meeting
- ☐ Notices sent or waivers filed
- ☐ Officers present at meeting
- ☐ Others present at meeting
- ☐ Officers presiding over meeting
- ☐ Calling of meeting to order and quorum present

Annual Matters

- ☐ Date last state corporate tax return filed
- ☐ Date last federal corporate tax return filed
- ☐ Date last state annual report filed
- ☐ Date any other required reports/returns filed
- ☐ Date of last financial statement
- ☐ Review stock transfer ledger
- ☐ Review current financial statement
- ☐ Review current year-to-date income and expenses
- ☐ Review current salaries

The Business Start-Up Toolkit

- ☐ Review current pension/profit-sharing plans
- ☐ Review other employee fringe benefit plans
- ☐ Review accounts receivable
- ☐ Determine if collection procedures are warranted
- ☐ Review status of any outstanding loans
- ☐ Ascertain net profit
- ☐ Determine if a stock dividend should be declared
- ☐ Discuss any major items requiring board action
- ☐ Discuss election and salaries of officers
- ☐ Discuss major purchases or leases (real estate or personal property)
- ☐ Discuss lawsuits
- ☐ Discuss loans
- ☐ Other business
- ☐ Adjournment of meeting
- ☐ Date and secretary signature on minutes

Notice of Annual Board of Directors Meeting

of _____

TO:

In accordance with the bylaws of this corporation, an annual meeting of the board of directors will be held on _____ , 20 _____ , at _____ o'clock ____ . m. , at the offices of the corporation located at _____ _____ .

Dated: _____ , 20 _____

Corporate Seal

_____
Signature of Secretary of Corporation

_____
Printed Name of Secretary of Corporation

Waiver of Notice of Annual Board of Directors Meeting

of _____

We, the undersigned directors of this corporation, waive any required notice and consent to the holding of the annual meeting of the board of directors of this corporation on _____ , 20 _____ , at _____ o'clock ____ . m., at the offices of the corporation located at _____
_____ .

Dated: _____ , 20 _____

Signature of Director/Printed Name of Director

_____ , _____
_____ , _____
_____ , _____
_____ , _____
_____ , _____
_____ , _____
_____ , _____

Minutes of Annual Board of Directors Meeting of _____

The annual meeting of the board of directors of this corporation was held on _____ , 20 _____ , at _____ o'clock ____ . m. , at the offices of the corporation located at _____ _____ .

Present at the meeting were the following people:
_____
_____
_____

all of whom are directors of this corporation.

The following persons were also present:
_____
_____
_____

_____ , the president of the corporation, presided over the meeting.
_____ , the secretary of the corporation, served as secretary for the meeting.

1. The president called the meeting to order. The president determined that a quorum was present and that the meeting could conduct business.

2. The secretary reported that notice of the meeting had been properly given or waived by each director in accordance with the bylaws.

   Upon motion made and carried, the secretary was ordered to attach the appropriate Affidavit of Mailing of Notice or Waiver of Notice to the minutes of this meeting.

3. The secretary distributed copies of the minutes of the previous meeting of the board of directors which had been held on _____ , 20 ____ .

Upon motion made and carried, these minutes were approved.

4. The president presented the annual President's Report.

   Upon motion made and carried, the President's Report was approved and the secretary was directed to attach a copy of the President's Report to these minutes.

5. The treasurer of the corporation presented the Treasurer's Report, which stated that as of _____ , 20 _____ , the corporation had a net profit of $ _____ .   Upon motion made and carried, the Treasurer's Report was approved and the secretary was directed to attach a copy of the Treasurer's Report to these minutes.

6. Upon motion made and carried, the board of directors RESOLVED that:

   A dividend of $ _____ per share of common stock is declared on the stock of this corporation. This dividend shall be paid to the shareholders of record as of _____ , 20 _____ , and shall be paid on _____ , 20 _____ . The officers of this corporation are directed to take all necessary actions to carry out this resolution.

7. Upon motion made and carried, the following persons were elected as officers of this corporation for a term of one (1) year:

   _____ ,President
   _____ ,Vice-President
   _____ ,Treasurer
   _____ ,Secretary

8. Upon motion made and carried, the salaries of the officers were fixed for the term of one (1) year at the following rates:

   President $ _____
   Vice-President $ _____
   Secretary $ _____
   Treasurer $ _____

9. The following other business was transacted:

There being no further business, upon motion made and carried, the meeting was adjourned.

Dated: _____ , 20 _____

Corporate Seal

_____
Signature of Secretary of Corporation

_____
Printed Name of Secretary of Corporation

Corporate Shareholders Meeting

⚡ Warning!

You must hold at least an annual corporate shareholders meeting and keep accurate minutes of the meetings. Failure to do so could subject you to personal liability for corporate actions or debt.

The main responsibility of the shareholders of a corporation is to elect the directors of the business. This election is conducted at the annual meeting of the shareholders that is held on the date, time, and place as specified in the corporate bylaws. In addition, specific corporate business at other times of the year may occasionally need shareholder approval. For example, shareholders must vote on the dissolution of the corporation, on amendments to the Bylaws or Articles of Incorporation, and on any extraordinary business transactions, such as the sale of all of the assets of the corporation. For these purposes, a special meeting of the shareholders must be held.

The initial meeting of the shareholders also has a slightly different agenda. At this meeting, the shareholders approve and ratify the adoption of the corporate bylaws, and ratify the election or appointment of the initial board of directors who will serve until the first annual meeting of the shareholders. The shareholders also approve the election of the first officers of the corporation by the board of directors.

On the following pages, there are checklists and forms for the initial, annual, and special shareholders meetings. Please follow the checklists in preparing the forms. The notice requirements for shareholders meetings are identical to those for directors meetings. However, the forms are slightly different.

Note: If your corporation will elect to be taxed as an S-corporation, you will need to use a different form for your first shareholders meeting in order to approve this election. Please see details in Chapter 10 on S-corporations.

First Shareholders Meeting Checklist

The following information should be covered and documented in the minutes of the first shareholders meeting:

- ☐ Name of corporation
- ☐ Date of meeting
- ☐ Location of meeting
- ☐ Officers present at meeting
- ☐ Others present at meeting
- ☐ Calling of meeting to order and quorum present
- ☐ Shareholders present at meeting
- ☐ Shareholders represented by proxy at meeting
- ☐ Name of president acting at meeting
- ☐ Name of secretary acting at meeting
- ☐ Name of chairperson elected to preside over meeting
- ☐ Proper notification of meeting
- ☐ Notice sent and affidavit filed /or waivers filed
- ☐ Reading of minutes of first directors meeting
- ☐ Approval and ratification of minutes of first directors meeting
- ☐ Approval and ratification of election of officers and directors
- ☐ Approval and ratification of adoption of corporate bylaws
- ☐ Any other business
- ☐ Meeting adjourned
- ☐ Dating and signing of minutes by secretary

Notice of First Shareholders Meeting

of _____

TO:

In accordance with the bylaws of this corporation, a first official meeting of the shareholders will be held on _____ , 20 _____ , at _____ o'clock ___ . m., at the offices of the corporation located at _____ _____ .

The purpose of this meeting is to approve adoption of the bylaws of this corporation, approve election of the officers, approve continuation of the directors of this corporation, and to transact any other necessary business.

The Stock Transfer Book of this corporation will remain closed from _____ _____ , 20 _____ , until _____ , 20 _____ .

Dated: _____ , 20 _____

Corporate Seal

_____
Signature of Secretary of Corporation

_____
Printed Name of Secretary of Corporation

Waiver of Notice of First Shareholders Meeting

of _____

We, the undersigned shareholders of this corporation, waive any required notice and consent to the holding of the first meeting of the shareholders of this corporation on _____ , 20 _____ , at _____ o'clock ___ . m., at the offices of the corporation located at _____ _____ .

Dated: _____ , 20 _____

Signature of Shareholder/Printed Name of Shareholder

_____ , _____
_____ , _____
_____ , _____
_____ , _____
_____ , _____
_____ , _____
_____ , _____

Authorization to Vote Shares (Proxy) _____

I, _____ , the record owner of this corporation's stock certificate # _____ , which represents ____ shares in this corporation, authorize _____ to vote all of these shares at the meeting of the shareholders of this corpora-tion which is scheduled to be held on _____ , 20 _____ , at _____ o'clock ___ . m., at the offices of this corporation located at _____ _____ .

Through the use of this proxy and authorization, _____ _____ has the right to vote these shares at any business conducted at this meeting as if I personally were present.

This proxy and authorization may be revoked by me at any time prior to the meeting and will be void if I personally attend the meeting.

Dated: _____ , 20 _____

_____
Signature of Shareholder

_____
Printed Name of Shareholder

Minutes of First Shareholders Meeting

of _____

The first meeting of the shareholders of this corporation was held on _____
_____ , 20 _____ , at _____ o'clock ____ . m., at the offices of the
corporation located at _____
_____ .

Present were:

_____ , President
_____ , Vice-President
_____ , Treasurer
_____ , Secretary

Other than shareholders of this corporation, the following persons were
also present:

_____
_____
_____
_____

1. The president of this corporation called the meeting to order. The president determined that a quorum was present, either in person or by proxy, and that the meeting could conduct business.

   The following shareholders were present in person:

   Name of Shareholder/Number of Shares

   _____
   _____
   _____
   _____
   _____
   _____
   _____

   The following shareholders were represented by proxy:

Name of Shareholder/Number of Shares

_____

_____

_____

_____

_____

_____

2. The secretary reported that notice of the meeting had been properly given or waived by each shareholder in accordance with the bylaws.

Upon motion made and carried, the secretary was ordered to attach the appropriate Affidavit of Mailing of Notice or Waiver of Notice to the minutes of this meeting.

3. _____ was then elected chairperson of this meeting.

4. The secretary read the minutes of the first meeting of the board of directors of this corporation which was held on _____ , 20 _____ .

Upon motion made and carried, the shareholders RESOLVED that:

All acts taken and decisions made at the first meeting of the board of directors of this corporation are approved and ratified, specifically that the shareholders approve and ratify the adoption of the bylaws of this corporation and that the shareholders approve and ratify the election of the following persons as officers for the terms as stated in the minutes of the first meeting of the board of directors:

_____ , President
_____ , Vice-President
_____ , Treasurer
_____ , Secretary

5. Upon motion made and carried, the shareholders

RESOLVED that:

The following persons are designated as the initial directors of this corporation in the Articles of Incorporation and the shareholders approve and ratify this designation of the following persons as directors of this corporation until the first annual meeting of the shareholders of this corporation:

_____ , Director
_____ , Director
_____ , Director

6. The following other business was transacted:

There being no further business, upon motion made and carried, the meeting was adjourned.

Dated: _____ , 20 _____

Corporate Seal

_____
Signature of Secretary of Corporation

_____
Printed Name of Secretary of Corporation

Annual Shareholders Meeting Checklist

The following information should be covered and documented in the minutes of the annual shareholders meetings:

- ☐ Name of corporation
- ☐ Date of meeting
- ☐ Location of meeting
- ☐ Officers present at meeting
- ☐ Others present at meeting
- ☐ Calling of meeting to order and quorum present
- ☐ Shareholders present at meeting
- ☐ Shareholders represented by proxy at meeting
- ☐ Name of president acting at meeting
- ☐ Name of secretary acting at meeting
- ☐ Name of chairperson elected to preside over meeting
- ☐ Proper notification of meeting
- ☐ Notices sent and affidavit filed /or waivers filed
- ☐ Reading of minutes of previous shareholders meeting
- ☐ Approval of minutes of previous shareholders meeting
- ☐ Reading and approval of President's Report and direction that it be attached to minutes
- ☐ Reading and approval of Treasurer's Report and direction that it be attached to minutes
- ☐ Nomination of persons to serve as directors
- ☐ Election of directors
- ☐ Any other business
- ☐ Meeting adjournment
- ☐ Dating and signing of minutes by secretary

Notice of Annual Shareholders Meeting

of _____

TO:

In accordance with the bylaws of this corporation, an official annual meeting of the shareholders will be held on _____ , 20 _____ , at _____ o'clock ___ . m., at the offices of the corporation located at _____
_____ .

The purpose of this meeting is to elect directors of this corporation and to transact any other necessary business.

The Stock Transfer Book of this corporation will remain closed from _____ , 20 _____ , until _____ , 20 _____ .

Dated: _____ , 20 _____

                                                    Corporate Seal

_____
Signature of Secretary of Corporation

_____
Printed Name of Secretary of Corporation

Waiver of Notice of Annual Shareholders Meeting

of _____

We, the undersigned shareholders of this corporation, waive any required notice and consent to the holding of the annual meeting of the shareholders of this corporation on _____ , 20 _____ , at _____ o'clock ____ . m., at the offices of the corporation located at _____

_____ .

Dated: _____ , 20 _____

Signature of Shareholder/Printed Name of Shareholder

_____ , _____
_____ , _____
_____ , _____
_____ , _____
_____ , _____
_____ , _____
_____ , _____

Minutes of Annual Shareholders Meeting

of _____

The annual meeting of the shareholders of this corporation was held on
_____ , 20 _____ , at _____ o'clock ____ . m., at the offices of the corporation located at _____ .

Present were:
_____ ,President
_____ ,Vice-President
_____ ,Treasurer
_____ ,Secretary

Other than shareholders of this corporation, the following persons were also present:

_____
_____
_____

1. The president of this corporation called the meeting to order. The president determined that a quorum was present, either in person or by proxy, and that the meeting could conduct business.

The following shareholders were present in person:

Name of Shareholder/Number of Shares

_____
_____
_____
_____

The following shareholders were represented by proxy:

Name of Shareholder/Number of Shares

_____
_____
_____

2. The secretary reported that notice of the meeting had been properly given or waived by each shareholder in accordance with the bylaws.

   Upon motion made and carried, the secretary was ordered to attach the appropriate Affidavit of Mailing of Notice or Waiver of Notice to the minutes of this meeting.

3. _____ was then elected chairperson of this meeting.

4. The secretary distributed copies of the minutes of the previous meeting of the shareholders which had been held on _____ , 20 _____ .

   Upon motion made and carried, these minutes were approved.

5. The president presented the annual President's Report.

   Upon motion made and carried, the President's Report was approved and the secretary was directed to attach a copy of the President's Report to these minutes.

6. The treasurer of the corporation presented the Treasurer's Report.

   Upon motion made and carried, the Treasurer's Report was approved and the secretary was directed to attach a copy of the Treasurer's Report to these minutes.

7. The following persons were nominated as directors of this corporation for a term of _____ year(s):

   Name of Nominee

   _____
   _____
   _____
   _____

8. In accordance with the bylaws of this corporation, an election of directors was held, with each shareholder stating their choices for director by secret ballot and the number of shares held personally or by proxy.

9. The votes were tallied by the secretary and, by a majority vote of the out-standing shares entitled to vote in this election, the following persons were elected as directors of this corporation for a term of _____ year(s):

_____ , Director
_____ , Director
_____ , Director

10. On motion made and carried, it was directed that a report of the election be filed with the Clerk of _____ County, State of _____ _____ , if required.

11. The following other business was transacted:

There being no further business, upon motion made and carried the meeting was adjourned.

Dated: _____ , 20 _____

Corporate Seal

_____
Signature of Secretary of Corporation

_____
Printed Name of Secretary of Corporation

Corporate Resolutions

Warning!

You must document major decisions by both the board of directors and the shareholders with corporate resolutions. Failure to do so could subject you to personal liability for corporate actions or debt.

Corporate resolutions are records of official acts of either the shareholders of the corporation or the board of directors. They are a permanent record of actions taken by either of these bodies as a group. In most situations and for most corporations, a majority vote of the directors or shareholders present at an official meeting (as long as the number present constitutes a quorum) is required to adopt a corporate resolution. The resolutions adopted should be kept permanently in the corporate record book. In some cases, a copy of the resolution will be required by a third party. For example, a financial institution will usually require a copy of the corporate resolution that authorizes an officer to bind the corporation in a loan transaction.

In recent years, the use of consent resolutions has increased among businesses. These resolutions are used in lieu of formal meetings and can simplify corporate management. They require, however, the written consent of all of the directors (or shareholders) of a corporation in order to be valid. Any of the resolutions in this chapter can be used as consent resolutions by adapting them using the consent resolution instructions located at the end of this chapter.

Two checklists follow that specify the general circumstances in which corporate resolutions are required. They are not required for all of the normal day-to-day transactions of a business. In general, directors resolutions are only necessary to document the major decisions or transactions of a corporation. Shareholders resolutions are even more rare, used only for extraordinary corporate matters. Note that many additional directors resolution forms for most situations that will arise in the general course of business have been included on the attached Forms-on-CD. This includes forms for all of the directors resolution situations that are included on the following Corporate Resolutions Checklist.

Corporate Resolutions Checklists

Directors Resolutions: Directors resolutions need to be adopted at official meetings of the board of directors of the corporation. The resolutions are necessary for the corporation or its officers to be specifically authorized to transact significant business transactions. The following items may be the subject of directors resolutions:

- ❏ Authorizing major contracts
- ❏ Authorizing the sale of corporate real estate
- ❏ Authorizing the purchase of real estate
- ❏ Authorizing the corporation to borrow money
- ❏ Authorizing the corporation to enter into a real estate lease
- ❏ Authorizing a lawsuit
- ❏ Authorizing the appointment of a lawyer
- ❏ Authorizing the appointment of an accountant
- ❏ Authorizing stock dividends
- ❏ Authorizing stock dividends to be declared and paid annually
- ❏ Authorizing stock dividends to be declared and paid quarterly
- ❏ Authorizing the reimbursement of expenses to an employee
- ❏ Authorizing employee stock option plans
- ❏ Authorizing the retention of corporate earnings
- ❏ Authorizing pension plans
- ❏ Authorizing profit-sharing plans
- ❏ Authorizing healthcare plans
- ❏ Authorizing group insurance plans
- ❏ Authorizing the payment of a bonus to employees
- ❏ Authorizing death benefit plans
- ❏ Authorizing other employee benefit plans

- ☐ Authorizing recision of prior resolutions
- ☐ Authorizing loans to directors or officers
- ☐ Authorizing the payment of officers' salaries
- ☐ Authorizing a restricted stock transfer
- ☐ Authorizing a registered office address change
- ☐ Authorizing the corporate president to make purchases

Shareholders Resolutions: Resolutions by shareholders are much rarer than those by directors. Shareholder resolutions are only necessary to approve major actions by the corporation, such as:

- ☐ Approving the sale of all the corporate assets
- ☐ Approving the election of S-corporation status if desired
- ☐ Approving the dissolution of the corporation
- ☐ Approving the sale of the corporation
- ☐ Approving the merger of the corporation with another company

Resolution of Board of Directors

of _____

A meeting of the board of directors of this corporation was duly called and held on _____ , 20 _____ , at _____ o'clock ___ . m., at the offices of the corporation located at _____

_____ .

A quorum of the board of directors was present and at the meeting it was decided, by majority vote, that it is necessary for the corporation to:

Therefore, it is
RESOLVED, that this corporation shall:

The officers of this corporation are hereby authorized to perform all necessary acts to carry out this resolution.

The undersigned, _____ , certifies that he or she is the duly elected secretary of this corporation and that the above is a true and correct copy of the resolution that was duly adopted at a meeting of the board of directors that was held in accordance with state law and the bylaws of the corporation on _____ , 20 _____ .
I further certify that such resolution is now in full force and effect.

Dated: _____ , 20 _____

Corporate Seal

_____
Signature of Secretary of Corporation

_____
Printed Name of Secretary of Corporation

Resolution of Shareholders of _____

A meeting of the shareholders of this corporation was duly called and held on _____ , 20 _____ , at _____ o'clock ____ . m., at the offices of the corporation located at _____ .

A quorum of the shareholders was present, in person or by proxy, and at the meeting it was decided, by majority vote, that it is in the best interests of the corporation that:

Therefore, it is
RESOLVED that this corporation:

The officers of this corporation are hereby authorized to perform all necessary acts to carry out this resolution.

The undersigned, _____ , certifies that he or she is the duly elected secretary of this corporation and that the above is a true and correct copy of the resolution that was duly adopted at a meeting of the shareholders that was held in accordance with state law and the bylaws of the corporation on _____ , 20 _____ . I further certify that such resolution is now in full force and effect.

Dated: _____ , 20 _____

Corporate Seal

_____
Signature of Secretary of Corporation

_____
Printed Name of Secretary of Corporation

Consent Resolutions

Any of the resolution forms that are contained in this chapter can easily be adapted for use as consent resolutions. First, however, it must be verified that the bylaws of the corporation allow the use of consent resolutions for directors and shareholders. The bylaws that are presented in this book contain the following clauses which allow consent resolutions to be used:

> [*For shareholders*]
>
> **Any action which may be taken at a shareholders meeting may be taken instead without a meeting if a resolution is consented to, in writing, by all shareholders who would be entitled to vote on the matter.**
>
> [*For directors*]
>
> **Any action which may be taken at a directors meeting may be taken instead without a meeting if a resolution is consented to, in writing, by all directors.**

> ⊘ **Definition:**
>
> **Consent Resolution:**
> This type of resolution allows decisions to be made without requiring face-to-face meetings of either directors or shareholders of corporations.

If you are operating under different bylaws, be certain that your bylaws contain a substantially similar authorization for consent resolutions.

The use of consent resolutions allows for a much greater flexibility in the management of corporations. Formal meetings are not necessary, although for many issues, meetings may be highly recommended as a method to record the remarks and positions of board members or shareholders who may oppose the action. Consent resolutions are most useful in those situations where the board of directors or number of shareholders is small and all of the directors or shareholders are in complete agreement regarding the action to be taken.

In order to adapt the standard resolutions in this and other chapters of this book for use as consent resolutions, simply alter the form in the following three ways (substitute "shareholders" where appropriate if you are preparing a shareholders consent resolution):

1. Add the word "Consent" to the title, for example:

   Consent Resolution of the Board of Directors of the ABCXYZ Corporation

2. Substitute the following for the first paragraph of the resolution:

   The undersigned, being all of the directors (or shareholders) of this corporation and acting in accordance with state law and the bylaws of this corporation, consent to the adoption of the following as if it was adopted at a duly called meeting of the board of directors (or shareholders) of this corporation. By unanimous consent of the board of directors (or shareholders) of this corporation, it is decided that:

3. Add signature lines for all of the directors (or shareholders) of the corporation. After all of the signatures, insert the following phrase:

   Being all of the directors (or shareholders) of the corporation.

4. Substitute the following for the last paragraph of the resolution:

   The undersigned, _____ , certifies that [he or she] is the duly elected secretary of this corporation and that the above is a true and correct copy of the resolution that was duly adopted by consent of the board of directors (or shareholders) in accordance with state law and the bylaws of the corporation on _____ , 20 ___ . I further certify that such resolution is now in full force and effect.

On the following page, you will find a general Consent Resolution of Board of Directors which has been adapted with these instructions from the general Resolution of Board of Directors form that was shown previously in this chapter.

Consent Resolution of Board of Directors

of _____

The undersigned, being all of the directors of this corporation and acting in accordance with state law and the bylaws of this corporation, consent to the adoption of the following as if it was adopted at a duly called meeting of the board of directors of this corporation. By unanimous consent of the board of directors of this corporation, it is decided that:

Therefore, it is
RESOLVED, that the corporation shall:

The officers of this corporation are hereby authorized to perform all necessary acts to carry out such resolution.

Dated: _____ , 20 _____

Signature of Directors of Corporation/Printed Name of Directors

_____ , _____

_____ , _____

_____ , _____

Being all of the directors of the corporation.

The undersigned, _____ , certifies that he or she is the duly elected secretary of this corporation and that the above is a true and correct copy of the resolution that was duly adopted by consent of the board of directors in accordance with state law and the bylaws of the corporation on _____ , 20 _____ . I further certify that such resolution is now in full force and effect.

Dated: _____ , 20 _____

Corporate Seal

_____
Signature of Secretary of Corporation

_____
Printed Name of Secretary of Corporation

Corporate Stock

Corporate stock represents the money or property that is invested in a corporation. It is a representation of the share of ownership in a corporate business. When a corporation files its Articles of Incorporation with the state, it states how many shares of stock it will be authorized to issue (for example, 500 shares). When the authorized shares are sold or transferred to a shareholder for something of value (money, property, or labor), the shares are said to be "issued and outstanding." All of the authorized shares need not be issued. The ownership of the shares in the corporation is then evidenced by a stock certificate describing the number of shares owned. The value of the shares can be a specific "par" value (for example, $1.00 per share) or they can be "no-par" value, which allows the board of directors to fix the value of the shares by resolution. If the shares are given a par value, the stock must be sold for at least the stated par value. The concept of par value is gradually being eliminated from modern business corporation acts, allowing board of directors discretion to fix the value of the shares. All states allow the use of no-par stock.

An example may best illustrate the use of stock: A corporation is formed and 500 shares of no-par value common stock are authorized in the Articles of Incorporation. Three people will form the initial shareholders of the corporation, with one desiring to own 50 percent of the shares and the other two desiring to own 25 percent each. All three comprise the board of directors. As a board, they decide to issue 300 shares of stock and they decide to fix the value per share at $10.00. Thus, the majority owner will pay the corporation $1,500.00 ($10.00 x 150 shares, or 50 percent of the issued and outstanding shares, *not* 50 percent of the authorized shares). The other two shareholders will pay $750.00 each for 75 shares apiece of the issued shares. The ownership of the shares that have been issued will be represented by stock certificates that will be delivered to each of the owners. The transactions will be recorded in the corporation's stock transfer book.

At the close of these transactions, the corporation will have three shareholders: one with 150 shares of issued and outstanding stock and two with 75 shares each of issued and outstanding stock. The corporation will have $3,000.00 of paid-in capital. Two hundred shares will remain as authorized, but not issued or outstanding. At shareholder meetings, each share of issued and outstanding stock will represent one vote.

The above scenario presents stock ownership at its most basic. The shares described were no-par value common stock. There are many, many variable characteristics that can be given to stock. The forms in this book are based on basic single-class common stock with voting rights. Classes of stock may, however, be created with non-voting attributes, with preferences for dividends, and with many other different characteristics. Most small business corporations can operate efficiently with a single class of common stock with voting rights. There is no requirement that the stock certificate be in a particular format. The stock certificate for use in this book is a simple generic form. If you desire, you may obtain fancy blank stock certificates from most office supply stores, but these are not required. For the issuance of stock, follow the steps shown next in the Corporate Stock Checklist. Each of the steps taken at a meeting of the board of directors must be documented with a board resolution. Also included in this chapter is a page for use in the stock transfer book, which should be included in your basic corporate record book.

> ⊘ **Definition:**
>
> **No-Par Value:**
> Stock with no-par value has no stated value noted on the stock certificate itself.

Corporate Stock Checklist

☐ Designate the number of authorized shares in the Articles of Incorporation and whether they are par or no-par value

☐ At the initial board of directors meeting, determine the number of shares to be issued

☐ If the shares are no-par, determine the value of the shares at the initial board of directors meeting

☐ At a board of directors meeting, determine who will purchase shares and how many will be sold to each person

☐ If necessary, at a board of directors meeting, the board of directors must fix the value of any property that will be accepted in exchange for shares of stock

☐ At a board of directors meeting, authorize officers to issue shares to persons designated

☐ The secretary will then prepare the appropriate stock certificates

☐ If there are restrictions on the transfer of stock, note the restrictions on the back of the certificate

☐ All of the officers of the corporation will sign the certificates

☐ The secretary will receive the money or property from the purchasers and deposit any funds in the corporate bank account

☐ The secretary will issue the certificates and receipts for money or property and record the transaction in the corporate stock transfer book

Certificate Number: _____   Number of Shares: _____

Corporate Stock Certificate

_____

Name of Corporation

A business corporation incorporated
under the laws of the State of: _____

Par Value of Shares: $ _____
Number of Shares Authorized: _____

This Certifies That _____ is the owner
of _____ shares of common stock of this corporation. The shares represented
are fully paid and are non-assessable. The shares represented by this certificate
are only transferable on the official books of the corporation by the holder of this
certificate, in person or by attorney. For transfer, this certificate must be properly
endorsed on the back and surrendered to the corporation. This certificate is signed
by all of the officers of this corporation.

Dated: _____ , 20 _____

_____   _____
Signature of President   Signature of Vice-President

_____   _____
Printed Name of President   Printed Name of Vice-President

_____   _____
Signature of Treasurer   Signature of Secretary

_____   _____
Printed Name of Treasurer   Printed Name of Secretary

For value received, I,

_____ ,

the owner of this certificate, transfer the number of shares represented by this certificate to

_____ ,

and I instruct the secretary of this corporation to record this transfer on the books of the corporation. Any restrictions on the transfer of these shares are shown below.

Dated: _____ , 20 _____

_____

Signature of Shareholder

_____

Printed Name of Shareholder

Restrictions on Transfer:

Corporate Stock Transfer Book

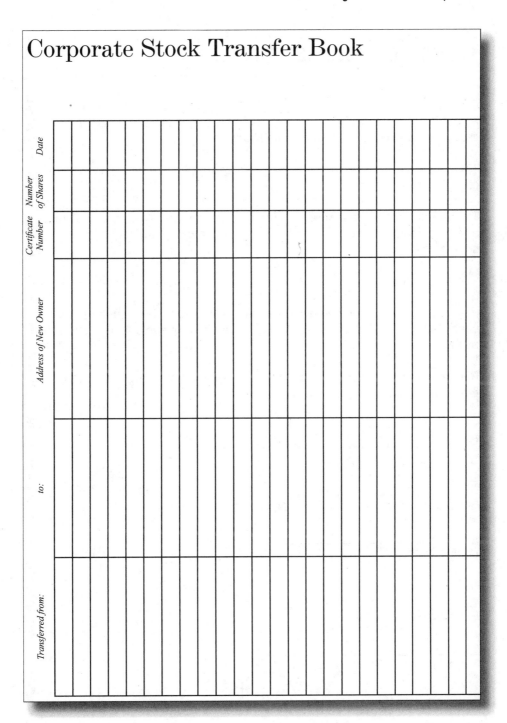

Date	Number of Shares	Certificate Number	Address of New Owner	to:	Transferred from:

Receipt for Stock Certificate of _____

On this date, _____ , 20 _____ , a shareholder in this corporation has purchased _____ shares of common stock in this corporation, represented by Stock Certificate Number _____ .

This certificate represents _____ percent (%) of ownership in this corporation.

The shareholder has transferred to the corporation the following assets, with a fair market value of $ _____ in consideration for the receipt of the shares of stock:

Payment in full has been received for these shares and the shares have been issued by the corporation, transferred to the shareholder, and received by the shareholder.

Record of this transaction has been recorded in the Stock Transfer Book of this corporation.

Dated: _____ , 20 _____

Corporate Seal

_____
Signature of Secretary of Corporation

_____
Printed Name of Secretary of Corporation

_____
Signature of Shareholder

_____
Printed Name of Shareholder

Chapter 10

Starting Business as an S-Corporation

Having completed your Business Plan, including the Marketing and Financial Plans, you are ready to begin to understand, in detail, the type of business entity that you have chosen. An S-corporation is a type of corporation that is recognized by the U.S. Internal Revenue Service and is treated differently than other corporations in terms of federal taxation. Some states also recognize S-corporation status for state income taxation purposes; some states do not. The only reason for becoming an S-corporation is to obtain a different method of taxation than other corporations.

For standard corporations, the corporation pays a federal and, perhaps, state corporate tax on the business profits. If the company's after-tax profit is distributed to the shareholders as dividends, the shareholders then pay an additional personal income tax on the dividends. The amount distributed to the shareholders as dividends is not a deduction for the corporation.

S-corporations, on the other hand, are taxed similarly to partnerships for tax purposes. The income, losses, and deductions generated by an S-corporation are "passed through" the corporate entity to the individual shareholders. Thus, there is no "double" taxation of an S-corporation. In addition, unlike a stan-

> **⊘ Definition:**
>
> **S-Corporation:** This is a type of business entity created by Subchapter S of the IRS Code, that provides rules for a type of corporation that is not subject to standard corporate taxation if it meets certain requirements.

dard corporation, shareholders of S-corporations can personally deduct any corporate losses. They act merely as a conduit for passing the income and deductions of the corporation directly to the individual shareholders in much the same manner as partnerships, or even sole proprietorships.

The S-corporation does not pay a corporate tax and files a different type of tax form than does a standard corporation (please see Chapter 15 for more information on taxation of S-corporations). Taxation of the profits of the S-corporation falls to the individuals who own shares in the corporation. This also allows for each individual shareholder to personally deduct their share of any corporate losses, as well as claim their share of S-corporation income personally.

> **⚡ Warning!**
>
> You must meet every single one of the IRS requirements in order to obtain the preferential tax treatment for your S-corporation.

As the purpose of an S-corporation is to allow small corporations to choose to be taxed, at the federal level, like a partnership, but to also enjoy many of the benefits of a corporation, S-corporations are, in many respects, similar to limited liability companies. The main difference lies in the rules that a company needs to meet in order to qualify as an S-corporation under federal law. (Note that there are also other differences between S-corporations and limited liability companies).

There are certain basic requirements for qualifying a corporation with the IRS for S-corporation status. Every requirement must be met before the IRS will recognize S-corporation status and allow for the different tax treatment.

- The corporation must have no more than 100 shareholders. (Wives and husbands, and/or immediate family members, even if they own stock separately, are considered as only one shareholder)

- Each of the corporation's shareholders must be a natural person or the estate of a natural person. Corporations and partnerships may not hold shares in the corporation. Each shareholder must also be a citizen or resident of the United States

- The corporation must have only one class of stock that is issued and outstanding. The corporation may have other classes of stock that are authorized, providing no shares are issued. Different voting rights within a class of stock (ie., voting and nonvoting) do not disqualify the corporation

- The corporation must already be incorporated in the United States or one of its possessions. Financial institutions, foreign corporations, and certain other very specialized corporations are not eligible

- The corporation must not have been qualified as an S-corporation within the previous five years. This restriction prevents abrupt shifting from one type of corporation to another in order to obtain the maximum tax benefits

- The corporation has a calendar tax year or has been approved by the IRS to have a tax year ending other than on December 31

- All shareholders consent to the election of S-corporation status on IRS Form 2553: Election by a Small Business Corporation which must then be filed with the IRS

If your corporation meets all of these requirements, S-corporation status may be elected. It may be prudent to obtain the advice of a competent accountant prior to making the election, however. The actual steps in electing S-corporation status are detailed at the end of this chapter in the S-Corporation Checklist. Please note that IRS Form 2553: Election by a Small Business Corporation is also provided on the enclosed Forms-on-CD. These forms and all other IRS forms can also easily be downloaded from the IRS website: www.irs.gov/formspubs/index.html

The steps in starting business as an S-Corporation are noted on the following checklist. After that are found Minutes of the First Shareholders Meeting for an S-Corporation and a Resolution of Shareholders Regarding S-Corporation Status. You will complete all of the steps for starting business as a corporation that were noted in Chapter 9, except for the first meeting of the shareholders. At that meeting you should use the minutes in this chapter and the checklist as your blueprint for qualifying as an S-corporation.

> **:ᵠ:Toolkit Tip!**
> You should prepare a pre-incorporation worksheet (from Chapter 9 regarding standard corporations) for your S-corporation.

S-Corporation Checklist

☐ Determine that the corporation has fewer than 100 shareholders

☐ Determine that all shareholders are natural persons or estates

☐ Determine that the corporation has only one class of stock issued and out standing

☐ Determine that the corporation is already incorporated in the U.S or in one of its possessions

☐ Determine that the corporation hasn't had "S" status within the past five years

☐ Determine that all of the other requirements noted on the latest version of the instructions for IRS Tax Form 2553 have been met

☐ Complete all of the forms for starting a standard corporation in Chapter 9, except for the First Meeting of the Shareholders

☐ At the first shareholders meeting, a resolution consenting to the election to be treated as an S-corporation must be presented and approved by all shareholders of record

☐ A shareholders resolution consenting to the election to be treated as an S-corporation should be signed by all shareholders of record

☐ All shareholders of record must sign IRS Form 2553: Election by a Small Business Corporation

☐ The secretary of the corporation should complete IRS Form 2553: Election by a Small Business Corporation no more than 2 months and 15 days after the beginning of the tax year in which the election will take place or any time in the year preceding the tax year in which the election is to take effect

Minutes of First Shareholders Meeting of S-Corporation

The first meeting of the shareholders of this corporation was held on _____ ,
20 ____ , at _____ o'clock ____ . m., at the offices of the corporation located at
_____ .

Present were:

_____ , President
_____ , Vice-President
_____ , Treasurer
_____ , Secretary

Other than shareholders of this corporation, the following persons were also
present:

_____
_____
_____

1. The president of this corporation called the meeting to order. The president
   determined that a quorum was present, either in person or by proxy, and
   that the meeting could conduct business.

   The following shareholders were present in person:

Name of Shareholder/Number of Shares

_____
_____
_____
_____
_____

   The following shareholders were represented by proxy:

Name of Shareholder/Number of Shares

_____
_____
_____
_____
_____

2. The secretary reported that notice of the meeting had been properly given or waived by each shareholder in accordance with the bylaws.

Upon motion made and carried, the secretary was ordered to attach the appropriate Affidavit of Mailing of Notice or Waiver of Notice to the minutes of this meeting.

3. _____ was then elected chairperson of this meeting.

4. The secretary read the minutes of the first meeting of the board of directors of this corporation which was held on _____ , 20 ____ .

Upon motion made and carried, the shareholders
RESOLVED that:

All acts taken and decisions made at the first meeting of the board of directors of this corporation are approved and ratified, specifically that the shareholders approve and ratify the adoption of the bylaws of this corporation and that the shareholders approve and ratify the election of the following persons as officers for the terms as stated in the minutes of the first meeting of the board of directors:

_____ , President
_____ , Vice-President
_____ , Treasurer
_____ , Secretary

5. Upon motion made and carried, the shareholders
RESOLVED that:

The following persons are designated as the initial directors of this corporation in the Articles of Incorporation and the shareholders approve and ratify this designation of the following persons as directors of this corporation until the first annual meeting of the shareholders of this corporation:

_____ , Director
_____ , Director
_____ , Director

6. Upon motion made and carried, the following resolution was approved unanimously by the shareholders of all outstanding shares of the corporation:

RESOLVED that:

This corporation elects to be treated and taxed as an S-Corporation under IRS Code Section 1362.

The president declared that this shareholders resolution was duly adopted.

7. The following other business was transacted:

There being no further business, upon motion made and carried, the meeting was adjourned.

Dated: _____ , 20 _____

Corporate Seal

_____
Signature of Secretary of Corporation

_____
Printed Name of Secretary of Corporation

Resolution of Shareholders Regarding S-Corpration Status

A meeting of the shareholders of this corporation was duly called and held on _____ , 20 _____ , at _____ o'clock ____ . m., at the offices of the corporation located at _____ .

All of the shareholders of this corporation were present, in person or by proxy.

At the meeting it was decided, by unanimous vote, that it is in the best interests of the corporation that the corporation elect to be treated as an S-corporation under the provisions of IRS Code Section 1362.

Therefore, it is unanimously
RESOLVED, that this corporation elects to be treated as an S-corporation under the provisions of IRS Code Section 1362. The officers of this corporation are hereby authorized to perform all necessary acts to carry out this resolution.

The undersigned, _____ , certifies that he or she is the duly elected secretary of this corporation and that the above is a true and correct copy of the resolution that was duly adopted at a meeting of the shareholders that was held in accordance with state law and the bylaws of the corporation on _____ , 20 _____ . I further certify that such resolution is now in full force and effect.

Dated: _____ , 20 _____

Corporate Seal

_____
Signature of Secretary of Corporation

_____
Printed Name of Secretary of Corporation

Signature of Shareholder/Printed Name of Shareholder

_____ , _____
_____ , _____
_____ , _____
_____ , _____
_____ , _____
_____ , _____

Being all of the shareholders of this corporation.

Form **2553**
(Rev. December 2007)
Department of the Treasury
Internal Revenue Service

Election by a Small Business Corporation
(Under section 1362 of the Internal Revenue Code)
▶ See Parts II and III on page 3 and the separate instructions.
▶ The corporation can fax this form to the IRS (see separate instructions).

OMB No. 1545-0146

Note. This election to be an S corporation can be accepted only if all the tests are met under **Who May Elect** on page 1 of the instructions; all shareholders have signed the consent statement; an officer has signed below; and the exact name and address of the corporation and other required form information are provided.

Part I	Election Information

Type or Print

Name (see instructions)	**A** Employer identification number
Number, street, and room or suite no. (If a P.O. box, see instructions.)	**B** Date incorporated
City or town, state, and ZIP code	**C** State of incorporation

D Check the applicable box(es) if the corporation, after applying for the EIN shown in **A** above, changed its ☐ name or ☐ address

E Election is to be effective for tax year beginning (month, day, year) (see instructions) . . . . . ▶ ____/____/____

Caution. A corporation (entity) making the election for its first tax year in existence will usually enter the beginning date of a short tax year that begins on a date other than January 1.

F Selected tax year:

(1) ☐ Calendar year

(2) ☐ Fiscal year ending (month and day) ▶ _____

(3) ☐ 52-53-week year ending with reference to the month of December

(4) ☐ 52-53-week year ending with reference to the month of ▶ _____

If box (2) or (4) is checked, complete Part II

G If more than 100 shareholders are listed for item J (see page 2), check this box if treating members of a family as one shareholder results in no more than 100 shareholders (see test 2 under **Who May Elect** in the instructions) ▶ ☐

H Name and title of officer or legal representative who the IRS may call for more information

I Telephone number of officer or legal representative
( )

If this S corporation election is being filed with Form 1120S, I declare that I had reasonable cause for not filing Form 2553 timely, and if this election is made by an entity eligible to elect to be treated as a corporation, I declare that I also had reasonable cause for not filing an entity classification election timely. See below for my explanation of the reasons the election or elections were not made on time (see instructions).

Sign Here

Under penalties of perjury, I declare that I have examined this election, including accompanying schedules and statements, and to the best of my knowledge and belief, it is true, correct, and complete.

▶ _____   _____   _____
Signature of officer   Title   Date

For Paperwork Reduction Act Notice, see separate instructions.   Cat. No. 18629R   Form **2553** (Rev. 12-2007)

Form 2553 (Rev. 12-2007)

Page **2**

Part I — Election Information (continued)

J Name and address of each shareholder or former shareholder required to consent to the election. (See the instructions for column K.)	K Shareholders' Consent Statement. Under penalties of perjury, we declare that we consent to the election of the above-named corporation to be an S corporation under section 1362(a) and that we have examined this consent statement, including accompanying schedules and statements, and to the best of our knowledge and belief, it is true, correct, and complete. We understand our consent is binding and may not be withdrawn after the corporation has made a valid election. (Sign and date below.)		L Stock owned or percentage of ownership (see instructions)		M Social security number or employer identification number (see instructions)	N Shareholder's tax year ends (month and day)
	Signature	Date	Number of shares or percentage of ownership	Date(s) acquired		

Form **2553** (Rev. 12-2007)

Form 2553 (Rev. 12-2007)   Page **3**

Part II   **Selection of Fiscal Tax Year** (see instructions)

Note. All corporations using this part must complete item O and item P, Q, or R.

O   Check the applicable box to indicate whether the corporation is:

    1. ☐   A new corporation **adopting** the tax year entered in item F, Part I.

    2. ☐   An existing corporation **retaining** the tax year entered in item F, Part I.

    3. ☐   An existing corporation **changing** to the tax year entered in item F, Part I.

P   Complete item P if the corporation is using the automatic approval provisions of Rev. Proc. 2006-46, 2006-45 I.R.B. 859, to request **(1)** a natural business year (as defined in section 5.07 of Rev. Proc. 2006-46) or **(2)** a year that satisfies the ownership tax year test (as defined in section 5.08 of Rev. Proc. 2006-46). Check the applicable box below to indicate the representation statement the corporation is making.

    1. Natural Business Year ► ☐   I represent that the corporation is adopting, retaining, or changing to a tax year that qualifies as its natural business year (as defined in section 5.07 of Rev. Proc. 2006-46) and has attached a statement showing separately for each month the gross receipts for the most recent 47 months (see instructions). I also represent that the corporation is not precluded by section 4.02 of Rev. Proc. 2006-46 from obtaining automatic approval of such adoption, retention, or change in tax year.

    2. Ownership Tax Year ► ☐   I represent that shareholders (as described in section 5.08 of Rev. Proc. 2006-46) holding more than half of the shares of the stock (as of the first day of the tax year to which the request relates) of the corporation have the same tax year or are concurrently changing to the tax year that the corporation adopts, retains, or changes to per item F, Part I, and that such tax year satisfies the requirement of section 4.01(3) of Rev. Proc. 2006-46. I also represent that the corporation is not precluded by section 4.02 of Rev. Proc. 2006-46 from obtaining automatic approval of such adoption, retention, or change in tax year.

Note. If you do not use item P and the corporation wants a fiscal tax year, complete either item Q or R below. Item Q is used to request a fiscal tax year based on a business purpose and to make a back-up section 444 election. Item R is used to make a regular section 444 election.

Q   Business Purpose—To request a fiscal tax year based on a business purpose, check box Q1. See instructions for details including payment of a user fee. You may also check box Q2 and/or box Q3.

    1. Check here ► ☐   if the fiscal year entered in item F, Part I, is requested under the prior approval provisions of Rev. Proc. 2002-39, 2002-22 I.R.B. 1046. Attach to Form 2553 a statement describing the relevant facts and circumstances and, if applicable, the gross receipts from sales and services necessary to establish a business purpose. See the instructions for details regarding the gross receipts from sales and services. If the IRS proposes to disapprove the requested fiscal year, do you want a conference with the IRS National Office?

    ☐ Yes   ☐ No

    2. Check here ► ☐   to show that the corporation intends to make a back-up section 444 election in the event the corporation's business purpose request is not approved by the IRS. (See instructions for more information.)

    3. Check here ► ☐   to show that the corporation agrees to adopt or change to a tax year ending December 31 if necessary for the IRS to accept this election for S corporation status in the event (1) the corporation's business purpose request is not approved and the corporation makes a back-up section 444 election, but is ultimately not qualified to make a section 444 election, or (2) the corporation's business purpose request is not approved and the corporation did not make a back-up section 444 election.

R   Section 444 Election—To make a section 444 election, check box R1. You may also check box R2.

    1. Check here ► ☐   to show that the corporation will make, if qualified, a section 444 election to have the fiscal tax year shown in item F, Part I. To make the election, you must complete **Form 8716**, Election To Have a Tax Year Other Than a Required Tax Year, and either attach it to Form 2553 or file it separately.

    2. Check here ► ☐   to show that the corporation agrees to adopt or change to a tax year ending December 31 if necessary for the IRS to accept this election for S corporation status in the event the corporation is ultimately not qualified to make a section 444 election.

Part III   **Qualified Subchapter S Trust (QSST) Election Under Section 1361(d)(2)***

Income beneficiary's name and address	Social security number
Trust's name and address	**Employer identification number**

Date on which stock of the corporation was transferred to the trust (month, day, year)   . . . . ►   /   /

In order for the trust named above to be a QSST and thus a qualifying shareholder of the S corporation for which this Form 2553 is filed, I hereby make the election under section 1361(d)(2). Under penalties of perjury, I certify that the trust meets the definitional requirements of section 1361(d)(3) and that all other information provided in Part III is true, correct, and complete.

_____   _____
Signature of income beneficiary or signature and title of legal representative or other qualified person making the election   Date

*Use Part III to make the QSST election only if stock of the corporation has been transferred to the trust on or before the date on which the corporation makes its election to be an S corporation. The QSST election must be made and filed separately if stock of the corporation is transferred to the trust **after** the date on which the corporation makes the S election.

                      ✿   **Printed on recycled paper**   Form **2553** (Rev. 12-2007)

Instructions for Form 2553

Department of the Treasury
Internal Revenue Service

(Rev. December 2007)
Election by a Small Business Corporation

Section references are to the Internal Revenue Code unless otherwise noted.

What's New

For tax years ending on or after December 31, 2007, certain corporations (entities) with reasonable cause for not timely filing Form 2553 can request to have the form treated as timely filed by filing Form 2553 as an attachment to Form 1120S, U.S. Income Tax Return for an S Corporation. An entry space for an explanation of reasonable cause was added to page 1 of the form. See *Relief for Late Elections.*

General Instructions

Purpose of Form

A corporation or other entity eligible to elect to be treated as a corporation must use Form 2553 to make an election under section 1362(a) to be an S corporation. An entity eligible to elect to be treated as a corporation that meets certain tests discussed below will be treated as a corporation as of the effective date of the S corporation election and does not need to file Form 8832, Entity Classification Election.

The income of an S corporation generally is taxed to the shareholders of the corporation rather than to the corporation itself. However, an S corporation may still owe tax on certain income. For details, see *Tax and Payments* in the Instructions for Form 1120S.

Who May Elect

A corporation or other entity eligible to elect to be treated as a corporation may elect to be an S corporation only if it meets all the following tests.

1. It is (a) a domestic corporation, or (b) a domestic entity eligible to elect to be treated as a corporation, that timely files Form 2553 and meets all the other tests listed below. If Form 2553 is not timely filed, see *Relief for Late Elections* on page 2.

2. It has no more than 100 shareholders. You can treat a husband and wife (and their estates) as one shareholder for this test. You can also treat all members of a family (as defined in section 1361(c)(1)(B)) and their estates as one shareholder for this test. For additional situations in which certain entities will be treated as members of a family, see Notice 2005-91, 2005-51 I.R.B. 1164. All others are treated as separate shareholders. For details, see section 1361(c)(1).

3. Its only shareholders are individuals, estates, exempt organizations described in section 401(a) or 501(c)(3), or certain trusts described in section 1361(c)(2)(A).

For information about the section 1361(d)(2) election to be a qualified subchapter S trust (QSST), see the instructions for Part III. For information about the section 1361(e)(3) election to be an electing small business trust (ESBT), see Regulations section 1.1361-1(m). For guidance on how to convert a QSST to an ESBT, see Regulations section 1.1361-1(j)(12). If these elections were not timely made, see Rev. Proc. 2003-43, 2003-23 I.R.B. 998.

4. It has no nonresident alien shareholders.

5. It has only one class of stock (disregarding differences in voting rights). Generally, a corporation is treated as having only one class of stock if all outstanding shares of the corporation's stock confer identical rights to distribution and liquidation proceeds. See Regulations section 1.1361-1(l) for details.

6. It is not one of the following ineligible corporations.

   a. A bank or thrift institution that uses the reserve method of accounting for bad debts under section 585.

   b. An insurance company subject to tax under subchapter L of the Code.

   c. A corporation that has elected to be treated as a possessions corporation under section 936.

   d. A domestic international sales corporation (DISC) or former DISC.

7. It has or will adopt or change to one of the following tax years.

   a. A tax year ending December 31.

   b. A natural business year.

   c. An ownership tax year.

   d. A tax year elected under section 444.

   e. A 52-53-week tax year ending with reference to a year listed above.

   f. Any other tax year (including a 52-53-week tax year) for which the corporation establishes a business purpose.

   For details on making a section 444 election or requesting a natural business, ownership, or other business purpose tax year, see the instructions for Part II.

8. Each shareholder consents as explained in the instructions for column K.

See sections 1361, 1362, and 1378, and their related regulations for additional information on the above tests.

A parent S corporation can elect to treat an eligible wholly-owned subsidiary as a qualified subchapter S subsidiary. If the election is made, the subsidiary's assets, liabilities, and items of income, deduction, and credit generally are treated as those of the parent. For details, see Form 8869, Qualified Subchapter S Subsidiary Election.

When To Make the Election

Complete and file Form 2553:
• No more than two months and 15 days after the beginning of the tax year the election is to take effect, or
• At any time during the tax year preceding the tax year it is to take effect.

For this purpose, the 2 month period begins on the day of the month the tax year begins and ends with the close of the day before the numerically corresponding day of the second calendar month following that month. If there is no corresponding day, use the close of the last day of the calendar month.

Example 1. No prior tax year. A calendar year small business corporation begins its first tax year on January 7. The two month period ends March 6 and 15 days after that is March 21. To be an S corporation beginning with its first tax year, the corporation must file Form 2553 during the period that begins January 7 and ends March 21. Because

Cat. No. 49978N

The Business Start-Up Toolkit

The type and rule above prints on all proofs including departmental reproduction proofs. MUST be removed before printing.

the corporation had no prior tax year, an election made before January 7 will not be valid.

Example 2. Prior tax year. A calendar year small business corporation has been filing Form 1120 as a C corporation but wishes to make an S election for its next tax year beginning January 1. The two month period ends February 28 (29 in leap years) and 15 days after that is March 15. To be an S corporation beginning with its next tax year, the corporation must file Form 2553 during the period that begins the first day (January 1) of its last year as a C corporation and ends March 15th of the year it wishes to be an S corporation. Because the corporation had a prior tax year, it can make the election at any time during that prior tax year.

Example 3. Tax year less than 2 1/2 months. A calendar year small business corporation begins its first tax year on November 8. The two month period ends January 7 and 15 days after that is January 22. To be an S corporation beginning with its short tax year, the corporation must file Form 2553 during the period that begins November 8 and ends January 22. Because the corporation had no prior tax year, an election made before November 8 will not be valid.

Relief for Late Elections

A late election to be an S corporation generally is effective for the tax year following the tax year beginning on the date entered on line E of Form 2553. However, relief for a late election may be available if the corporation can show that the failure to file on time was due to reasonable cause.

To request relief for a late election when the tax year beginning on the date entered on line E ends on or after December 31, 2007, a corporation that meets the following requirements can explain the reasonable cause in the designated space on page 1 of Form 2553.
• The corporation fails to qualify to elect to be an S corporation (see *Who May Elect* on page 1) solely because of the failure to timely file Form 2553.
• The corporation has reasonable cause for its failure to timely file Form 2553.
• The corporation has not filed a tax return for the tax year beginning on the date entered on line E of Form 2553.
• The corporation files Form 2553 as an attachment to Form 1120S no later than 6 months after the due date of Form 1120S (excluding extensions) for the tax year beginning on the date entered on line E of Form 2553.
• No taxpayer whose tax liability or tax return would be affected by the S corporation election (including all shareholders of the S corporation) has reported inconsistently with the S corporation election on any affected return for the tax year beginning on the date entered on line E of Form 2553.
Similar relief is available for an entity eligible to elect to be treated as a corporation (see the instructions for Form 8832) electing to be treated as a corporation as of the date entered on line E of Form 2553. For more details, see Rev. Proc. 2007-62, 2007-41 I.R.B. 786.

To request relief for a late election when the above requirements are not met, the corporation generally must request a private letter ruling and pay a user fee in accordance with Rev. Proc. 2008-1, 2008-1 I.R.B. 1 (or its successor). However, the ruling and user fee requirements may not apply if relief is available under the following revenue procedures.
• If an entity eligible to elect to be treated as a corporation (a) failed to timely file Form 2553, and (b) has not elected to be treated as a corporation, see Rev. Proc. 2004-48, 2004-32 I.R.B. 172.
• If a corporation failed to timely file Form 2553, see Rev. Proc. 2003-43, 2003-23 I.R.B. 998.

• If Form 1120S was filed without an S corporation election and neither the corporation nor any shareholder was notified by the IRS of any problem with the S corporation status within 6 months after the return was timely filed, see Rev. Proc. 97-48, 1997-43 I.R.B. 19.

Where To File

Generally, send the original election (no photocopies) or fax it to the Internal Revenue Service Center listed below. If the corporation files this election by fax, keep the original Form 2553 with the corporation's permanent records. However, certain late elections can be filed attached to Form 1120S. See *Relief for Late Elections* above.

If the corporation's principal business, office, or agency is located in:	Use the following address or fax number:
Connecticut, Delaware, District of Columbia, Illinois, Indiana, Kentucky, Maine, Maryland, Massachusetts, Michigan, New Hampshire, New Jersey, New York, North Carolina, Ohio, Pennsylvania, Rhode Island, South Carolina, Vermont, Virginia, West Virginia, Wisconsin	Department of the Treasury Internal Revenue Service Center Cincinnati, OH 45999 Fax: (859) 669-5748
Alabama, Alaska, Arizona, Arkansas, California, Colorado, Florida, Georgia, Hawaii, Idaho, Iowa, Kansas, Louisiana, Minnesota, Mississippi, Missouri, Montana, Nebraska, Nevada, New Mexico, North Dakota, Oklahoma, Oregon, South Dakota, Tennessee, Texas, Utah, Washington, Wyoming	Department of the Treasury Internal Revenue Service Center Ogden, UT 84201 Fax: (801) 620-7116

Acceptance or Nonacceptance of Election

The service center will notify the corporation if its election is accepted and when it will take effect. The corporation will also be notified if its election is not accepted. The corporation should generally receive a determination on its election within 60 days after it has filed Form 2553. If box Q1 in Part II is checked, the corporation will receive a ruling letter from the IRS that either approves or denies the selected tax year. When box Q1 is checked, it will generally take an additional 90 days for the Form 2553 to be accepted.

Care should be exercised to ensure that the IRS receives the election. If the corporation is not notified of acceptance or nonacceptance of its election within 2 months of the date of filing (date faxed or mailed), or within 5 months if box Q1 is checked, take follow-up action by calling 1-800-829-4933.

If the IRS questions whether Form 2553 was filed, an acceptable proof of filing is (a) a certified or registered mail receipt (timely postmarked) from the U.S. Postal Service, or its equivalent from a designated private delivery service (see Notice 2004-83, 2004-52 I.R.B. 1030 (or its successor)); (b) Form 2553 with an accepted stamp; (c) Form 2553 with a stamped IRS received date; or (d) an IRS letter stating that Form 2553 has been accepted.

-2-

The type and rule above prints on all proofs including departmental reproduction proofs. MUST be removed before printing.

 Do not file Form 1120S for any tax year before the year the election takes effect. If the corporation is now required to file Form 1120, U.S. Corporation Income Tax Return, or any other applicable tax return, continue filing it until the election takes effect.

End of Election

Once the election is made, it stays in effect until it is terminated or revoked. IRS consent generally is required for another election by the corporation (or a successor corporation) on Form 2553 for any tax year before the 5th tax year after the first tax year in which the termination or revocation took effect. See Regulations section 1.1362-5 for details.

Specific Instructions

Part I

Name and Address

Enter the corporation's true name as stated in the corporate charter or other legal document creating it. If the corporation's mailing address is the same as someone else's, such as a shareholder's, enter "C/O" and this person's name following the name of the corporation. Include the suite, room, or other unit number after the street address. If the Post Office does not deliver to the street address and the corporation has a P.O. box, show the box number instead of the street address. If the corporation changed its name or address after applying for its employer identification number, be sure to check the box in item D of Part I.

Item A. Employer Identification Number (EIN)

Enter the corporation's EIN. If the corporation does not have an EIN, it must apply for one. An EIN can be applied for:
• Online–Click on the EIN link at *www.irs.gov/businesses/small*. The EIN is issued immediately once the application information is validated.
• By telephone at 1-800-829-4933.
• By mailing or faxing Form SS-4, Application for Employer Identification Number.

If the corporation has not received its EIN by the time the return is due, enter "Applied For" and the date you applied in the space for the EIN. For more details, see the Instructions for Form SS-4.

Item E. Effective Date of Election

 Form 2553 generally must be filed no later than 2 months and 15 days after the date entered for item E. For details and exceptions, see When To Make the Election *on page 1.*

A corporation (or entity eligible to elect to be treated as a corporation) making the election effective for its first tax year in existence should enter the earliest of the following dates: (a) the date the corporation (entity) first had shareholders (owners), (b) the date the corporation (entity) first had assets, or (c) the date the corporation (entity) began doing business.

 When the corporation (entity) is making the election for its first tax year in existence, it will usually enter the beginning date of a tax year that begins on a date other than January 1.

A corporation (entity) not making the election for its first tax year in existence that is keeping its current tax year should enter the beginning date of the first tax year for which it wants the election to be effective.

A corporation (entity) not making the election for its first tax year in existence that is changing its tax year and wants to be an S corporation for the short tax year needed to switch tax years should enter the beginning date of the short tax year. If the corporation (entity) does not want to be an S corporation for this short tax year, it should enter the beginning date of the tax year following this short tax year and file Form 1128, Application To Adopt, Change, or Retain a Tax Year. If this change qualifies as an automatic approval request (Form 1128, Part II), file Form 1128 as an attachment to Form 2553. If this change qualifies as a ruling request (Form 1128, Part III), file Form 1128 separately. If filing Form 1128, enter "Form 1128" on the dotted line to the left of the entry space for item E.

Item F

Check the box that corresponds with the S corporation's selected tax year. If box (2) or (4) is checked, provide the additional information about the tax year, and complete Part II of the form.

Signature

Form 2553 must be signed and dated by the president, vice president, treasurer, assistant treasurer, chief accounting officer, or any other corporate officer (such as tax officer) authorized to sign.

If Form 2553 is not signed, it will not be considered timely filed.

Column K. Shareholders' Consent Statement

For an election filed before the effective date entered for item E, only shareholders who own stock on the day the election is made need to consent to the election.

For an election filed on or after the effective date entered for item E, all shareholders or former shareholders who owned stock at any time during the period beginning on the effective date entered for item E and ending on the day the election is made must consent to the election.

If the corporation timely filed an election, but one or more shareholders did not timely file a consent, see Regulations section 1.1362-6(b)(3)(iii). If the shareholder was a community property spouse who was a shareholder solely because of a state community property law, see Rev. Proc. 2004-35, 2004-23 I.R.B. 1029.

Each shareholder consents by signing and dating either in column K or on a separate consent statement. The following special rules apply in determining who must sign.
• If a husband and wife have a community interest in the stock or in the income from it, both must consent.
• Each tenant in common, joint tenant, and tenant by the entirety must consent.
• A minor's consent is made by the minor, legal representative of the minor, or a natural or adoptive parent of the minor if no legal representative has been appointed.
• The consent of an estate is made by the executor or administrator.
• The consent of an electing small business trust (ESBT) is made by the trustee and, if a grantor trust, the deemed owner. See Regulations section 1.1362-6(b)(2)(iv) for details.
• If the stock is owned by a qualified subchapter S trust (QSST), the deemed owner of the trust must consent.
• If the stock is owned by a trust (other than an ESBT or QSST), the person treated as the shareholder by section 1361(c)(2)(B) must consent.

The Business Start-Up Toolkit

The type and rule above prints on all proofs including departmental reproduction proofs. MUST be removed before printing.

Continuation sheet or separate consent statement. If you need a continuation sheet or use a separate consent statement, attach it to Form 2553. It must contain the name, address, and EIN of the corporation and the information requested in columns J through N of Part I.

Column L

Enter the number of shares of stock each shareholder owns on the date the election is filed and the date(s) the stock was acquired. Enter -0- for any former shareholders listed in column J. An entity without stock, such as a limited liability company (LLC), should enter the percentage of ownership and date(s) acquired.

Column M

Enter the social security number of each individual listed in column J. Enter the EIN of each estate, qualified trust, or exempt organization.

Column N

Enter the month and day that each shareholder's tax year ends. If a shareholder is changing his or her tax year, enter the tax year the shareholder is changing to, and attach an explanation indicating the present tax year and the basis for the change (for example, an automatic revenue procedure or a letter ruling request).

Part II

Complete Part II if you checked box (2) or (4) in Part I, Item F.

Note. Corporations cannot obtain automatic approval of a fiscal year under the natural business year (box P1) or ownership tax year (box P2) provisions if they are under examination, before an appeals (area) office, or before a federal court without meeting certain conditions and attaching a statement to the application. For details, see section 7.03 of Rev. Proc. 2006-46, 2006-45 I.R.B. 859.

Box P1

A corporation that does not have a 47-month period of gross receipts cannot automatically establish a natural business year.

Box Q1

For examples of an acceptable business purpose for requesting a fiscal year, see section 5.02 of Rev. Proc. 2002-39, 2002-22 I.R.B. 1046, and Rev. Rul. 87-57, 1987-2 C.B. 117.

Attach a statement showing the relevant facts and circumstances to establish a business purpose for the requested fiscal year. For details on what is sufficient to establish a business purpose, see section 5.02 of Rev. Proc. 2002-39.

If your business purpose is based on one of the natural business year tests provided in section 5.03 of Rev. Proc. 2002-39, identify which test you are using (the 25% gross receipts, annual business cycle, or seasonal business test). For the 25% gross receipts test, provide a schedule showing the amount of gross receipts for each month for the most recent 47 months. For either the annual business cycle or seasonal business test, provide the gross receipts from sales and services (and inventory costs, if applicable) for each month of the short period, if any, and the three immediately preceding tax years. If the corporation has been in existence for less than three tax years, submit figures for the period of existence.

If you check box Q1, you will be charged a user fee of $3,200 ($1,500 if your request is received before February 2, 2008) (subject to change by Rev. Proc. 2009-1 or its successor). Do not pay the fee when filing Form 2553. The service center will send Form 2553 to the IRS in Washington, DC, who, in turn, will notify the corporation that the fee is due.

Box Q2

If the corporation makes a back-up section 444 election for which it is qualified, then the section 444 election will take effect in the event the business purpose request is not approved. In some cases, the tax year requested under the back-up section 444 election may be different than the tax year requested under business purpose. See Form 8716, Election To Have a Tax Year Other Than a Required Tax Year, for details on making a back-up section 444 election.

Boxes Q3 and R2

If the corporation is not qualified to make the section 444 election after making the item Q2 back-up section 444 election or indicating its intention to make the election in item R1, and therefore it later files a calendar year return, it should write "Section 444 Election Not Made" in the top left corner of the first calendar year Form 1120S it files.

Part III

In Part III, the income beneficiary (or legal representative) of certain qualified subchapter S trusts (QSSTs) may make the QSST election required by section 1361(d)(2). Part III may be used to make the QSST election only if corporate stock has been transferred to the trust on or before the date on which the corporation makes its election to be an S corporation. However, a statement can be used instead of Part III to make the election. If there was an inadvertent failure to timely file a QSST election, see the relief provisions under Rev. Proc. 2003-43.

Note. Use Part III only if you make the election in Part I. Form 2553 cannot be filed with only Part III completed.

The deemed owner of the QSST must also consent to the S corporation election in column K of Form 2553.

Paperwork Reduction Act Notice. We ask for the information on this form to carry out the Internal Revenue laws of the United States. You are required to give us the information. We need it to ensure that you are complying with these laws and to allow us to figure and collect the right amount of tax.

You are not required to provide the information requested on a form that is subject to the Paperwork Reduction Act unless the form displays a valid OMB control number. Books or records relating to a form or its instructions must be retained as long as their contents may become material in the administration of any Internal Revenue law. Generally, tax returns and return information are confidential, as required by section 6103.

The time needed to complete and file this form will depend on individual circumstances. The estimated average time is:

Recordkeeping . . . . 9 hr., 48 min.

Learning about the law or the form . . . . 2 hr., 33 min.

Preparing, copying, assembling, and sending the form to the IRS . . . . 4 hr., 1 min.

If you have comments concerning the accuracy of these time estimates or suggestions for making this form simpler, we would be happy to hear from you. You can write to Internal Revenue Service, Tax Products Coordinating Committee, SE:W:CAR:MP:T:T:SP, 1111 Constitution Ave. NW, IR-6526, Washington, DC 20224. Do not send the form to this address. Instead, see *Where To File* on page 2.

-4-

242

Chapter 11

Starting Business as a Limited Liability Company

Limited liability companies are a relatively new form of business organization, first recognized in the United States by the state of Wyoming in 1977. Since then, legislation has been enacted in all 50 states and the District of Columbia (Washington D.C.) to allow businesses to organize as limited liability companies. A limited liability company is a separate legal entity, as is a corporation. The business structure is actually a hybrid type of business entity—between a corporation and a partnership. It is organized in a fashion similar, but not identical, to that of corporations. It also offers owners the limits on personal liability that were previously available only to shareholders in corporations. Like the shareholders of a corporation, the *members* (or owners) are not liable for the debts and obligations of the company beyond their actual contributions to the company. In addition, in most cases, if the company is organized properly, it is taxed at the federal level as a partnership, or even possibly as a sole proprietorship. This means that there will only be one level of taxation. The profits and losses of the company are passed through to the individual owners, in the same manner as in the taxation of partnerships. Corporations, on the other hand, are subject to a double taxation—first at the corporate level and then at the individual level—after corporate profits in the form of dividends are passed on to shareholders.

> **⊘ Definition:**
>
> **Members:**
> The owners of a limited liability company, equivalent to shareholders in a corporation.

Another flexibility that limited liability companies are afforded is the ability to distribute profits and losses to its members in any proportion that they choose. For common corporations, this flexibility is not present. Shareholders in corporations do not share directly in the profits or losses of the corporation. They only receive dividends if so decided by the directors of the corporation. S-type corporations pass their profits and losses through to the shareholders, but are generally restricted to dividing the profits and losses on the basis of percentage of ownership of each individual shareholder. Limited liability companies have the greater flexibility to choose to distribute their profits and losses in any manner that they wish, regardless of the percentage of ownership of the members. There are a few restrictions on such distributions, however, if a limited liability company is to be treated as a partnership for Federal tax purposes. They must abide by two particular partnership distribution rules: that the distribution allocations must have some "substantial economic" relation to the actual economic risks or rewards of the members and that the members may be subject to income tax on their contribution of future services to the limited liability company. If you wish for the manner in which your limited liability company distributes its profits and losses to its members to deviate far from the actual proportionate contributions of its members, a competent tax professional should be consulted to avoid any problems.

Toolkit Tip!

Limited liability companies are subject to certain state default rules unless the company chooses to alter how those rules impact the company.

The limited liability company also offers management possibilities that are more flexible than those of either corporations or limited partnerships. These unique characteristics make this form of business operation one of the fastest growing forms of organization. Many of the actual operational characteristics of limited liability companies are set by what are termed *default rules*, which are rules that are set by statute in each state. A default rule is essentially a rule that governs the affairs of the company, *unless* the rule has officially been changed by the company in its official documents. Thus, in all states, there are certain rules that will govern the limited liability company but there is also, in all states, a manner by which a limited liability company can change these rules. Thus, by creatively using the formation and operating documents of the limited liability company, members can choose to operate the limited liability company in a wide variety of manners. How these default rules come into play as you plan your limited liability company will be examined below.

Organization of a Limited Liability Company

Limited liability companies are, in some ways, organized in a manner similar to corporations. The shareholders of a corporation have their counterpart in limited liability companies as its *members*. These members are the owners of the company, in much the same way that shareholders are the actual owners of a corporation. Most states now allow a limited liability company to be formed by one member, and that member need not always be a natural person. *Note*: One-member limited liability companies are generally taxed as sole proprietorships, not partnerships. One of the management capabilities of a limited liability company is that the members may choose to manage the company themselves or they can select managers to manage the company. Most states have a default rule that the members are the managers of the company. This is unlike corporations, in which the shareholders elect the directors, who, in turn select the officers of the corporation, who then manage the company. In limited liability companies, the members may either remain as the managers or they can select managers to run the company. If management is desired by managers, these managers may either be members of the limited liability company or they can be nonmembers. In addition, the managers of a limited liability company need not necessarily be *natural* (actual) persons, unlike the requirement that corporate directors must be natural persons. This affords the limited liability company a flexibility of management styles that is not available in other forms of business.

> ⏻ **Definition:**
>
> **Articles of Organization:** This document contains the formal rules that govern the operation of a limited liability company. They are equivalent to the Articles of Incorporation of a corporation.

Articles of Organization

Similar to a corporation, there are two initial forms that outline the actual operation of the limited liability company. The first form is known in most states as the Articles of Organization. A few states refer to this central organizing document by another name: for instance, the state of Washington calls it a Certificate of Formation. For ease of understanding, the title "Articles of Organization" will be used throughout this book. Please check the Appendix on the enclosed CD to verify the particular usage in your own state. This form parallels, in many ways, the function of the Articles of Incorporation of the business corporation. Its function is to provide the state with information regarding the framework of the business. All states require that it be filed, generally, with the Secretary of State or a similar state agency. There will be a filing fee for such filing, which may range from $40.00 to upwards of $500.00, depending on your particular state. In addition, some states base this fee on the capitalization of the company, generally charging more for companies with capitalization of over $50,000. Finally, there may be an additional initial fee charged for an annual or biennial report for the company. These are generally in the $100.00 range. For details of the fee requirements for your state, check the Appendix on the enclosed CD.

> **⚡ Warning!**
>
> Most states now require that you use their own pre-printed forms for filing your Articles of Organization. Please check the Appendix on the enclosed CD for your state's requirements.

Each state also has requirements that certain information be provided in the Articles of Organization. This is to enable the state to keep tabs on specific information regarding the company. Most states also require that such information be updated on a regular basis, either annually or biennially. In general, the basic requirements for information are similar to those required of corporations. Most states do not require all of the information listed below to be provided. Some states require a bare minimum of information. Most states will also provide a pre-printed fill-in-the-blanks Articles of Organization form. A very few states, notably Arizona and New York, also require that notice of filing the Articles of Organization be published in a newspaper. Please note that you should check your state's listing in the Appendix for the specific requirements. How to prepare your Articles of Organization is outlined later. Following is a list of most of the basic information requirements for Articles of Organization:

- Name of the company
- Duration of the company, if less than perpetual
- Purpose of the company
- Registered agent's name and address
- Initial members' names and addresses
- Any reservation of the right to admit new members
- The right of the company to continue business following an act of dissolution
- Whether the company will be managed by members or managers
- Managers' names and addresses, if managed by managers
- Contributions by members to the company
- Future contributions to the company required of members

Operating Agreement

The second important document for a limited liability company is the Operating Agreement. This document is the limited liability company equivalent of a set of corporate bylaws. Within this document, the basic rights and responsibilities of the members or managers are defined. If matters relating to these areas are not covered by an adequate Operating Agreement, the state's default rules will, generally, take effect. It is within the Operating Agreement that the limited liability company management structure will be decided, the division of profits and losses will be laid out, the members' contributions of money, services, or property will be defined, and members' voting and other rights will be laid out. This document is the key to the success of the limited liability company and must be prepared with care and foresight. Instructions for preparing your limited liability company Operating Agreement are contained later in this chapter.

> **⊘ Definition:**
>
> **Operating Agreement:** These are the internal rules that specify how a limited liability company will actually be managed. They are equivalent to the bylaws of a corporation.

Management

Basically, there are three methods by which a limited liability company can be managed: by members only, by members and nonmembers, or by nonmember managers only. The reasons for selecting each of these methods is set out below.

Management by Members Only

This is, by far, the most common approach taken to managing a limited liability company. Most small business owners prefer to take the hands-on approach and manage their own companies. However, if there is a large number of members of the limited liability company, this approach can become unwieldy. It is possible under this approach that not all members will manage the company and that some of the investing members will choose that the company be run by other members. However, even non-voting non-managing members of a member-managed limited liability company will be considered to have earned the profits of the company and, thus, will be required to pay personal income tax on any limited liability company income that passes to them.

However, there is a special tax situation that may arise regarding those members who do not participate in the management of the company. They may avoid paying self-employment taxes on their share of the company's profits if they work for 500 hours or less at the company's business. If one or more of your members fall into this category, a competent tax professional should be consulted. In addition, in limited liability companies that are managed entirely by members and in which all members participate, the ownership interests are generally not considered to be securities under state and Federal law. This eliminates an enormous amount of paperwork and regulation from the operation of the member-managed limited liability company. In most situations, this will be the management style with the most flexibility.

Management by Members and Nonmember Managers

> **Toolkit Tip!**
>
> Nearly all limited liability companies are managed by their own members. Non-member management is advised only if non-members have certain expertise that none of the members have.

It is possible to run a limited liability company by a combination of members and non-members. This choice may be appropriate for limited liability companies that desire to have an outsider (nonmember) with particular expertise participate in the management decisions. For any number of reasons, the nonmember manager may be desired: so that all profits are passed only to members, so that all losses are sustained only by members, or for any other reasons specific to your particular business situation. Again, there is a special tax situation that may arise regarding those members who do not participate in the management of the company. They may also avoid paying any self-employment taxes on their share of the company profits if they work at the company's business for 500 hours or less. If one or more of your members fall into this category, a competent tax professional should be consulted. Finally, the ownership and transfer of membership interests in a limited liability company that is managed, even in part, by managers may possibly subject the limited liability company to regulation under state and federal securities laws. If you choose this type of management structure, a competent tax professional should be consulted.

Management by Nonmember Managers Only

Although this type of management style is possible, it is chosen in relatively few companies. This style may be chosen if the members have little or no expertise in the particular business and desire a skilled manager or management team to handle all the affairs of the business. Again, for this form of management, there is a special tax situation that may arise regarding members who do not participate in the management of the company. They may avoid paying self-employment taxes on their share of the company's profits if they work for 500 hours or less at the company's business. Finally, the ownership and transfer of membership interests in a limited liability company that is managed solely by nonmember managers may possibly subject the limited liability company to regulation under state and Federal securities laws. If you choose this type of management structure, a competent tax professional should be consulted.

Limited Liability Company Existence

A limited liability company is a separate legal entity that offers its members a manner by which to assure that the personal assets of the owners are not at risk in the business. In a sole proprietorship or partnership, an owner's personal property and real estate can be accessed by creditors and courts to fulfill the legal obligations of the business. For corporations and limited liability companies, this is generally not true. Special care must be taken at the time of formation of the business to be certain as to when this limit on liability takes effect. States have several different general times when the limited liability company is considered to be officially formed for the purposes of determining liability. In general, a limited liability company is formed when either:

*   Its Articles of Organization are filed with the state

*   Its Articles of Organization have been state-approved

*   The Articles of Organization have been approved by the state, but the official formation date may be made retroactive to the date of original submission

> **Toolkit Tip!**
>
> The date on which a limited liability company begins its existence is when the member's actual liability for company debts or obligations becomes limited.

- The company has chosen to delay the date of effectiveness to a date later than the filing or approval of the company's submission of the Articles of Organization

If your company will be involved in an enterprise that will have potential liability immediately upon formation, it will be wise to understand the particulars of your state's rules in this area. Please check the Appendix on the enclosed CD for information on your state.

Division of Profits and Losses

Toolkit Tip!

A benefit of the limited liability company form of business is the ability to set the member's division of profits and losses in any reasonable manner.

As noted earlier, one of the principal flexibilities of the limited liability company is the ability to structure the division of profits and losses to members in any reasonable manner. Members may be provided their distribution of profits and losses in direct proportion to their contributions of money, services, or property to the company. This, in fact, is most often the clearest method by which to structure distribution. However, this form of business entity allows endless possibilities to tailor such distributions to the circumstances of your business. If a member is contributing a particular expertise, they may be compensated by a greater percentage of share in the profits of the business. If members choose not to participate in the management of the company, those members who do manage may earn a greater percentage share in the profits and losses. Look closely at your particular business organization and contributions to decide the fairest manner in which to distribute the proceeds or losses of your limited liability company.

Voting Rights of Members

The default rules that are in effect in most states provide that a member's right to vote is allocated in proportion to the member's contributions to the limited liability company. A few states provide that member's voting rights are *per-capita*, in other words, each member gets only one vote. In some states, managers are also given one vote in the affairs of the company. State default rules also typically provide that limited liability company matters be decided by either a majority or unanimous vote of the members. In all states, the Operating Agreement of the company may override most of these provisions and provide for voting divisions in any proportions desired, including denying voting rights to certain members. However, in many states, the default rules may not be overridden with regard to decisions on major company matters, such as the sale of all company assets, the dissolution of the company, or amendments to the Operating Agreement or Articles of Organization. Also note that in order to place any such restrictions in the Operating Agreement or Articles of Organization, it will be necessary to abide by the state default rules in order to adopt the original version of each document. Please consult the Appendix on the enclosed CD for the situation in your particular state.

Membership and Management Meetings

Most states do not require regular membership or management meetings. However, it is often prudent for the members and/or managers to meet at least on an annual basis to review the conduct of the company and plan for the future. In addition, meetings may be necessary more often in order to handle major affairs of the business that are beyond the scope of the managers alone, such as dissolving the company.

Member and Manager Liability to Others

One of the most important benefits of forming a limited liability company is that the owners are not personally liable for any debts or obligations of the company. Every state statute has this provision included in it. In addition, many states also extend such limited liability to others in the company, such as employees, nonmember managers, and agents of the company. However, please note that anyone who is shielded from personal liability for the normal debts and obligations of a company, whether he or she is director of a corporation or member of a limited liability company, is *not* shielded from personal liability for his or her own negligence, recklessness, or criminal activity. If this issue is critical, please check your state limited liability statute directly

> **⚡ Warning!**
>
> A limited liability company does *not* shield its members from liability for negligence, recklessness or criminal activity.

for information on the rules regarding the limits of the liability shield in your state.

Additional Default Rules

Each state's statute regarding limited liability companies contains additional default rules that will apply to your limited liability company unless it is officially altered in either the Articles of Organization or the Operating Agreement. Each state may have a different version of each of these rules. Please check the statutes in your state if these issues are critical. These rules generally cover the following items:

- **Continuity of the company:** This default rule states whether or not the company will be automatically dissolved if a member withdraws from the company

- **Transferability of interests:** This default rule governs the ability of a member to transfer his or her ownership interest in the limited liability company to another person by gift, sale, or otherwise. Most states require either a majority or unanimous vote of the members in order to obtain consent to transfer a limited liability company ownership interest

- **Operating distributions:** The method by which operating distributions are to be distributed to the members of an limited liability company are noted under this default rule in most states. The variations on this particular rule are distribution on a per-capita basis, a proportionate basis based on each member's contribution, or a per-profit share basis

Taxation of Limited Liability Companies

Toolkit Tip!

Limited liability companies have a choice regarding how they wish to be taxed—this choice may be the most important decision members make.

In general, the owners of limited liability companies have a choice regarding how they are to be taxed. If the company has only one member, it will be treated as a sole-proprietorship for federal tax purposes, unless the member/owner elects otherwise. Being taxed as a sole proprietorship means that all of the profits and losses of the company will be reported on the member/owner's personal income tax return, using IRS Schedule C (Form 1040): *Profit or Loss from Business (Sole Proprietorship)*. The single-member limited liability company may, however, choose to be taxed as a corporation by filing IRS Form 8832: *Entity Classification Election*, and selecting "A domestic eligible entity electing to be classified as an association taxable as a corporation." If the company makes this election, the company must file a normal corporate tax form, IRS Form 1120: *U.S. Corporation Income Tax Return*, and pay corporate income tax on any profits.

If the limited liability company has two or more members, it will be taxed as a partnership under IRS rules, unless it elects to be taxed otherwise. Being taxed as a partnership means that all of the profits and losses of the company will be passed through to the members in the proportion determined by the Articles of Organization or the Operating Agreement of the company. This pass-through will be reported on IRS Schedule K-1 (Form 1065): *Partner's Share of Income, Credits, Deductions, etc.* A multiple-member limited liability company may also, however, choose to be taxed as a corporation by filing IRS Form 8832: *Entity Classification Election*, and selecting "A domestic eligible entity electing to be classified as an association taxable as a corporation." If the company makes this election, the company must file a normal corporate tax form, IRS Form 1120: *U.S. Corporation Income Tax Return*, and pay corporate income tax on any profits. Additional information and schedules on taxation of limited liability companies are contained in Chapter 15.

> **Toolkit Tip!**
>
> Very few limited liability companies elect to be taxed as a corporation, subject to corporate income tax.

Series Limited Liability Companies

A relatively new development in LLC law is the 'series' limited liability company. This is a single limited liability company (the master LLC) that has multiple 'series' LLC (like mini-LLCs) under its control, each of which may be separate for liability purposes (with separate members, managers, profit allocations and operating agreements), but are a single entity for state filing purposes. This type of limited liability company arrangement is often used for multiple real estate holdings. This type of limited liability company structure is not available in all states. Its main advantage is to pay less state filing fees. Only the Master LLC is actually registered with the state. If you wish to set up a series-type LLC, you are advised to consult an attorney with experience with this type of complex business structure.

Pre-Organization Activities

The planning stage is vital to the success of any limited liability company. The structure of a new limited liability company, including the number of members, distribution of profits and losses, and other matters, must be carefully tailored to the specific needs of the business. Attorneys typically use a Pre-Organization Worksheet to assemble all of the necessary information from which to plan the organization process.

By filling out a Pre-Organization Worksheet, potential business owners will be able to have before them all of the basic data to use in preparing the necessary organization paperwork. The process of preparing this worksheet will also help uncover any potential differences of opinion among the persons who are desiring to form the limited liability company. Often conflicts and demands are not known until the actual process of determining the company's structure begins. Frank discussions regarding the questions of voting rights, distribution of profits, amounts of contributions, and other management decisions often will enable potential associates to resolve many of the difficult problems of company management in advance. The use of a written worksheet will also provide all persons involved with a clear and permanent record of the information. This may provide the principals of the limited liability company with vital support for later decisions that may be required.

All persons involved in the planned limited liability company should participate in the preparation of the following worksheet. Please take the time to carefully and completely fill in all of the spaces. Following the worksheet, there is a Pre-Organization Checklist that provides a clear listing of all of the actions necessary to organize a limited liability company business. Follow this checklist carefully as the organization process proceeds. After this Pre-Organization Checklist, there is a Document Filing Checklist that provides a listing of the documents that are normally required to be filed with the state agency or office that handles limited liability companies. Finally, there is a discussion and form for reserving the company name with the state limited liability company department. If desired or required, this will be the first form filed with the state.

Unfamiliar terms relating to limited liability companies are explained in the glossary of this book. As the Pre-Organization Worksheet is filled in, please refer to the following explanations:

Address of state limited liability company department: The appendix of this book on the enclosed CD provides this address. You should contact this department immediately, requesting all available information on organization of a business limited liability company in your state. Although the forms provided on the enclosed CD are state-specific and the appendix provides up-to-date information on state requirements, state laws, and fees charged for organization are subject to change. Having the latest available information will save you time and trouble. Many of the state-specific forms are fill-in the-blank that make filing the Articles of Organization a simple task. However, you will still need to prepare this worksheet to determine how best to complete any state-supplied forms.

Toolkit Tip!

The enclosed CD provides state-specific forms for filing Articles of Organization and for reserving a company name.

Company name: The selection of a name is often crucial to the success of a limited liability company. The name must not conflict with any existing company names, nor must it be deceptively similar to other names. It is often wise to clearly explain the business of the limited liability company through the choice of name. All states allow for a reservation of the company name in advance of actual organization and most state forms are provided on the enclosed CD. Check the Appendix on the enclosed CD listing for your state.

Toolkit Tip!

The name chosen for the company must not be deceptively similar to that of another company doing business in your state.

Parties involved: This listing should provide the names, addresses, and phone numbers of all of the people who are involved in the planning stages of the limited liability company.

Principal place of business: This must be the address of the actual physical location of the main business. It may not be a post office box. If the limited liability company is home-based, this address should be the home address.

Purpose of limited liability company: All states provide for the use of an "all-purpose" business purpose clause in describing the main activity of the business; for example, to conduct any lawful business. The Articles of Organization that are used in this book provide this type of clause.

State/local licenses required: Here you should note any specific requirements for licenses to operate your type of business. Most states require obtaining a tax ID number and a retail, wholesale, or sales tax license. A Federal tax ID number (FEIN) must be obtained by all limited liability companies. Additionally, certain types of businesses will require health department approvals, state board licensing, or other forms of licenses. If necessary, check with a competent local attorney for details regarding the types of licenses required for your locality and business type.

Patents/copyrights/trademarks: If patents, copyrights, or trademarks will need to be transferred into the limited liability company, they should be noted here.

State of organization: In general, the limited liability company should be organized in the state in which it will conduct business.

Company existence: The choices here are perpetual (forever) or limited to a certain length. In virtually all cases, you should choose perpetual.

Proposed date to begin company business: This should be the date on which you expect the limited liability company to begin its legal existence. Until this date (actually, until the state formally accepts the Articles of Organization), the organizers of your limited liability company will continue to be legally liable for any business conducted on behalf of the proposed limited liability company.

Organizers: This should be the person (or persons) who will prepare and file the Articles of Organization.

> **💡 Toolkit Tip!**
>
> Every limited liability company must obtain a federal employer identification number using IRS Form SS-4.

Number of members: Most states allow a limited liability company to have a single member. Please check the Appendix on the enclosed CD for the requirements in your particular state.

Proposed members: Here you should list the names and addresses of the proposed members of the company. Although not a requirement in every state, the Articles of Organization used in this book provide that these persons be listed.

Limited liability company's registered agent and address: Here you should list the name and actual street address of the person who will act as the registered agent of the limited liability company. All states require that a specific person be available as the agent of the limited liability company for the service of process (accepting subpoenas or summons on behalf of the limited liability company). The person need not be a member of the limited liability company. The registered agent need not be a lawyer. Normally, the main owner or the attorney of the limited liability company is selected as the registered agent.

> **Toolkit Tip!**
> Every limited liability company must have a registered agent on record with the state to accept served legal papers.

Initial investment: This figure is the total amount of money or property that will be transferred to the limited liability company upon its beginning business. This transfer will be in exchange for ownership interests in the limited liability company. This is also referred to as "paid-in-capital." List also the dates on which the contributions are to be made.

Additional contributions by members: If there are to be planned additional member contributions of money, services, or property, list them here.

Initial indebtedness: If there is to be any initial indebtedness for the limited liability company, please list it here.

Share of profits and losses: Under this heading is noted how the members decide in what proportions the profits and losses of the business will be distributed to the members. This may, but need not, be based on the amount of the contributions of the members to the company.

Distribution of profits and losses: Here decide how the

limited liability company will distribute its profits and losses to each partner. If the company will retain a portion of the profits for reinvestment, note that here.

Management of the limited liability company: If the business is to be managed by members only, members and managers, or managers only, note the decision here. Also note who will actually comprise the management of the company.

Date of first members meeting: This will be the date proposed for holding the first meeting of the members, at which the company Operating Agreement will be officially adopted.

:ϙ:Toolkit Tip!

You should select a bank for company business prior to filing your Articles of Organization.

Proposed bank for company bank account: In advance of organization, you should determine the bank that will handle the company accounts. Obtain from the bank the necessary bank resolution form, which will be signed by the members at the first members meeting.

Cost of organization: The state fees for organization are listed in the Appendix on the enclosed CD. This cost should also reflect the cost of obtaining professional assistance (legal or accounting), the cost of procuring the necessary supplies, and any other direct costs of the organization process.

Out-of-state qualification: If the limited liability company desires to actively conduct business in a state other than the main state of organization, it is necessary to "qualify" the limited liability company in that state. This generally requires obtaining a Certificate of Authority to Transact Business from the other state. In this context, a limited liability company from another state is referred to as a "foreign" limited liability company. If you desire that your limited liability company qualify for activities in another state, you are advised to consult a competent business attorney.

Required quorum for members: This is the percentage of ownership shares in the limited liability company that must be represented at a members meeting in order to officially transact any company business. This is normally set at a majority (more than 50 percent), although this figure can be set higher.

Annual members meeting: The date, time, and place of the annual members meeting should be specified.

Required vote for member action: Once it is determined that a quorum of members is present at a meeting, this is the percentage of ownership shares of the limited liability company that must vote in the affirmative in order to officially pass any member business. This is normally set at a majority (more than 50 percent), although this figure can be set higher and can be made to be unanimous.

Fiscal year and accounting type: For accounting purposes, the fiscal year and accounting type (cash or accrual) of the limited liability company should be chosen in advance. Please see the discussion in Chapter 13 and consult with a competent accounting professional, if necessary

Financial authority: Here list the authority of each proposed member to sign checks, borrow money in the company name, or sign documents in the name of the limited liability company.

Loans to members: In this item, decide if you wish the company to have the ability to make loans directly to its members.

Salaries to members: Here you should decide if the members will earn a salary for their work on behalf of the company.

Transfer of membership interests: Under this listing, a decision should be noted as to whether and how members are to be allowed to transfer their ownership interests in the limited liability company to third parties. This may range from "not at all" to "freely" or may be by unanimous or majority consent of the other members.

Expulsion of members: Here you should consider the terms and conditions for the removal of members.

Insurance: Various types of insurance may be needed, ranging from general casualty to various business liability policies. Also, consider the need for the members or the company to provide the members with life and/or disability insurance.

> **🛈 Toolkit Tip!**
>
> For more details about accounting periods and types, please see Chapter 13: Business Financial Recordkeeping.

New members: Will new members be allowed in the company? Here note the terms and conditions for their entry.

Termination of limited liability company: How will the company end? Here list any considerations relating to the dissolution of the limited liability company that you may wish to be considered.

Amendments to Articles of Organization: Here should be the determination of how the limited liability company will amend the Articles of Organization. The forms in this book are designed to allow the Articles of Organization to be amended by unanimous or majority approval of the members of the company.

Amendments to Operating Agreement: Here should be the determination of how the limited liability company will amend its Operating Agreement. The forms in this book are designed to allow the Operating Agreement to be amended by unanimous or majority approval of the members of the company.

Following the Pre-Organization Worksheet are a Pre-Organization Checklist and a Document Filing Checklist. Please use these checklists to be certain that you have completed all of the necessary steps for organization. Once all of the persons involved have completed the Pre-Organization Worksheet, agreed on all of the details, and reviewed the Pre-Organization and Document Filing Checklists, the actual process of organization may begin.

If the choice for a company name may be similar to that of another business or if the incorporators wish to insure that the name will be available, an Application for Reservation of Limited Liability Company Name may be filed. This is a simple form that requests that the state limited liability company department hold a chosen company name until the actual Articles of Organization are filed, at which time the name will become the official registered name of the limited liability company. At the end of this chapter, there is a sample of this form. There will be a fee required for the filing of this form, and some states prefer that preprinted state forms be used. Please check in the Appendix on the enclosed CD and with the specific state limited liability company department for information. In any event, the information required will be the same as is necessary for this sample form.

> **⎯ऀ Toolkit Tip!**
>
> Forms for the amendment of limited liability company documents and for the termination of the company are contained at the end of this chapter.

> **⎯ऀ Toolkit Tip!**
>
> You may wish to reserve your company name in advance of filing your Articles of Organization. If so, please check the Appendix on the enclosed CD for requirements in your state.

Pre-Organization Worksheet

Name/Address of State Limited Liability Company Department

_____

_____

_____

Proposed Name of the Limited Liability Company

First choice: _____

Alternate choices: _____

_____

Parties Involved in Forming the Limited Liability Company

Name/Address/Phone

_____

_____

_____

_____

_____

Location of Business

Address of principal place of business: _____

_____

Description of principal place of business: _____

_____

_____

Ownership of principal place of business (own or lease?): _____

_____

Other places of business: _____

_____

_____

Type of Business

Purpose of limited liability company: _____
_____
_____
_____

State/local licenses required: _____
_____

Patents/copyrights/trademarks: _____
_____
_____

Organization Matters

State of organization: _____

Company existence (limited or perpetual?): _____

Proposed date to begin company business: _____

Names and addresses of those who will act as organizers:

Name/Address
_____
_____
_____
_____
_____

Number of proposed members: _____

Proposed members of the company:

Name/Address/Phone
_____
_____
_____
_____

Limited liability company's registered agent and office address: _____

_____

_____

Initial investment total: $_____

Date when due: _____

Name/ Cash, Property or Services/Value

_____

_____

_____

_____

_____

Additional contributions: $ _____

Date when due: _____

Name/ Cash, Property or Services/Value

_____

_____

_____

_____

_____

Members' Share of Profits and Losses:

Name/Proportionate Share of Profits and Losses

_____

_____

_____

_____

Distribution and retention of profits and losses: _____

_____

Initial indebtedness: $ _____

Management of the company:

Name/Proportionate Share of Management

_____

_____

_____

_____

_____

Proposed date of first members meeting: _____

Proposed bank for company bank account: _____

_____

Cost of organization: _____

Is qualification in other states necessary? _____

Company Operating Agreement

Required quorum for members meetings: _____

Annual members meeting

Place/Date/Time

_____

_____

Required vote for members actions: (majority/%/unanimous?): _____

Fiscal year: _____

Accounting type (cash or accrual?): _____

Financial Authority:

Name/ Type of Authority

_____

_____

_____

Loans to members:

_____

_____

_____

Salaries of members:

Name/ Salary

_____

_____

_____

_____

_____

Transfer of membership interests: _____

_____

Expulsion of members: _____

_____

Insurance needs: _____

_____

New members: _____

_____

_____

Termination of limited liability company: _____

_____

Amendments to Articles of Organization (majority/%/unanimous?): _____

_____

Amendments to Operating Agreement (majority/%/unanimous?): _____

_____

Pre-Organization Checklist

☐ Contact state limited liability company office for information (see Appendix on the enclosed CD)

☐ Complete Pre-Organization Worksheet

☐ Check annual fees and filing requirements

☐ Reserve company name, if desired, by filing with the state

☐ Prepare Articles of Organization

☐ Prepare Operating Agreement

☐ If desired, have attorney review Articles of Organization prior to filing

☐ Review tax impact of organization with an accountant

☐ Check state tax, employment, licensing, unemployment, and workers' compensation requirements

☐ Check insurance requirements

☐ Prepare company accounting ledgers

☐ Prepare company record book (looseleaf binder)

Document Filing Checklist

- ☐ Application for Reservation of Limited Liability Company Name (if desired)
- ☐ Articles of Organization (mandatory)
- ☐ Amendment to Articles of Organization (mandatory, if applicable)
- ☐ Annual or Biennial Company Reports (generally, mandatory)
- ☐ Change of Address of Registered Agent (mandatory)
- ☐ Articles of Dissolution (mandatory, if applicable)
- ☐ Any other required state forms (see Appendix on the enclosed CD)

Application for Reservation of Limited Liability Company Name

TO:

I, _____ , with an office located at:

acting as an organizer, apply for reservation of the following company name:
_____ .

This company name is intended to be used for a limited liability company in the
State of _____ , County of _____ .

I request that this company name be reserved for a period of _____ days. Please issue a certificate of reservation of this company name.

Enclosed please find our check in the amount of $ _____ to cover the registration fee.

Dated: _____ , 20 _____

_____
Signature of Organizer

_____
Printed Name of Organizer

Articles of Organization

The central legal document for any limited liability company is the Articles of Organization. In some states, this document may be called a Certificate of Formation or a Certificate of Organization. Please check the Appendix on the enclosed CD for the requirements in your particular state. For clarity, however, this book will refer to the organizer-prepared document as the Articles of Organization. This form outlines the basic structure of the limited liability company and details those matters that are relevant to the public registration of the limited liability company. The name, purpose, owners, registered agent, address, and other vital facts relating to the existence of the limited liability company are filed with the state by using this form. Upon filing of the Articles of Organization, payment of the proper fee, and acceptance by the state limited liability company department, the limited liability company officially begins its legal existence. Until the state has accepted the Articles, the organizers are not shielded from personal liability by the limited liability company form.

There are a number of items that are required to be noted in all Articles of Organization. The Articles may also include many other details of the limited liability company's existence. Please check the Appendix on the enclosed CD and with your state department for specific details. Following is a checklist of items that are generally included in the Articles of Organization.

> ⛯ Toolkit Tip!
>
> Nearly all states now provide preprinted Articles of Incorporation that are required to be used for filing. The information required, however, will be the same as is noted in this chapter. Please check the appendix listing for your state's requirement.

Articles of Organization Checklist
The details for Articles of Organization under most state laws are:

☐ The name of the limited liability company

☐ The principal place of business of the company (optional in some states)

☐ The purpose and powers of the limited liability company

☐ The duration of the limited liability company

☐ The name and address of each member of the limited liability company

☐ The name and address of the registered agent of the limited liability company

☐ Amount of initial and future contributions to capital of the limited liability company (optional in most states)

☐ Provisions outlining the management of the company (optional in some states)

☐ Reservation of the right to admit new members (optional in some states)

☐ Right of the company to continue business following an act of dissolution or dissociation (optional in some states)

☐ Standard Industrial Code [SIC] for the company (optional in most states)

☐ Title and introduction

☐ The number of members of the limited liability company

☐ Federal Employer Identification Number [FEIN] for the company (optional in most states)

☐ The signature(s) of the organizer(s)

☐ The signature of the registered agent

☐ Additional articles

Preparing Your Articles of Organization

The Articles of Organization for your limited liability company should include all of the required information. Since Articles are a public record, all of the information in them will be available for inspection. Much of the information that is not required in the Articles may instead be put into the Operating Agreement of the limited liability company. In this manner, the actual management structure and details will remain unavailable for public inspection.

Note: All states (except Colorado and Georgia, which provides online LLC forms) now provide official forms for Articles of Organization that are required to be used for filing. The information required, however, will be the same as noted in the sample Articles of Organization in this chapter and it will be helpful to read through this chapter and fill in the information as noted on the sample forms. Transferring it to the state form will then be a simple task. In addition, some states supply forms listing the requirements for filing the particular documents. Please check the Appendix on the enclosed CD and the state-specific forms that are also included on the Forms-on-CD.

> **⚡Toolkit Tip!**
> State-specific forms for filing Articles of Organization are provided on the enclosed CD.

Articles of Organization may be amended at any time. However, this generally requires a formal filing with the state and the issuance of a Certificate of Amendment of Articles of Organization. It also normally requires the payment of a fee. For these reasons, it is often a good idea to put only those items in the original Articles that are unlikely to require changes in the near future.

This chapter contains instructions for preparing Articles of Organization. You should check the Appendix on the enclosed CD and any information noted on your state-specific form to be certain that you have included all of the necessary information for your state. A few states may require additional Articles. Most of the information required for preparing this form will be on your Pre-Organization Worksheet, which you prepared earlier in this chapter. Optional clauses may be added to state-supplied forms where necessary.

☀️Toolkit Tip!

Although you should have already done so, please check the Appendix listing for your state's requirement.

The Articles must then be properly signed. Although not required by all states, the form in this book is designed to be notarized. In addition, a few states require that the Articles be published as legal notices in newspapers. Please check the Appendix on the enclosed CD for the requirements in your particular state. The signed Articles of Organization and the proper fee should be sent to the proper state office. Upon receipt, the state department will check for duplication or confusing conflicts with the names of any other registered companies. They will also check to be certain that all of the statutory requirements have been fulfilled and that the proper fee has been paid. If there is a problem, the Articles will be returned with an explanation of the difficulty. Correct the problem and refile the Articles. If everything is in order, the business will officially be organized and able to begin to conduct business as a limited liability company entity. Some states have different procedures for indicating the beginning of existence of a limited liability company.

Name of Limited Liability Company

The name of the limited liability company should be unique. It should not be confusingly similar to any other business name in use within your state. In addition, it should not contain any terms that might lead people to believe that it is a government or financial institution. Finally, it must generally contain an indication that the business is a limited liability company, such as "LLC," "Llc," "limited liability company," or "Limited." Some states allow the use of the word "Company" in the names of limited liability companies. Others do not. If you wish to use a term of designation other than "limited liability company" or "limited" (or abbreviations of these), please check the Appendix on the enclosed CD and with your state limited liability company department.

Principal Place of Business

This should be the street address of the planned principal place of business of the limited liability company. Post office box addresses are not sufficient. It must be an actual street address.

Purpose and Powers of the Limited Liability Company

Many states allow a general statement of purpose: "to transact any and all lawful business for which limited liability companies may be organized under the Business Limited Liability Company Act of the State of _____ ." Others may require that you specifically state the purpose of your limited liability company. If you are required to state a specific purpose, try to be broad enough to allow your business flexibility without the necessity of later amending the Articles of Organization to reflect a change in direction of your business. Choose the clause appropriate for your state and circumstances (please note that Kentucky and Massachusetts are referred to as "Commonwealths," rather than "States").

Duration of Limited Liability Company

Most states allow for a perpetual duration for limited liability companies, meaning that the limited liability company can continue in existence forever. Unless there is a specific business reason to indicate otherwise, this is generally the safest choice.

Number of Members

The minimum number of members allowed is generally one. However, a few states require two. Please check the Appendix on the enclosed CD.

Name and Addresses of Initial Members

This clause provides for listing the initial members of the limited liability company.

Name of Registered Agent

The registered agent for a limited liability company is the person upon whom service of process (summons, subpoena, etc.) can be served. This person must be an adult who is a resident of the state of organization. The usual choice is the main owner or manager of the limited liability company. Please see the Appendix on the enclosed CD and check with your state limited liability company department. There is generally a place at the end of the Articles of Organization for the registered agent to sign.

Address of Registered Agent

This address must be an actual place, generally the offices of the limited liability company. It may not be a post office box or other unmanned location.

Capitalization

This refers to the amount of capital that will form the initial basis for operating the limited liability company. Several states require that specific dollar amounts of capital to be contributed to a limited liability company be noted for the purpose of collecting additional fees for organization. Other states have no such requirement. Please check the Appendix and with your state limited liability company department.

Management of the Company

Under this clause, which is mandatory in several states, you will outline whether the management of the company will be by members only, by members and non-member managers, or by nonmember managers only. Check your state's listing in the Appendix on the enclosed CD and choose the appropriate clause.

Reservation of Right to Admit New Members

In this clause, which is optional in most states, the company can reserve the right to admit new members. In most states, this information may instead be listed in the Operating Agreement of the limited liability company, if preferred. If you wish to add this to your Articles of Organization, insert the following clause:

The company reserves the right to admit new members at any time.

Right of Company to Continue

This clause allows the company to reserve the right to continue, without dissolution, upon an act of dissolution or dissociation under the laws of the particular state. This clause is optional in most states. Please check the Appendix on the enclosed CD. If you wish to add this to your Articles of Organization, insert the following clause:

The company reserves the right to continue without dissolution, under the terms as set forth in the company Operating Agreement, upon any act that might otherwise cause the dissolution of the company or the dissociation of a member under the laws of the State of _____ .

Standard Industrial Code

Some states require the Standard Industrial Code, or SIC, for the company. Please contact your appropriate state office for the listing of SIC codes.

Additional Articles

Most states allow you to add additional articles to the state-provided forms.

Operating Agreement

The Operating Agreement of a limited liability company is the third part of the triangle that provides the framework for the management of company business. Along with state law and the Articles of Organization, the Operating Agreement provides a clear outline of the rights and responsibilities of all parties to a limited liability company. In particular, the Operating Agreement provides the actual details of the operational framework for the business. The Agreement is the internal document that will contain the basic rules for how the limited liability company is to be run. Every limited liability company must have an Operating Agreement. Many of the provisions cover relatively standard procedural questions relating, for example, to quorums or voting. Other provisions may need to be specifically tailored to the type of business for which the Operating Agreement is intended. The provisions are able to be amended by vote of the members.

The Operating Agreement can contain very specific or very general provisions for the internal management of the company. Typically, the Agreement covers five general areas:

- Rights and responsibilities of the members

- Rights and responsibilities of the managers

- Financial matters

- Methods for amending the Operating Agreement

- Member withdrawal and dissolution of the company

This chapter contains sample clauses for preparing your limited liability company Operating Agreement. If you are using a computer and word processing program, simply select those clauses from the Forms-on-CD that you wish to use in your Operating Agreement. Your completed Operating Agreement should be formally adopted at the first members meeting. Following is a checklist for use in preparing your Operating Agreement:

Operating Agreement Checklist

- ☐ The name of the limited liability company
- ☐ Power to designate the location of the principal office of the limited liability company
- ☐ Power to designate the registered agent and agent's office of the limited liability company
- ☐ The name and address of each member of the limited liability company
- ☐ Liability of members and managers of the company
- ☐ Tax treatment of the company
- ☐ Amount of contributions and initial capital to the limited liability company
- ☐ Any additional planned contributions to the limited liability company
- ☐ Penalties on failure to make contributions
- ☐ Interest on capital contributions
- ☐ Loans to the limited liability company
- ☐ Each member's share in the profits or losses of the company
- ☐ Distribution of profits and losses of the limited liability company
- ☐ Management of the limited liability company
- ☐ Authority of manager(s) of the limited liability company
    - ☐ Signature for checking
    - ☐ Authorization to borrow money
    - ☐ Authorization to sign documents
- ☐ Date and time of annual meetings
- ☐ Place of annual members meeting
- ☐ Members quorum
- ☐ Members proxies
- ☐ Members voting
- ☐ Members consent agreements

- ☐ Powers of the members
- ☐ Fiduciary duties of members and managers
- ☐ Accounting matters
    - ☐ Cash or accrual accounting
    - ☐ Calendar or other fiscal periods
- ☐ Financial matters
- ☐ Bank account
- ☐ Loans to managers or members
- ☐ Draws to members
- ☐ Salaries to members
- ☐ Expense accounts
- ☐ Transfer of limited liability company interests
- ☐ Expulsion of member
- ☐ Automatic expulsion of member
- ☐ Limit on remedies of expelled member
- ☐ Insurance
    - ☐ Life insurance
    - ☐ Disability insurance
- ☐ Mediation or binding arbitration for dispute resolution
- ☐ Admission of new member
- ☐ Responsibility of new member
- ☐ Withdrawal from limited liability company
- ☐ Agreement not to compete
- ☐ Termination of limited liability company
- ☐ Amendments to Operating Agreement
- ☐ Amendments to Articles of Organization
- ☐ Additional provisions
- ☐ General provisions
- ☐ Signature(s) of member(s)

Operating Agreement

This Limited Liability Company Operating Agreement is for the
_____,
organized under the laws of the State of _____, by the filing
of its organizational documents on _____ ,20 _____.

The parties to this agreement agree to operate a limited liability company under the following terms and conditions:

1. The members have the power to determine the location of the limited liability company's principal place of business. The members also have the power to designate the limited liability company's registered agent, who may be a member.

The company's principal place of business shall be:

The name and address of the company's registered agent shall be:

2. The initial members of the company are as follows:

Name   Address

_____   _____
_____   _____
_____   _____
_____   _____
_____   _____

3. No members or managers of the limited liability company shall be personally liable for any debts, obligations, expenses, liabilities, or any claims made against the company.

4. The members of the limited liability company elect to have the company treated as a _____for state and federal income tax purposes. The members agree to execute and file any documents necessary to secure this tax treatment.

5. The start-up capital will be a total of $_____. Each member of the limited liability company agrees to contribute the following property, services, or cash to this total amount on or before the date indicated:

Name	Cash/Services/Property	Value	Date Due
_____	_____	____	____
_____	_____	____	____
_____	_____	____	____
_____	_____	____	____

6. If additional capital is required by the limited liability company and is determined by a _____vote of the members, then each member shall be required to contribute to such additional capital in such proportions and by a certain date as determined by such vote.

7. If any member shall fail to make his or her initial or additional contributions as indicated by this agreement, any amendment to this agreement, or any additional agreement between the members, then this company shall continue as a limited liability company of only those members who have satisfied their contribution requirements. Any member who has failed to satisfy his or her contribution requirements will not be a member of this limited liability company. Each member who has made a contribution shall then be entitled to a share of limited liability company profits and losses in proportion to the amount of their contribution to the total contributions. If any additional limited liability company contributions are necessary, such additional contributions shall be determined by the remaining members as specified under the terms of this agreement regarding "Additional Contributions " above.

8. Interest at the rate of _____percent (_____%) per annum shall be paid on each member's capital contributions that were paid in cash. The interest shall be an expense of the limited liability company and paid on an annual basis to the member who is entitled to it.

9. In addition to capital contributions, the following cash or property will be loaned to the limited liability company under the terms specified:

Name of Member	Cash/Property Loaned	Terms of Loan
_____	_____	_____
_____	_____	_____
_____	_____	_____
_____	_____	_____

10. Each member's proportionate share of the profits and losses of the limited liability company shall be as follows:

Name	Percent of Ownership of Limited Liability Company
_____	_____
_____	_____
_____	_____
_____	_____

11. Any profits or losses of the limited liability company shall be determined and distributed to the members on a _____ basis according to their proportionate share of the profits and losses of the limited liability company. However, the first _____ percent (_____%) of the profits for each such period shall be retained by the limited liability company for reinvestment in the limited liability company.

12. The management of the company shall be exclusively by_____. The actual person(s) to manage the company and the salary of an such person(s) shall be determined by a _____ vote of the members of the limited liability company, and the management may be removed at any time, with or without cause, by a like vote.

13. One or more managers may be selected under the terms of this agreement. If a single individual is selected to manage the company, such person shall have exclusive authority to make all management decisions. Otherwise, all limited liability company decisions will be made by _____ vote among the persons selected to manage the company, except the major company decisions noted below, which must be decided by unanimous vote of the persons selected to manage the company. The manager(s) shall have the authority to conduct the day-to-day business of the limited liability company, without consultation with the other members. This shall include hiring and firing employees, signing limited liability company checks, withdrawing funds from limited liability company accounts, borrowing money up to the amount of $_____, and maintaining the books and records of the limited liability company. Major decisions are defined as follows:

14. The annual limited liability company meeting will be held on the _____ of every year at _____ o 'clock ___ .m. This meeting is for the purpose of assessing the current status of the limited liability company and transacting any necessary business. If this day is a legal holiday, the meeting will be held on the next day.

15. The place for the annual members meeting will be the principal office of the limited liability company, located at:

16. A quorum for a members meeting will be a majority of the members. Once a quorum is present, business may be conducted at the meeting, even if members leave prior to adjournment.

17. At all meetings of members, a member may vote by signed proxy or by power of attorney. To be valid, a proxy must be filed with the limited liability company prior to the stated time of the meeting. No proxy may be valid for more than 11 months, unless the proxy specifically states otherwise. A proxy may always be revoked prior to the meeting for which it is intended. Attendance at the meeting for which a proxy has been authorized always revokes the proxy.

18. A _____ vote of the members entitled to vote will be sufficient to decide any matter, unless a greater number is required by this agreement or by state law. Adjournment shall be by majority vote of those shares entitled to vote.

19. Any action that may be taken at a company meeting may be taken instead without a meeting if an agreement is consented to, in writing, by all members who would be entitled to vote.

20. The members will, jointly, have all powers available under state law, including the power to: appoint and remove managers and employees; change the offices; borrow money on behalf of the limited liability company, including the power to execute any evidence of indebtedness on behalf of the limited liability company; and enter into contracts on behalf of the limited liability company. Such powers may be exercised by a single member only upon unanimous approval of all of the members.

21. Each member and manager owes a fiduciary duty of good faith and reasonable care with regard to all actions taken on behalf of the limited liability company. Each member and manager must perform his or her duties in good faith in a manner that he or she reasonably believes to be in the best interests of the limited liability company, using ordinary care and prudence.

22. The limited liability company will maintain accounting records that will be open to any member for inspection at any reasonable time. These records

will include separate income and capital accounts for each member. The accounting will be on the _____ basis and on a _____ -year basis. The capital account of each member will consist of no less than the value of the property, cash, or services that the member shall have contributed with his or her initial or additional contributions to the limited liability company.

23. All notes, mortgages, or other evidence of indebtedness shall be signed by all of the members of the limited liability company, unless otherwise allowed under the terms of this agreement.

24. The limited liability company will maintain a business checking bank account at:

25. The limited liability company may not lend any money to a manager or member of the limited liability company unless the loan has been approved by a _____ vote of all members of the limited liability company.

26. All members are entitled to _____ draws from the expected profits of the limited liability company. The draws will be debited against the income account of the member. The dollar amount of the draws shall be determined by a _____ vote of the members.

27. All members are eligible to be paid reasonable salaries for work or services they perform in the limited liability company business, unless such work is in the capacity of a manager or is to be considered as a contribution to the company.

28. Each member shall receive an expense account for up to $_____ per month for the payment of reasonable and necessary business expenses in the regular course of limited liability company business. Each member shall provide the limited liability company with a written record of such expenses in order to obtain reimbursement.

29. A member may transfer all or part of his or her interest in the limited liability company to any other party only with the unanimous consent of the other members. In addition, the limited liability company has the right of first refusal to purchase the member's interest on the same terms and conditions as the member's offer from the third party. This option to buy must be exercised by the limited liability company within 30 days from notice of the offer to buy by a third party.

30. A member may be expelled from the limited liability company at any time by the unanimous consent of the other members. Upon expulsion, the expelled member shall cease to be a member and shall have no interest, rights, authority, power, or ownership in the limited liability company or any limited liability company property. The expelled member shall be entitled to receive value for his or her interest in the limited liability company as determined by the terms of this agreement. The limited liability company shall continue in business without interruption without the expelled member.

31. A member is automatically expelled from the limited liability company at any time upon the occurrence of any of the following:

(a) A member files a petition for or becomes subject to an order for relief under the Federal Bankruptcy Code

(b) A member files for or becomes subject to any order for insolvency under any state law

(c) A member makes an assignment for the benefit of creditors

(d) A member consents to or becomes subject to the appointment of a receiver over a substantial portion of his or her assets

(e) A member consents to or becomes subject to an attachment or execution of a substantial portion of his or her assets

On the date of any of the above events, the expelled member shall cease to be a member and shall have no interest, rights, authority, power, or ownership in the limited liability company or any limited liability company property. The expelled member shall be entitled to receive value for his or her interest in the limited liability company as determined by the terms of this agreement. The limited liability company shall continue in business without interruption without the expelled member.

32. The expulsion of a member shall be final and shall not be subject to mediation, arbitration, or review by any court of any jurisdiction.

33. The limited liability company shall buy and maintain life insurance on the life of each member in the amount of $_____. The limited liability company shall also buy and maintain disability insurance on each other member in the amount of $_____. Such life and disability insurance shall be considered assets of the company. On the withdrawal, termination, or expulsion of any member for any reason other than his or her death or disability, any insurance policies on the member's life or health on which the limited liability company

paid premiums shall become the personal property of the departing member and the cash value (if any) of such policy shall be considered as a draw against the departing member's income account.

34. Except as otherwise provided by this agreement, the members agree that any dispute arising related to this agreement will be settled by _____ _____ . The person hired for such dispute resolution shall be chosen by a _____vote of the members. All costs of such dispute resolution will be shared equally by all members involved in the dispute.

35. A new member may be admitted to the limited liability company by _____ _____ consent of the members. Admission of a new member shall not cause the termination of the original limited liability company entity, but rather, it shall continue with the additional member.

36. Any new member to the limited liability company shall be responsible for and assume full personal liability equal to all other members for all limited liability company debts, liabilities, and obligations whenever incurred for which the other members of the company have assumed personal liability.

37. If any member withdraws from the limited liability company for any reason (including the death or disability of the member), the limited liability company shall continue and be operated by the remaining members. The withdrawing member or his or her personal representative will be obligated to sell that member's interest to the remaining members and those remaining members will be obligated to buy that interest. The value of the withdrawing member's interest will be his or her proportionate share of the total value of the limited liability company. If necessary, the total value of the limited liability company will be assessed by an independent appraisal made within 90 days of the member's withdrawal. The costs of the appraisal will be shared equally by all members, including the withdrawing member.

38. No member, during or after the operation of the limited liability company, shall engage in any business that is in competition in any manner with the limited liability company. The prohibition against competition shall continue for a period of _____ years after the member leaves the limited liability company and for any business within _____ miles of the limited liability company's principal place of business. This non competition agreement shall end with the termination of the limited liability company.

39. The limited liability company may be terminated at any time by unanimous consent of the members. Upon termination, the members agree to apply the assets and money of the limited liability company in the following order:

(a) To pay all the debts and obligations of the limited liability company
(b) To distribute the members' income accounts to them in their proportionate share
(c) To distribute the members' capital accounts to them in their proportionate share
(d) To distribute any remaining assets to them in their proportionate share

40. This Operating Agreement may be amended in any manner by _____ vote of the members.

41. This Articles of Organization may be amended in any manner by _____ vote of the members.

42. The following additional provisions are part of this agreement:

No modification of this agreement shall be effective unless it is in writing and approved by the required number of members set forth in this agreement. This agreement binds and benefits all members and any successors, inheritors, assigns, or representatives of the members. Time is of the essence of this agreement. This document is the entire agreement between the members. Any attached papers that are referred to in this agreement are part of this agreement. Any alleged oral agreements shall have no force or effect. This agreement is governed by the laws of the State of _____.
If any portion of this agreement is held to be invalid, void, or unenforceable by any court of law of competent jurisdiction, the rest of the agreement shall remain in full force and effect.

Dated _____, 20 _____

Signature of Member   Printed Name of Member

_____   _____
_____   _____
_____   _____
_____   _____
_____   _____

Members Meetings

The members of a limited liability company transact business as a group. Each individual member has no authority to bind the limited liability company (unless the members as a group have previously authorized him or her to exercise that power). Although it is not required, it is a good idea to hold official meetings to transact company business.

Members should, at a minimum, hold an annual meeting to handle any of the following business:

- Select managers for the coming year, if the company is to be run by managers

- Decide if any changes are necessary to the Articles of Organization or Operating Agreement

- Make any other annual decisions regarding the financial matters of the business

- Generally, review the operation of the company

All of the documents necessary to conduct and record a first and an annual members meeting are contained in this chapter.

> **♀ Toolkit Tip!**
>
> At a minimum, you should hold annual meetings and prepare annual minutes, even if there is only one member of the limited liability company.

First Members Meeting Checklist

The following information should be covered and documented in the minutes of the first members meeting:

- ☐ Name of limited liability company
- ☐ Date of meeting
- ☐ Location of meeting
- ☐ Members at meeting
- ☐ Others present at meeting
- ☐ Name of temporary chairperson presiding over meeting
- ☐ Name of temporary secretary acting at meeting
- ☐ Calling of meeting to order and determination of quorum present
- ☐ Articles of Organization filed with state
- ☐ Date of filing of Articles of Organization
- ☐ Effective date of organization of limited liability company
- ☐ Approval and ratification of any acts of organizers taken on behalf of limited liability company prior to effective date of organization of limited liability company
- ☐ Election of managers of limited liability company
- ☐ Decisions on annual salaries of managers
- ☐ Direction that any organizational expenses be reimbursed to organizers
- ☐ Authorization to open company bank account
- ☐ Approval of Operating Agreement
- ☐ Contributions of members
- ☐ Designation of fiscal year dates
- ☐ Designation of accounting basis (cash or accrual)
- ☐ Documentation of any other necessary business
- ☐ Adjournment of meeting
- ☐ Dating and signing of minutes by secretary

Minutes of First Members Meeting of

_____

The first meeting of the members of this limited liability company was held on
_____ , 20 _____ , at _____ o'clock ___ . m., at the offices of
the company located at _____ .

Present at the meeting were the following people: _____
_____
_____
_____
_____ ,

all of whom are designated as members of this limited liability company in the
Articles of Organization of this company.

The following other persons were also present:_____
_____
_____ .

1. _____was elected as the temporary
   chairperson of the meeting.

   _____ was elected as the temporary secretary of the meeting.

2. The chairperson announced that the meeting had been duly called by the
   organizer(s) of the limited liability company, called the meeting to order,
   and determined that a quorum was present.

3. The chairperson reported that the Articles of Organization of the company
   had been duly filed with the State of _____ on _____
   _____ , 20 _____ , and that the organization of the company was
   effective as of _____ , 20 _____ .

   Upon motion made and carried, a copy of the Articles of Organization of the
   company was ordered to be attached to the minutes of this meeting.

4. Upon motion made and carried, the members AGREED that:
The joint and individual acts of _____
and _____ , the organizer(s) of
this limited liability company, that were taken on behalf of the limited liability
company are approved, ratified, and adopted as acts of the limited liability
company.

5. The following persons were elected as managers of the limited liability company to serve until the first annual members meeting:

Name/Address

_____

_____

_____

6. Upon motion made and carried, the annual salaries of the managers were fixed at the following rates until the next annual meeting of the members:

Name/Salary

_____

_____

_____

7. Upon motion made and carried, it was AGREED that:
The organizer(s) of the company be reimbursed, from company funds, the following amounts for organizational expenses:

Name/Reimbursement

_____

_____

_____

8. Upon motion made and carried, it was AGREED that:
The company would open a business checking account at the following banking institution _____
_____ .

9. A copy of the proposed Operating Agreement of the limited liability company was presented at the meeting and read by each member.

Upon motion made and carried, the members AGREED that:
The proposed Operating Agreement of this limited liability company is approved and adopted. A copy of this Operating Agreement is ordered to be attached to the minutes of this meeting.

10. The following persons have offered to transfer the property or money listed below to the limited liability company in exchange for the following shares of ownership in the limited liability company:

Name/Property or Money/Ownership

_____

_____

_____

_____

Upon motion made and carried, the members AGREED that:
The assets proposed for transfer are good and sufficient consideration.

11. Upon motion made and carried, the members AGREED that:
The fiscal year of this limited liability company shall begin on _____, 20 _____ , and end on _____ , 20 _____ . This limited liability company shall report its income and expenses on a(n) _____ basis.

12. The following other business was conducted:

There being no further business, upon motion made and carried, the meeting was adjourned.

Dated _____ , 20 _____

_____
Signature of Secretary of Company

_____
Printed Name of Secretary of Company

Annual Members Meeting Checklist

The following information should be covered and documented in the minutes of the annual members meeting:

- ❏ Name of limited liability company
- ❏ Date of meeting
- ❏ Location of meeting
- ❏ Members present at meeting
- ❏ Others present at meeting
- ❏ Name of chairperson presiding over meeting
- ❏ Name of secretary presiding over meeting
- ❏ Calling of meeting to order and determination of quorum present
- ❏ Distribution and approval of minutes of previous meeting
- ❏ Presentation of Annual Financial Report
- ❏ Election of managers of limited liability company
- ❏ Decision on annual salaries of managers
- ❏ Other business (see next page for possible business discussions)
- ❏ Adjournment of meeting
- ❏ Dating and signing of minutes by secretary

Other Possible Business Discussions

- ❏ Date last state and Federal Tax returns filed
- ❏ Date last state annual report filed
- ❏ Date any other required reports/returns filed
- ❏ Date of last Financial Statement
- ❏ Review current employment agreements
- ❏ Review current insurance coverage

- ☐ Review current Financial Statement
- ☐ Review current year-to-date income and expenses
- ☐ Review current salaries
- ☐ Review current pension/profit-sharing plans
- ☐ Review accounts receivable
- ☐ Determination of necessity of collection procedures
- ☐ Review status of any outstanding loans
- ☐ Ascertainment of net profit
- ☐ Discussion of any major items requiring member action
- ☐ Major purchases or leases (real estate or personal property)
- ☐ Lawsuits
- ☐ Loans

Minutes of Annual Members Meeting of

_____

The annual meeting of the members of this limited liability company was held on _____ , 20 _____ , at _____ o'clock ____ . m., at the offices of the company located at _____ .

Present at the meeting were the following people: _____
_____
_____
_____
_____ ,

all of whom are members of this limited liability company.

The following other persons were also present: _____
_____
_____
_____ .

1. _____ was elected as the chairperson of the meeting.
   _____ was elected as the secretary of the meeting.

2. The chairperson announced that the meeting had been duly called by the organizer(s) of the limited liability company, called the meeting to order, and determined that a quorum was present.

3. The secretary distributed copies of the minutes of the previous meeting of the members that had been held on _____ , 20 _____ .

   Upon motion made and carried, these minutes were approved.

4. An Annual Financial Report was presented that stated that as of the date of _____ , 20 _____ , the limited liability company had a net profit of $ _____ .

Upon motion made and carried, the Annual Financial Report was approved and the secretary was directed to attach a copy of the Annual Financial Report to these minutes.

5. Upon motion made and carried, the following persons were elected as managers of this limited liability company for a term of one year:

Name/Address

_____

_____

_____

_____

_____

6. Upon motion made and carried, the salaries of the managers were fixed for the term of one year at the following rates:

Name/Rate

_____

_____

_____

_____

_____

7. The following other business was conducted:

There being no further business, upon motion made and carried, the meeting was adjourned.

Dated _____ , 20 _____

_____
Signature of Secretary of Company

_____
Printed Name of Secretary of Company

Amendments to Articles of Organization or Operating Agreement

At some time in the course of your limited liability company, changed conditions may require that you *amend* (or alter) certain portions of your Articles of Organization or Operating Agreement. In general, members may agree to alter or amend these documents in any manner, as changed conditions may dictate. However, state law in all states restricts the right to change certain general conditions and rules of limited liability company law and liability. Contact the state office in your state to obtain information regarding amendments to the Articles of Organization. They may even provide fill-in-the-blank forms for your use. There will generally be a fee required for filing Amendments to Articles of Organization. To make amendments to your original Articles of Organization or Operating Agreement, use one of the following forms for amending these limited liability company documents, if your state does not provide these forms.

Amendment to Articles of Organization of

_____

This Amendment to Articles of Organization is made on _____ , 20 _____ .
It is intended to permanently amend the Articles of Organization, filed on_____
____, 20 _____ , on behalf of _____ , a limited
liability company organized under the laws of the State of _____ .

The above-noted Articles of Organization are hereby amended to read as
follows:

All other portions of the original Articles of Organization dated _____
, 20 _____ , not changed by this Amendment to Articles of Organization, remain
in full force and effect and are ratified and confirmed.

Signature of Member/Printed Name of Member

_____   _____
_____   _____
_____   _____
_____   _____
_____   _____
_____   _____
_____   _____
_____   _____

Amendment to Operating Agreement of

_____

This Amendment to Operating Agreement is made on _____ , 20 _____ . It is intended to permanently amend the Operating Agreement of _____ , a limited liability company organized under the laws of the State of _____ .

The above noted Operating Agreement is hereby amended to read as follows:

All other portions of the original Operating Agreement dated _____ , 20 _____ , not changed by this Amendment to Operating Agreement, remain in full force and effect and are ratified and confirmed.

Signature of Member/Printed Name of Member

_____   _____

_____   _____

_____   _____

_____   _____

_____   _____

_____   _____

_____   _____

_____   _____

Termination of a Limited Liability Company

In many limited liability companies, there will come a time when the members will desire that the company cease to exist. In order for the dissolution of the limited liability company to proceed as amicably as possible, it is wise to carefully consider all aspects of the impending end of the company and to draft a comprehensive Termination of Limited Liability Company Agreement that will cover each aspect of dissolution of the business to each member's satisfaction. The termination of a limited liability company is, perhaps, one of the most difficult business situations to confront.

The following worksheet is designed to assist you in understanding the factors that will be important as you proceed to terminate your limited liability company. Following the worksheet is a Termination of Limited Liability Company Agreement that you may use as an outline to prepare your own customized agreement. Please note that in most states, you will also need to file Articles of Dissolution of a Limited Liability Company with your state's registration office. Please check your state's official website (as noted in the Appendix on the enclosed CD) for information on your state's requirements.

> **Toolkit Tip!**
>
> In order to understand the possible end of your company, It may be wise to review the following termination documents before you even set up your company.

Limited Liability Company Termination Worksheet

Date proposed for termination: _____

Reason for termination: _____
_____
_____

Valuation of limited liability company business: $ _____

Appraisal of limited liability company property: $ _____

Who will appraise the limited liability company property? _____
_____

Does anyone hold a right of first refusal or option to purchase the business?
_____
_____

Is an outside purchase or lease of the business involved? _____
_____

If so, what are the proposed terms of the outside purchaser's offer to buy or lease the business? _____
_____
_____

Are these terms unanimously acceptable to the members? _____

Is the business to be sold or leased to an existing member? _____

If so, what are the proposed terms of the existing purchaser's offer to buy or lease the business? _____
_____
_____

Are these terms unanimously acceptable to the members? _____

Will the limited liability company business be discontinued with no purchase of limited liability company assets? _____

What disposition will be made of the limited liability company name? _____
_____
_____

What date is set for the sale/lease/liquidation of the limited liability company? __
_____

What are the proportionate shares of profits and losses of each member? _____
_____
_____

What is the liquidation or sale value of all of the limited liability company assets?
_____
_____

What is the value of all of the limited liability company liabilities, other than to the members? _____
_____

What will be the remaining limited liability company assets after all limited liability company liabilities have been met? _____
_____

How much will be distributed to each member's income account? _____

How much will be distributed to each member's capital account? _____

How much additional limited liability company funds will be distributed to each member?
_____
_____

Who will wind up the limited liability company business? _____
_____

What is the estimated date for the distribution of the final limited liability company assets?
_____

Termination of Limited Liability Company

_____

This Termination of Limited Liability Company Agreement is made on _____ _____ , 20 _____ , by and between_____ _____ , of: (address) and _____ , of: (address)

It is intended to permanently terminate the limited liability company created by the Articles of Organization between the above parties that was dated _____ , 20 _____ , and filed with the State of _____ , on _____ , 20 _____ .

The above noted members agree to terminate their limited liability company under the following terms and conditions:

1. After _____ , 20 _____ , no member shall engage in any further limited liability company business nor incur any further limited liability company obligations, other than to liquidate the assets of the limited liability company and, in general, wind up the limited liability company's affairs.

2. The members agree that each asset of the limited liability company has a present fair market value equal to the asset's value as shown on the financial records of the limited liability company. However, if an asset is sold, the members agree that asset shall be deemed to have a fair market value equal to its sale price.

3. The members agree that their proportionate shares of the assets and liabilities of the limited liability company are as follows:

4. The limited liability company shall proceed to have an accounting made of all of the assets and liabilities of the limited liability company. The equities of the limited liability company creditors and members shall be determined on the date of the accounting, that shall be no later than _____ , 20 _____ . Any liabilities incurred or funds received by the limited liability company after this date shall be distributed to the members according to their proportionate shares.

5. Any limited liability company assets shall be sold. Any member shall have the right to purchase any limited liability company asset before any sale

to an outside purchaser. The proceeds from the sale of the limited liability company assets, along with any limited liability company funds, shall be applied to the limited liability company liabilities in the following order:

a. To pay all the debts and obligations of the limited liability company
b. To the members' income accounts to the members in their proportionate share
c. To the members' capital accounts to the members in their proportionate share
d. To any remaining assets to the members in their proportionate share

6. Every member hereby represents that he or she has not obligated the limited liability company in any way that does not appear on the records of the limited liability company, nor has he or she received any funds or assets that do not appear on the records of the limited liability company.

7. The limited liability company name shall be disposed of as follows:

8. No modification of this agreement shall be effective unless it is in writing and signed by a majority of the members. This agreement binds and benefits all members and any successors, inheritors, assigns, or representatives of the members. Time is of the essence of this agreement. This document is the entire agreement between the members. Any attached papers that are referred to in this agreement are part of this agreement. Any alleged oral agreements shall have no force or effect. This agreement is governed by the laws of the State of _____ . If any portion of this agreement is held to be invalid, void, or unenforceable by any court of law of competent jurisdiction, the rest of the agreement shall remain in full force and effect.

Dated _____ , 20 _____

Signature of Member/Printed Name of Member

_____   _____
_____   _____
_____   _____
_____   _____
_____   _____

Chapter 12

Employee Documents

The legal forms in this chapter cover a variety of situations that arise in the area of employment. From hiring an employee to subcontracting work on a job, written documents that outline each person's responsibilities and duties are important for keeping an employment situation on an even keel. The employment contract contained in this chapter may be used and adapted for virtually any employment situation. As job skills and salaries rise and employees are allowed access to sensitive and confidential business information, written employment contracts are often a prudent business practice. An independent contractor may also be hired to perform a particular task. As opposed to an employee, this type of worker is defined as one who maintains his or her own independent business, uses his or her own tools, and does not work under the direct supervision of the person who has hired him or her. A contract for hiring an independent contractor is provided in this chapter.

General Employment Contract

This form may be used for any situation in which an employee is hired for a specific job. The issues addressed by this contract are as follows:

- That the employee will perform a certain job and any incidental further duties
- That the employee will be hired for a certain period and for a certain salary
- That the employee will be given certain job benefits (for example: sick pay, vacations, etc.)
- That the employee agrees to abide by the employer's rules and regulations
- That the employee agrees to sign agreements regarding confidentiality and

inventions
- That the employee agrees to submit any employment disputes to mediation and arbitration

The information necessary to complete this form is as follows:

- The names and addresses of the employer and employee
- A complete description of the job
- The date the job is to begin and the length of time that the job will last
- The amount of compensation and benefits for the employee (salary, sick pay, vacation, bonuses, and retirement and insurance benefits)
- Any additional documents to be signed
- Any additional terms
- The state whose laws will govern the contract
- Signatures of employer and employee

Independent Contractor Agreement

This form should be used when hiring an independent contractor. It provides a standard form for the hiring out of specific work to be performed within a set time period for a particular payment. It also provides a method for authorizing extra work under the contract. Finally, this document provides that the contractor agrees to indemnify (reimburse or compensate) the owner against any claims or liabilities arising from the performance of the work. To complete this form, fill in a detailed description of the work; dates by which certain portions of the job are to be completed; the pay for the job; the terms and dates of payment; and the state whose laws will govern the contract.

Contractor/Subcontractor Agreement

This form is intended to be used by an independent contractor to hire a subcontractor to perform certain work on a job that the contractor has agreed to perform. It provides for the "farming out" of specific work to be performed by the subcontractor within a set time period for a particular payment. It also provides a method for authorizing extra work under the contract. Finally, this document provides that the subcontractor agrees to indemnify the contractor against any claims or liabilities arising from the performance of the work. To complete this form, fill in a detailed description of the work; dates by which portions of the job are to be completed; the pay for the job; the terms and dates of payment; and the state whose laws will govern the contract.

General Employment Contract

This contract is made on _____ , 20 _____ , between
_____ , employer,
of _____ , City of _____ ,
State of _____ , and _____
_____ , employee, of _____ , City of
_____ , State of _____ .

For valuable consideration, the employer and employee agree as follows:

1. The employee agrees to perform the following duties and job descrip-
    tion:

    The employee also agrees to perform further duties incidental to the general
    job description. This is considered a full-time position.

2. The employee will begin work on _____ , 20 _____ .

    This position shall continue for a period of _____ .

3. The employee will be paid the following:

    Weekly salary: $ _____

    The employee will also be given the following benefits:

    Sick pay: $ _____
    Vacations: $ _____
    Bonuses: $ _____
    Retirement benefits: $ _____
    Insurance benefits: $ _____

4. The employee agrees to abide by all rules and regulations of the employer
    at all times while employed.

5. This contract may be terminated by:

(a) Breach of this contract by the employee
(b) The expiration of this contract without renewal
(c) Death of the employee
(d) Incapacitation of the employee for over _____ days in any one (1) year

6. The employee agrees to sign the following additional documents as a condition to obtaining employment:

7. Any dispute between the employer and employee related to this contract will be settled by voluntary mediation. If mediation is unsuccessful, the dispute will be settled by binding arbitration using an arbitrator of the American Arbitration Association.

8. Any additional terms of this contract:

9. No modification of this contract will be effective unless it is in writing and is signed by both the employer and employee. This contract binds and benefits both parties and any successors. Time is of the essence of this contract. This document is the entire agreement between the parties. This contract is governed by the laws of the State of _____ .

Dated: _____ , 20 _____

_____
Signature of Employer

_____
Printed Name of Employer

_____
Signature of Employee

_____
Printed Name of Employee

Independent Contractor Agreement

This agreement is made on _____ , 20 _____ , between _____
_____ , owner, of _____
, City of _____ , State of _____ , and _____
_____ , contractor, of _____
_____ , City of _____ , State of _____ .

For valuable consideration, the owner and contractor agree as follows:

1. The contractor agrees to furnish all of the labor and materials to do the following work for the owner as an independent contractor:

2. The contractor agrees that the following portions of the total work will be completed by the dates specified:

Work:

Dates: _____

3. The contractor agrees to perform this work in a workmanlike manner according to standard practices. If any plans or specifications are part of this job, they are attached to and are part of this agreement.

4. The owner agrees to pay the contractor as full payment $ _____ , for doing the work outlined above. This price will be paid to the contractor on satisfactory completion of the work in the following manner and on the following dates:

Work:

Dates: _____

5. The contractor and the owner may agree to extra services and work, but any such extras must be set out and agreed to in writing by both the contractor and the owner.

6. The contractor agrees to indemnify and hold the owner harmless from any claims or liability arising from the contractor's work under this agreement.

7. No modification of this agreement will be effective unless it is in writing and is signed by both parties. This agreement binds and benefits both parties and any successors. Time is of the essence of this agreement. This document, including any attachments, is the entire agreement between the parties. This agreement is governed by the laws of the State of _____.

Dated: _____ , 20 _____

_____
Signature of Owner

_____
Printed Name of Owner

_____
Signature of Contractor

_____
Printed Name of Contractor

Contractor/Subcontractor Agreement

This agreement is made on_____ , 20_____ , between
_____, contractor, of _____ ,
City of _____State of _____ , and _____,
subcontractor, of _____ , City of _____ ,
State of _____ .

1. The subcontractor, as an independent contractor, agrees to furnish all of the labor and materials to do the following portions of the work specified in the agreement between the contractor and the owner dated _____, 20 _____ .

2. The subcontractor agrees that the following portions of the total work will be completed by the dates specified:

   Work:

   Dates: _____

3. The subcontractor agrees to perform this work in a workmanlike manner according to standard practices. If any plans or specifications are part of this job, they are attached to and are part of this agreement.

4. The contractor agrees to pay the subcontractor as full payment $ _____ , for doing the work outlined above. This price will be paid to the subcontractor on satisfactory completion of the work in the following manner and on the following dates:

   Work:

   Dates: _____

5. The contractor and subcontractor may agree to extra services and work, but any such extras must be set out and agreed to in writing by both the contractor and the subcontractor.

6. The subcontractor agrees to indemnify and hold the contractor harmless from any claims or liability arising from the subcontractor's work under this agreement.

7. No modification of this agreement will be effective unless it is in writing and is signed by both parties. This agreement binds and benefits both parties and any successors. Time is of the essence of this agreement. This document, including any attachments, is the entire agreement between the parties. This agreement is governed by the laws of the State of _____ .

Dated: _____ , 20 _____

_____
Signature of Contractor

_____
Printed Name of Contractor

_____
Signature of Subcontractor

_____
Printed Name of Subcontractor

Chapter 13

Business Financial Recordkeeping

Each year, thousands of small businesses fail because their owners have lost control of their finances. Many of these failures are brought on by the inability of the business owners to understand the complex accounting processes and systems that have become relatively standard in modern business. Accounting and bookkeeping have, in most businesses, been removed from the direct control and, therefore, understanding of the business owners themselves. If business owners cannot understand the financial situation of their own businesses, they have little chance of succeeding.

Keeping accurate and clear business financial records can, for many business owners, be the most difficult part of running a business. For most business owners, understanding those records is, at best, a struggle. And yet, maintaining a set of clear and understandable financial records is perhaps the single most important factor that separates successful businesses from those that fail.

Modern business practices have tended to complicate many areas of business when, in many cases, simplification is what most business owners need. In law, in management, and in accounting, many important business functions have been obscured from their owners by intricate systems and complex terminology. Business owners must then turn the handling of these affairs over to specialized professionals in a particular field. The result, in many cases, is that business owners lose crucial understanding of those portions of their business. With this loss of understanding comes the eventual and almost inevitable loss of control.

This is particularly true for small business owners and their financial records. It is absolutely vital that emerging small business owners intimately understand their financial position. Daily decisions must be made that can make or break a fledgling business. If the financial records of a small business are delegated to an outside accountant or bookkeeper, it is often difficult, if not impossible, for a novice business owner to understand the current financial position of the business on a day-to-day basis. Critical business decisions are then made on the basis of incomplete or often unknown financial information.

There are numerous computer-based accounting programs on the market, such as QuickBooks®, that can provide the framework for a company accounting system. However, in order to understand and use any of the computer accounting systems, it is necessary to first have an understanding of the basics of financial recordkeeping.

As a business grows and becomes more complex, and a business owner becomes more comfortable with financial recordkeeping, other more sophisticated and complex accounting systems may become appropriate.

> **Toolkit Tip!**
>
> Even if you choose to use a computer-based accounting program (such as QuickBooks®), you will need to understand the basics of financial records.

Understanding Financial Records

The purpose of any business financial recordkeeping system is to provide a clear vision of the relative health of the business, both on a day-to-day basis and periodically. Business owners themselves need to know whether they are making a profit, why they are making a profit, which parts of the business are profitable, and which are not. This information is only available if the business owner has a clear and straight-forward recordkeeping system. Business owners also need to be able to produce accurate financial statements for income tax purposes, for loan proposals, and for the purpose of selling the business. Clear, understandable, and accurate business records are vital to the success of any small business. In order to design a good recordkeeping system for a particular business, an understanding of certain fundamental ideas of accounting is necessary. For those unfamiliar with the terms and concepts of accounting, grasping these basic ideas may be the most difficult part of accounting, even simplified accounting.

First, let's get some of the terminology clarified. Accounting is the design of the recordkeeping system that a business uses and the preparation and interpretation of reports based on the information that is gathered and put into the system. Bookkeeping is the actual inputting of the financial information into the recordkeeping system. The purpose of any business recordkeeping system is to allow the business owner to easily understand and use the information gathered. Certain accounting principles and terms have been adopted as standard over the years to make it easier to understand a wide range of business transactions. In order to understand what a recordkeeping system is trying to accomplish, it is necessary to define some of the standard ways of looking at a business. There are two standard reports that are the main sources of business financial information: the balance sheet and the profit-and-loss statement.

The Balance Sheet

Ø Definition:

Balance Sheet: A statement of a business's financial position; a summary of the company's assets, liabilities and equity.

The purpose of the balance sheet is to look at what the business owns and owes on a specific date. By seeing what a business owns and owes, anyone looking at a balance sheet can tell the relative financial position of the business at that point in time. If the business owns more than it owes, it is in good shape financially. On the other hand, if it owes more than it owns, the business may be in trouble. The balance sheet is the universal financial document used to view this aspect of a business. It provides this information by laying out the value of the assets and the liabilities of a business. One of the most critical financial tasks that a small business owner must confront is keeping track of what the business owns and owes. Before the business buys or sells anything or makes a profit or loss, the business must have some assets.

The assets of a business are anything that the business owns. These can be cash on hand or in a bank account; personal property, like office equipment, vehicles, tools, or supplies; inventory, or material that will be sold to customers; real estate, buildings, and land; and money that is owed to the business. Money that is owed to a business is called its accounts receivable, basically the money that the business hopes to eventually receive. The total of all of these things that a business owns are the business's assets.

The liabilities of a business are anything that the business owes to others. These consist of long-term debts, such as a mortgage on real estate or a long-term loan. Liabilities also consist of any short-term debts, such as money owed for supplies or taxes. Money that a business owes to others is called its accounts payable, basically the money that the business hopes to eventually pay. In addition to money owed to others, the equity of a business is also considered a liability.

> **⊘ Definition:**
> **Assets and Liabilities:**
> In simplest terms: Assets are what a business owns and liabilities are what a business owes.

The equity of a business is the value of the ownership of the business. It is the value that would be left over if all of the debts of the business were paid off. If the business is a partnership or a sole proprietorship, the business equity is referred to as the net worth of the business. If the business is a corporation, the owner's equity is called the capital surplus or retained capital. All of the debts of a business and its equity are together referred to as the business's liabilities.

The basic relationship between assets and liabilities is shown in a simple equation:

> **⊘ Definition:**
> **Equity:**
> In simplest terms: The equity of a business is the total of its assets minus its liabilities.

Assets = Liabilities

This simple equation is the basis of business accounting. When the books of a business are said to balance, it is this equation that is in balance: the assets of a business must equal the liabilities of a business. Since the liabilities of a business consist of both equity and debts, the equation can be expanded to read:

Assets = Debts + Equity

Rearranging the equation can provide a simple explanation of how to arrive at the value of a business to the owner, or its equity:

Equity = Assets – Debts

A basic tenet of recordkeeping is that both sides of this financial equation must always be equal. The formal statement of the assets and liabilities of a specific business on a specific date is called a balance sheet. A balance sheet is usually prepared on the last day of a month, quarter, or year. A balance sheet simply lists the amounts of the business's assets and liabilities in a standardized format.

☼ Toolkit Tip!

Understand-ing the basics of accounting is crucial in understanding the financial health of your business.

On a balance sheet, the assets of a business are generally broken down into two groups: current assets and fixed assets. Current assets consist of cash, accounts receivable (remember, money that the business intends to receive; basically, bills owed to the business), and inventory. Current assets are generally considered anything that could be converted into cash within one year. Fixed assets are more permanent-type assets and include vehicles, equipment, machinery, land, and buildings owned by the business.

The liabilities of a business are broken down into three groups: current liabilities, long-term liabilities, and owner's equity. Current liabilities are short-term debts, generally those that a business must pay off within one year. This includes accounts payable (remember, money that the business intends to pay; basically, bills the business owes), and taxes that are due. Long-term liabilities are long-term debts such as mortgages or long-term business loans.

Owner's equity is whatever is left after debts are deducted from assets. Thus, the owner's equity is what the owner would have left after all of the debts of the business were paid off. Owner's equity is the figure that is adjusted to make the equation of as-sets and liabilities balance.

Let's look at a simple example: a basic sales business.

Smith's Gourmet Foods has the following assets: Smith has $500.00 in a bank account, is owed $70.00 by customers who pay for their food monthly, has $200.00 worth of food supplies, and owns food preparation equipment worth $1,300.00.

These are the assets of Smith's Gourmet Foods and they are shown on a balance sheet as follows:

⋅♡˙Toolkit Tip!

In order to use computer bookkeeping systems effectively, you will still need an understanding of basic accounting principles.

Cash	$ 500.00
+ Accounts owed to it	$ 70.00
+ Inventory	$ 200.00
+ Equipment	$1,300.00
= Total assets	$2,070.00

Smith also has the following debts: $100.00 owed to the supplier of the food, $200.00 owed to the person from whom she bought the food equipment, and $100.00 owed to the state for sales taxes that have been collected on food sales. Thus, the debts of Smith's Gourmet Foods are shown as follows:

Accounts it owes	$100.00
+ Loans it owes	$ 200.00
+ Taxes it owes	$ 100.00
= Total debts	$ 400.00

To find what Smith's equity in this business is, we need to subtract the amount of the debts from the amount of the assets. Remember: assets – debts = equity. Thus, the owner's equity in Smith's Gourmet Foods is as follows:

Total assets	$2,070.00
– Total debts	$ 400.00
= Owner's equity	$1,670.00

That's it. The business of Smith's Gourmet Foods has a net worth of $1,670.00. If Smith paid off all of the debts of the business, there would be $1,670.00 left. This basic method is used to determine the net worth of businesses worldwide, from the smallest to the largest: **assets = debts + equity**, or **assets – debts = equity**. Remember, both sides of the equation always have to be equal.

The Profit and Loss Statement

The other main business report is the profit and loss statement. This report is a summary of the income and expenses of the business during a certain period. Profit and loss statements are sometimes referred to as income statements or operating statements. You may choose to prepare a profit and loss statement monthly, quarterly, or annually, depending on your particular needs. You will, at a minimum, need to have an annual profit and loss statement in order to streamline your tax return preparation.

A profit and loss statement, however, provides much more than assistance in easing your tax preparation burdens. It allows you to clearly view the performance of your business over a particular time period. As you begin to collect a series of profit and loss statements, you will be able to conduct various analyses of your business. For example, you will be able to compare monthly performances over a single year to determine which month was the best or worst for your business. Quarterly results will also be able to be contrasted. The comparison of several annual expense and revenue figures will allow you to judge the growth or shrinkage of your business over time. Numerous other comparisons are possible, depending on your particular business. How have sales been influenced by advertising expenses? Are production costs higher this quarter than last? Do seasons have an impact on sales? Are certain expenses becoming a burden on the business? The profit and loss statement is one of the key financial statements for the analysis of your business.

Generally, income for a business is any money that it has received or will receive during a certain period. Expenses are any money that it has paid or will pay out during a certain period. Simply put, if the business has more income than expenses during a certain period, it has made a profit. If it has more expenses than income, then the business has a loss for that period of time.

Income can be broken down into two basic types: service income and sales income. The difference between the two types of income lies in the need to consider inventory costs. Service income is income derived from performing a service for someone (cutting hair, for example). Sales income is revenue derived from selling a product of some type. With service income, the profit can be determined simply by deducting the expenses that are associated with making the income. With sales income, however, in addition to deducting the expenses of making the income, the cost of the product that was sold must also be taken into account. This is done through inventory costs. Thus, for sales income, the income from selling a product is actually the sales income minus the cost of the product to the seller. This inventory cost is referred to as the cost of goods sold.

A profit and loss statement begins with a sale. Back to the food business as an example: Smith had the following transactions during the month of July: $250.00 worth of food was sold, the wholesale cost of the food that was sold was $50.00, the cost of napkins, condiments, other supplies, and rent amounted to $100.00, and interest payments on the equipment loan were $50.00. Thus, Smith's profit and loss statement would be prepared as follows:

Gross sales income	$ 250.00
– Cost of food	$ 50.00
= Net sales income	$ 200.00
Operating expenses	$100.00
+ Interest payments	$ 50.00
= Net expenses	$150.00

Thus, for the month of July, Smith's business performed as follows:

Net sales income	$ 200.00
– Net expenses	$ 150.00
= Net profit	$ 50.00

Again, this simple setup reflects the basics of profit and loss statements for all types of businesses, no matter what their size. For a pure service business, with no inventory of any type sold to customers: income – expenses = net profit. For a sales-type business or a sales/service combined business: income – cost of goods sold – expenses = profit.

> **⚡ Toolkit Tip!**
>
> For any business with inventory, you must calculate the 'cost of goods sold' for your profit and loss statement. This is the cost (to you) of the inventory that you have sold over a period of time.

These two types of summary reports—the balance sheet and the profit and loss statement—are the basic tools for understanding the financial health of any business. The figures on them can be used for many purposes to understand the operations of a business. The balance sheet shows what proportion of a business's assets are actually owned by the business owner and what proportion is owned or owed to someone else.

Looking at Smith's balance sheet, we can see that the owner's equity is $1,670.00 of assets of $2,070.00. Thus, we can see that the owner has more than 80 percent ownership of the business, a very healthy situation. There are numerous ways to analyze the figures on these two financial statements. Understanding what these figures mean and how they represent the health of a business are keys to keeping control of the finances of any business.

Accounting Methods

⊘ Definition:

Cash Method:
In 'cash' accounting, income and expenses are recorded when they are actually received or paid.

There are a few more items that must be understood regarding financial recordkeeping. First is the method for recording the records. There are two basic methods for measuring transactions: the *cash method* and the *accrual method*. Cash-method accounting is a system into which income is recorded when it is received and expenses are recorded when they are paid. With cash accounting, there is no effective method to accurately reflect inventory costs. Thus, Internal Revenue Service regulations require that the cash method of accounting may only be used by those few businesses that are solely service businesses and do not sell any materials to their customers at all, even a few spare parts. If a business sells any type of product or material whatsoever, it must use the accrual method of accounting. (An exception to this general rule is allowed for any corporation or partnership with annual gross receipts of under $5 million.)

The accrual method of accounting counts income and expenses when they are due to the business. Income is recorded when the business has a right to receive the income. In other words, accounts receivable (bills owed to the business) are considered as income that has already been received by the business. Expenses are considered and recorded when they are due, even if they are not yet paid. In other words, accounts payable (bills owed by the business) are considered expenses to the business when they are received, not when they are actually paid. The vast majority of businesses will wish to use the accrual method of accounting. A business must choose to keep its records either on the accrual basis or on the cash basis. Once this decision is made, approval from the IRS must be obtained before the method can be changed. After you select the type of accounting you will use, please consult a tax professional if a change in the system must be made.

Accounting Systems

In addition, there are two basic types of recordkeeping systems: *single-entry* and *double-entry*. Both types are able to be used to keep accurate records, although the double-entry system has more ways available to double-check calculations. Double-entry recordkeeping is, however, much more difficult to master, in that each and every transaction must be entered in two separate places in the records. Most modern computer-based accounting systems have greatly simplified the use of double-entry accounting. If you will be keeping your own book, however, the benefits of ease of use of a single-entry system far outweigh the disadvantages of this system. The IRS recommends single-entry records for beginning small businesses, and states that this type of system can be "relatively simple...used effectively...and is adequate for income tax purposes." Many accountants will disagree with this and insist that only double-entry accounting is acceptable. For the small business owner who wishes to understand his or her own company's finances, the advantages of single-entry accounting far outweigh the disadvantages.

Accounting Periods

A final item to consider is the accounting period for your business. A business is allowed to choose between a *fiscal-year* accounting period and a *calendar-year* period. A fiscal year consists of 12 consecutive months that do not end on December 31st. A

> **⊘ Definition:**
> **Accrual Method:**
> This type of accounting records income and expenses when they are either earned or billed, as opposed to when they are actually received or paid, as with the cash method.

> **⊘ Definition:**
> **Calendar Year:**
> An accounting period from January 1 to December 31.

⊘ Definition:

Fiscal Year:
An accounting period of 12 consecutive months, beginning on the 1st of any month, such as July 1st.

calendar year consists of 12 consecutive months that do end on December 31st. There are complex rules relating to the choice of fiscal-year accounting. Partnerships and S-corporations may generally choose to report on a fiscal-year basis only if there is a valid business purpose that supports the use of a fiscal year. This generally complicates the reporting of income and should be avoided unless there is an important reason to choose a fiscal-year accounting period. If a fiscal-year period is considered necessary, please consult a tax or accounting professional as there are complicated rules to comply with.

For the majority of small businesses, the choice of a calendar-year period is perfectly adequate and, in most cases, will simplify the tax reporting and accounting recordkeeping. In the year in which a business is either started or ended, the business year for reporting may not be a full year. Thus, even for those who choose to use a calendar year, the first year may actually start on a date other than January 1st.

Chart of Accounts

The backbone of the recordkeeping system is the Chart of Accounts for your business. A *chart of accounts* will list each of the income, expense, asset, or debt categories that you wish to keep track of. Every business transaction that you make and every financial record that you create will fit into one of these four main categories. Your transactions will either be money coming in (income) or money going out (expenses). Your records will also track things the business owns (assets) or things the business owes (debts). The chart of accounts that you create will allow you to itemize and track each of these four broad categories in detail.

Setting up an account for each of these categories consists of the simple task of deciding which items you will need to categorize, selecting a name for the account, and assigning a number to the account.

Before you can set up your accounts, you need to understand the reason for setting up these separate accounts. It is possible, although definitely not recommended, to run a business and merely keep track of your income and expenses without any itemization at all. However, you would be unable to analyze how the business is performing beyond a simple check to see if you have any money left after paying the expenses. You would also be unable to properly fill in the necessary information for business income tax returns. A major reason for setting up separate accounts for many business expense and income transactions is to separate and itemize the amounts spent in each category so that this information is available at tax time. This insures that a business is taking all of its allowable business deductions.

The main reason, however, to set up individual accounts is to allow the business owner to have a clear view of the financial health of the business. With separate accounts for each type of transaction, a business owner can analyze the proportional costs and revenues of each aspect of the business. Is advertising costing more than labor expenses? Is the income derived from sale items worth the discount of the sale? Only by using the figures obtained from separate itemized accounts can these questions be answered.

> **Toolkit Tip!**
>
> A chart of accounts customized for your business will be necessary even if you use a computer-based accounting system.

Take some time to analyze your specific business to decide how you wish to set up your accounts. Ask yourself what type of information you will want to extract from your financial records. Do you need more details of your income sources? Then you should set up several income accounts for each type and possibly even each source of your income. Would you like more specific information on your expenses? Then you would most likely wish to set up clear and detailed expense accounts for each type of expense that you must pay.

Be aware that you may wish to alter your Chart of Accounts as your business grows. You may find that you have set up too many accounts and unnecessarily complicated your recordkeeping tasks. You might wish to set up more accounts once you see how your Balance Sheets and Profit and Loss Statements look. You can change, add, or delete accounts at any time. Remember, however, that any transactions that have been recorded in an account must be transferred to any new account or accounts that take the place of the old account.

Income Accounts

These are accounts that are used to track the various sources of your company's income. There may be only a few sources of income for your business or you may wish to track your income in more detail. The information which you collect in your income accounts will be used to prepare your Profit and Loss Statements periodically. Recall that a Profit and Loss Statement is also referred to as an Income and Expense Statement.

Income may be separated into several categories. You can choose the income account categories which best suit your type of business. If your business is a service business, you may wish to set up accounts for labor income and for materials income. Or you may wish to set up income accounts in more detail, for example: sales income, markup income, income from separate properties, or income from separate sources in your business, etc. Non-sales income, such as bank account interest income or income on the sale of business equipment, should be placed in separate individual income accounts. You may also wish to set up separate income accounts for income from different ongoing projects or income from separate portions of your business.

Expense Accounts

These are the accounts that you will use to keep track of your expenses. Each separate category of expense should have its own account. Many of the types of accounts are dictated by the types of expenses which should be itemized for tax purposes. Consulting the tax return for your type of business entity is a good way to understand which expense should be tracked.

You will generally have separate accounts for advertising costs, utility expenses, rent, phone costs, etc. One or more separate accounts should also be set up to keep track of inventory expenses. These should be kept separate from other expense accounts as they must be itemized for tax purposes. You will need to analyze your business and determine which expense accounts would be best suited to select for your particular situation.

Asset and Liability Accounts

Asset and liability accounts are collectively referred to as Balance Sheet Chart of Accounts. This is because the information collected on them is used to prepare your business Balance Sheets. You will set up current and fixed asset accounts and current and long-term liability accounts. Types of current asset accounts are cash, short-term notes receivable, accounts receivable, inventory, and prepaid expenses. Fixed assets may include equipment, vehicles, buildings, land, long-term notes receivable, and long-term loans receivable.

Types of current liability accounts are short-term notes payable (money due within one year), short-term loans payable (money due on a loan within one year), unpaid taxes, and unpaid wages. Long-term liability accounts may be long-term notes payable (money due more than one year in the future) or long-term loans payable (money due on a loan more than one year in the future). Finally, you will need an owner's equity account to tally the ownership value of your business.

Tracking Business Assets

After setting up a Chart of Accounts, the next financial recordkeeping task for a business will consist of preparing a method to keep track of the assets of the business. Recall that the assets of a business are everything that is owned by the business and are either current assets that can be converted to cash within a year or fixed assets that are more long-term in nature. Each of these two main categories of assets will be discussed separately.

Current Assets

Typical current assets for a business are the business bank checking account, business bank savings account, cash (petty cash fund and cash on hand), accounts receivable (money owed to the company), and inventory.

> ⊘ **Definition:**
>
> **Current Assets:** Generally, assets of a business that can be converted into cash within one year.

A company may have other types of current assets such as notes or loans receivable, but the five listed above are the basic ones for most small businesses. In complex double-entry accounting systems, the current asset account balances are constantly being changed.

In a double-entry system, each time an item of inventory is sold, for example, the account balance for the inventory account must be adjusted to reflect the sale. In single-entry systems, all asset and liability accounts are updated only when the business owner wishes to prepare a Balance Sheet. This may be done monthly, quarterly, or annually. At a minimum, this updating must take place at the end of the year in order to have the necessary figures available for tax purposes.

Inventory

Toolkit Tip!

The value of your inventory on hand is considered a current asset of a business.

Any business that sells an item of merchandise to a customer must have a system in place to keep track of inventory. Inventory is considered any merchandise or materials that are held for sale during the normal course of your business. Inventory costs include the costs of the merchandise or products themselves and the costs of the materials and paid labor that go into creating a finished product. Inventory does not include the costs of the equipment or machinery that you need to create the finished product.

There are several reasons you will need a system of inventory control. First, if you are stocking parts or supplies to sell, you will need to keep track of what you have ordered, what is in stock, and when you will need to reorder. You will also need to keep track of the cost of your inventory for tax purposes. The amount of money that you spend on your inventory is not fully deductible in the year spent as a business deduction. The only portion of your inventory cost that will reduce your gross profit for tax purposes is the actual cost of the goods that you have sold during the tax year.

For tax purposes and for your own understanding of inventory management, you will need to determine the actual cost of the goods that were sold during a particular time period. There are numerous methods to determine the value of your inventory at the end of a time period. The three most important are the specific identification method, the first-in first-out (FIFO) method, and the last-in first-out (LIFO) method. Specific identification is the easiest to use if you have only a few items of inventory, or one-of-a-kind type merchandise. With this method, you actually keep track of each specific item of inventory. You keep track of when you obtained the item, its cost, and when you sold the specific item. With the FIFO method, you keep track only of general quantities of your inventory. Your inventory costs are calculated as though the oldest inventory merchandise was sold first. The first items that you purchased are the first items that you sell. With the LIFO method, the cost values are calculated as though you sold your most-recently purchased inventory first. It is important to note that you do not necessarily have to actually sell your first item first to use the FIFO method and that you don't have to actually sell your last item first to use the LIFO method of calculation.

Although there may be significant advantages in some cases to using the LIFO method, it is also a far more complicated system than the FIFO. The specific identification method allows you to simply track each item of inventory and deduct the actual cost of the goods that you sold during the year. The FIFO method allows you to value your inventory on hand at the end of a time period based on the cost of your most recent purchases.

Cost of Goods Sold

The basic method for keeping track of inventory costs for tax purposes is to determine the cost of goods sold. First, you will need to know how much inventory is on hand at the beginning of the year. To this amount, you add the cost of any additional inventory you purchased during the year. Finally, you determine how much inventory is left at the end of the year. The difference is essentially the cost (to you) of the inventory that you sold during the year. This amount is referred to as the cost of goods sold. Every year at tax time, you will need to figure the cost of goods sold. Additionally, you may need to determine your cost of goods sold monthly or quarterly for various business purposes.

> **Toolkit Tip!**
> At a minimum, you will need to calculate the cost of goods sold annually for income tax purposes.

Using our sample company, Smith's Gourmet Foods, we will start the owner's first year in business with an inventory of $0.00. When her business begins, there is no inventory. During the first year, she purchases $17,500.00 worth of products that are for selling to customers. At the end of the year, she counts all of the items that are left in her possession and determines her cost for these items. The cost of the items left unsold at the end of the year is $3,700.00.

The calculation of the cost of goods sold for the first year in business is as follows:

Inventory at beginning of first year	$ 00.00
+ Cost of inventory added during year	$ 17,500.00
= Cost of inventory	$ 17,500.00
− Inventory at end of first year	$ 3,700.00
= Cost of Goods Sold for first year	$ 13,800.00

For the second year in business, the figure for the inventory at the beginning of the year is the value of the inventory at the end of the previous year. Thus, if Smith's Gourmet Foods added $25,000.00 additional inventory during the second year of operation and the value of the inventory at the end of the second year was $4,800.00, the cost-of-goods-sold calculations for the second year would be as follows:

Inventory at beginning of second year	$ 3,700.00
+ Cost of inventory added during year	$ 25,000.00
= Cost of inventory	$ 28,700.00
− Inventory at end of second year	$ 4,800.00
= Cost of goods sold for second year	$ 23,900.00

Thus, for the second year in operation the cost of goods sold would be $23,900.00. This amount would be deducted from the gross revenues that Smith's Gourmet Foods took in for the year to determine the gross profit for the second year in business.

Fixed Assets

The final category of assets that you will need to track are your fixed assets. Fixed assets are the more permanent assets of your business, generally the assets that are not for sale to customers. The main categories of these fixed assets are:

- Buildings
- Land
- Machinery
- Tools
- Furniture and Equipment
- Vehicles

There are many more types of fixed assets, such as patents, copyrights, and goodwill. However, the six listed above are the basic ones for most small businesses. If your business includes other types of fixed assets, please consult an accounting professional. For those with basic fixed assets, you will need to keep track of the actual total costs to you to acquire them. These costs include sales taxes, transportation charges, installation costs, etc. The total cost of a fixed asset to you is referred to as the asset's cost basis.

With a major exception explained below, the costs of fixed assets are, generally, not immediately deductible as a business expense. Rather, except for land, their costs are deductible proportionately over a period of time. This proportionate deduction is referred to as depreciation. Since these assets generally wear out over time (except for land), each year you are allowed to deduct a portion of the initial cost as a legitimate business expense. Each type of fixed asset is given a specific time period for dividing up the cost into proportional amounts. This time period is called the recovery period of the asset. Depreciation is a very complex subject and one whose rules change nearly every year. The full details of depreciation are beyond the scope of this book. What follows is only a general outline of depreciation rules. It will allow you to begin to set up your fixed asset records. However, you will need to consult either an accounting or tax professional or consult specific tax preparation manuals for details on how your specific assets should be depreciated.

> **⊘ Definition:**
> **Fixed Assets:**
> Generally, assets of a business that cannot readily be converted into cash. Thus, they are all assets that are not *current* assets.

> **⌁ Toolkit Tip!**
>
> Depreciation rules are quite complex and you should consult with a tax professional to determine the depreciation rates for the initial fixed assets of your business.

The major exception to depreciation rules is that, under the rules of Internal Revenue Service Code Section 179, every year a total of $125,000.00 (after the tax year 2007, this amount will be adjusted annually for inflation) of your fixed asset costs can be immediately used as a business deduction. This means that if your total purchases of equipment, tools, vehicles, etc., during a year amounted to less than $125,000.00, you can deduct all of the costs as current expenses. If your total fixed asset costs are more than $125,000.00, you can still deduct the first $125,000.00 in costs and then depreciate the remaining costs over time. Here are some basic rules relating to depreciation:

1. The depreciation rules that were in effect at the time of the purchase of the asset will be the rules that apply to that particular asset.

2. The actual cost to you of the asset is the cost basis that you use to compute your depreciation amount each year.

3. Used assets that you purchase for use in your business can be depreciated in the same manner as new assets.

4. Assets that you owned prior to going into business and that you will use in your business can be depreciated. The cost basis will be the lower of their actual market value when you begin to use them in your business or their actual cost to you. For example, you start a carpentry business and use your personal power saw in the business. It cost $150.00 new, but is now worth about $90.00. You can depreciate $90.00 (or deduct this amount as an expense if the total of your fixed asset deductions is less than $125,000.00).

5. You may depreciate proportionately those assets that you use partially for business and partially for personal use. In the above example, if you use your saw 70 percent of the time in your business and 30 percent for personal use, you may deduct or depreciate 70 percent of $90.00, which is $63.00.

The tax depreciation rules set up several categories of asset types for the purpose of deciding how long a period you must use to depreciate the asset. Cars, trucks, computer equipment, copiers, and similar equipment are referred to as five-year property. Most machinery, heavy equipment, and office furniture are referred to as seven-year property. This means that for these types of property the actual costs are spread out and depreciated over five or seven years—that is, the costs are deducted over a period of five or seven years.

There are also several different ways to compute how much of the cost can be depreciated each year. There are three basic methods: straight-line, MACRS, and ACRS. Straight-line depreciation spreads the deductible amount equally over the recovery period.

Thus for the power saw that is worth $90.00 and is used 70 percent of the time in a business, the cost basis that can be depreciated is $63.00. This asset has a recovery period of seven years. Spreading the $63.00 over the seven-year period allows you to deduct a total of $9.00 per year as depreciation of the saw. After the first year, the saw will be valued on your books at $54.00. Thus, after seven years, the value of the saw on your books will be zero. It will have been fully depreciated. You will have finally been allowed to fully deduct its cost as a business expense. Of course, if you have fixed asset costs of less than $125,000.00 for the year you put the saw in service, you will be allowed to claim the entire $63.00 deduction that first year.

See the glossary for an explanation of MACRS and ACRS depreciations. Other methods of depreciation have more complicated rules that must be applied. For full details, please refer to a tax preparation manual or consult a tax or accounting professional.

Following are listed various types of property that are depreciable or deductible. Consult this list to determine which of your business purchases may be depreciated and which of them may be written off as an immediately deductible expense. Of course, also remember that tax laws are always subject to change.

> **Toolkit Tip!**
>
> Certain property that would normally be depreciable can be deducted as a Section 179 expense in its first year of use. Please see www.irs.gov for a more detailed explanation of this rule.

☼ Toolkit Tip!

There are special rules that apply to the deductibility of certain business expenses that relate to home businesses. Please see www.irs.gov for more details.

Deductible Expenses

Advertising
Bad debts
Bank charges
Books and periodicals
Car and truck expenses:
  Gas, repairs, licenses,
  insurance, maintenance
Commissions to salespersons
Independent contractor costs
Donations
Dues to professional groups
Educational expenses
Entertainment of clients
Freight costs
Improvements worth less than $100
Insurance
Interest costs
Laundry and cleaning
Licenses for business
Legal and professional fees
Maintenance

Office equipment worth less than $100
Office furniture worth less than $100
Office supplies
Pension plans
Postage
Printing costs
Property taxes
Rent
Repairs
Refunds, returns, and allowances
Sales taxes collected
Sales taxes paid on purchases
Telephone
Tools worth less than $100
Uniforms
Utilities
Wages paid

Depreciable Property

Business buildings (not land)
Office furniture worth over $100
Office equipment worth over $100
Business machinery
Tools worth over $100
Vehicles used in business

Tracking Business Debts

Business debts are also referred to as business liabilities. However, technically, business liabilities also include the value of the owner's equity in the business. Business debts can be divided into two general categories. First are current debts, those that will normally be paid within one year. The second general category is long-term debts. These are generally debts that will not be paid off within one year. Current debts for most small businesses consist primarily of accounts payable and taxes that are due during the year. For small businesses, the taxes that are due during a year fall into three main categories: estimated income tax payments, payment of collected sales taxes, and payroll taxes. Since the collection and payment of sales taxes are handled differently in virtually every state, you will need to contact your state's department of revenue or similar body to determine the specific necessary recordkeeping requirements for that business debt. Payroll taxes will be explained in the next chapter.

Accounts payable are the current bills that your business owes. They may be for equipment or supplies that you have purchased on credit or for items that you have ordered on account. Long-term debts are, generally, debts based on business loans for equipment, inventory, business-owned vehicles, or business property. Regardless of the source of the debt, you will need a clear system to record the debt and keep track of how much you still owe on the debt, and the current principal and interest for these debts.

> **⌀ Definition:**
>
> **Accounts Payable:**
> These are simply the bills that your business currently owes to others.

Tracking Business Expenses

The expenses of a business are all of the transactions of the business where money is paid out of the business, with one general exception. Money paid out of the business to pay off the principal of a loan is not considered an expense of a business. Because of the tax deductibility of the cost of most business expenses, it is crucial for a business to keep careful records of what has been spent to operate the business. But even beyond the need for detailed expense records for tax purposes, a small business needs a clear system that will allow a quick examination of where money is being spent. The tracking of business expenses will allow you to quickly see where your money is flowing.

Tracking Business Income

The careful tracking of your business income is one of the most important accounting activities you will perform. It is essential for your business that you know intimately where your income comes from. Failure to accurately track income and cash is one of the most frequent causes of business failure. You must have in place a clear and easily understood system to track your business income. There are three separate features of tracking business income that must be incorporated into your accounting system. You will need a system in place to handle cash, a system to track all of your sales and service income, and a system to handle credit sales.

The first system you will need is a clear method for handling cash on a periodic basis. This is true no matter how large or small your business may be and regardless of how much or how little cash is actually handled. You must have a clear record of how much cash is on hand and how much cash is taken in during a particular time period. Most businesses will have to handle cash in some form. Here we are not talking about the use of petty cash but rather the daily handling of cash used to take money in from customers or clients and the use of a cash drawer or some equivalent. You must have some method to accurately account for the cash used in your business in this regard. Petty cash is the cash that a business has on hand for the payment of minor expenses that may crop up and for which the use of a business check is not convenient.

The second feature of your business income tracking system should be a method to track your actual income from sales or services. This differs from your cash tracking. With these records you will track taxable and nontaxable income whether the income is in the form of cash, check, credit card payment, or payment on an account. For sales tax information, please contact your state's sales tax revenue collection agency. If your state has a sales tax on the product or service that you provide, you will need accurate records to determine your total taxable and nontaxable income and the amount of sales tax that is due. Please note that when nontaxable income is referred to, it means only that income which is not subject to any state or local sales tax.

The third feature of your business income tracking consists of a method to track and bill credit sales. With this portion of income tracking, you will need to track all of your sales to customers that are made on account or on credit. The accounts that owe you money are referred to as your *accounts receivable*. These are the accounts from whom you hope to receive payment. The actual billing of these credit sales will require you to prepare and incorporate invoices, statements, and past due statements.

These basic accounting principles and practices are used in all types of businesses, large or small. They also form the frameworks of all of the various computer-based accounting and bookkeeping software that you may choose to use. Understanding these basics will help you make sure that your new business is as successful as possible. Following is a checklist for setting up your business financial recordkeeping:

⊘ **Definition:**

Accounts Receivable: These are the debts that are currently owed to your business by others.

Financial Recordkeeping Checklist

❏ Set up your business chart of accounts

❏ Open a business checking account

❏ Prepare a check register

❏ Set up a business petty cash fund

❏ Prepare a petty cash register

❏ Set up asset accounts

❏ Prepare current asset account records

❏ Prepare fixed asset account records

❏ Set up expense account records

❏ Set up income account records

❏ Set up payroll system

❏ Prepare payroll time sheets

❏ Prepare payroll depository records

❏ Determine proper tax forms for use in the business

Chapter 14

Business Payroll

One of the most difficult and complex accounting functions that small businesses face is their payroll. Because of the various state and federal taxes that must be applied and the myriad government forms that must be prepared, the handling of a business payroll often causes accounting nightmares. Even if there is only one employee; there is a potential for problems.

First, let's examine the basics. If your business is a corporation or limited liability company, all pay must be handled as payroll, even if you are the only employee. The corporation is a separate entity and the corporation or limited liability company itself will be the employer. You and any other people that you hire will be the employees. If you are operating as a sole proprietorship, you may still hire employees. A business payroll entails a great deal of paperwork and has numerous government tax filing deadlines. You will be required to make payroll tax deposits, file various quarterly payroll tax returns, and make additional end-of-the-year reports.

Initially, you must take certain steps to set up your payroll and official status as an employer. The following information contains the instructions only for meeting federal requirements. Please check with your particular state and local governments for information regarding any additional payroll tax, state unemployment insurance, or workers' compensation requirements.

☿ Toolkit Tip!

You must check with your state's payroll tax department and unemployment insurance department if you will be hiring any employees.

Setting up Your Payroll

1. The first step in becoming an employer is to file Internal Revenue Service Form SS-4: Application for Employer Identification Number. This will officially register your business with the Federal government as an employer. This form and instructions are included on the Forms-on-CD.

2. Next, each employee must fill in an IRS Form W-4: Employee's Withholding Allowance Certificate. This will provide you with the necessary information regarding withholding allowances to enable you to prepare your payroll.

3. You must then determine the gross salary or wage that each employee will earn. For each employee, complete an Employee Payroll Record and prepare a Quarterly Payroll Time Sheet as explained later in this chapter.

4. You will then need to consult the tables in IRS Circular E: Employer's Tax Guide. From the tables in this publication, you will be able to determine the proper deductions for each employee for each pay period. If your employees are paid on an hourly basis and the number of hours worked is different each pay period, you will have to perform these calculations for each pay period. You will need to obtain the latest version of this guide from www.irs.gov.

5. Before you pay your employee, you should open a separate business bank account for handling your business payroll tax deductions and payments. This will allow you to immediately deposit all taxes due into this separate account and help prevent the lack of sufficient money available when the taxes are due.

6. Next you will pay your employee and record the deduction information on the Employee Payroll Record.

7. When you have completed paying all of your employees for the pay period, you will write a separate check for the total amount of all of your employees' deductions and any employer's share of taxes. You will then deposit this check

into your business payroll tax bank account that you set up following the instructions above.

8. At the end of every month, you will need to transfer the information regarding employee deductions to your Payroll Depository Record and Annual Payroll Summary. Copies of these forms and instructions are included later in this chapter. You will then calculate your employer share of Social Security and Medicare taxes. Each month (or quarter if your tax liability is more than $2,500 per quarter), you will need to deposit the correct amount of taxes due to the Federal government. This is done by making a monthly payment to your bank for the taxes due using IRS Form 8109: Federal Tax Deposit Coupon (If your liability is below $2500 per quater then you make the payment on a quarterly basis when you file IRS Form 941: Employer's Quarterly Federal Tax Return. Copies of these forms are contained on the Forms-on-CD.

> **Toolkit Tip!**
>
> Failure to pay payroll taxes on time is one of the most common reasons for business tax problems.

9. On a quarterly or annual basis, you will also need to make a tax payment for Federal Unemployment Tax, using IRS Form 940: Employer's Annual Federal Unemployment (FUTA) Tax Return. This tax is solely the responsibility of the employer and is not deducted from the employee's pay. Also on a quarterly basis, you will need to file IRS Form 941: Employer's Quarterly Federal Tax Return. If you have made monthly deposits of your taxes due, there will be no quarterly taxes to pay, but you will still need to file these forms quarterly.

10. Finally, to complete your payroll, at the end of the year you must do the following:

   • Prepare IRS Form W-2: Wage and Tax Statement for each employee
   • File IRS Form W-3: Transmittal of Wage and Tax Statements

Remember that your state and local tax authorities will generally have additional requirements and taxes that will need to be paid. In many jurisdictions, these requirements are tailored after the Federal requirements and the procedures and due dates are similar.

Payroll Checklist

❑ File IRS Form SS-4: Application for Employer Identification Number and obtain Federal Employer Identification Number.

❑ Obtain IRS Form W-4: Employee's Withholding Allowance Certificate for each employee.

❑ Set up Payroll Record and Quarterly Payroll Time sheet for each employee.

❑ Open separate business Payroll Tax Bank Account.

❑ Consult IRS Circular E: Employer's Tax Guide and use tables to determine withholding tax amounts.

❑ Obtain information on any applicable state or local taxes.

❑ List withholding, Social Security, Medicare and any state or local deductions on employee's Payroll Record.

❑ Pay employees and deposit appropriate taxes in your Payroll Tax Bank Account.

❑ Fill in Payroll Depository Record and Annual Payroll Summary.

❑ Pay payroll taxes:

    ❑ Monthly using IRS Form 8109: Federal Tax Deposit Coupon, if your payroll tax liability is more than $2500 per quarter.

    ❑ Quarterly using IRS Form 941: Employer's Quarterly Federal Tax Return, if your payroll tax liability is less than $2500 per quarter.

    ❑ Annually, file IRS Form 940: Employer's Annual Federal Unemployment (FUTA) Tax Return.

❑ Annually, prepare and file IRS W-2 Forms: Wage and Tax Statement for each employee, and IRS Form W-3: Transmittal of Wage and Tax Statements.

Quarterly Payroll Time Sheet

On the following page is a Quarterly Payroll Time Sheet. If your employees are paid an hourly wage, you will prepare a sheet like this for each employee for each quarter during the year. On this sheet you will keep track of the following information:

• Number of hours worked (daily, weekly, and quarterly)
• Number of regular and overtime hours worked

The information from this Quarterly Payroll Time Sheet will be transferred to your individual Employee Payroll Record in order to calculate the employee's paycheck amounts. This is explained following the Quarterly Payroll Time Sheet.

Quarterly Payroll Time Sheet

Employee:

Week of	Sun	Mon	Tue	Wed	Thu	Fri	Sat	Reg	OT	Total
Quarterly TOTAL										

Employee Payroll Record

1. For each employee, fill in the following information at the top of the form:

    - Name and address of employee
    - Employee's Social Security number
    - Number of exemptions claimed by employee on Form W-4
    - Regular and overtime wage rates
    - Pay period (ie., weekly, biweekly, monthly, etc.)
    - Date check is written
    - Payroll check number

2. For each pay period, fill in the number of regular and overtime ("OT") hours worked by the employee from his or her Quarterly Payroll Time Sheet. Multiply this amount by the employee's wage rate to determine the gross pay. For example: 40 hours at the regular wage of $8.00/hour = $320.00; plus five hours at the overtime wage rate of $12.00/hour = $60.00. Gross pay for the period is $320.00 + $60.00 = $380.00.

3. Determine the Federal withholding tax deduction for the pay amount by consulting the withholding tax tables in IRS Circular E: Employer's Tax Guide. Enter this figure on the form in the "Fed. W/H" column.

4. Determine the employee's share of Social Security and Medicare deductions. As of 2008, the employee's Social Security share rate is 6.2 percent and the employee's Medicare share rate is 1.45 percent. Multiply these rates times the employee's gross wages and enter the figures in the appropriate places; the "S/S Ded." and "Medic. Ded." columns. For example: for $380.00, the Social Security deduction would be $380.00 x .062 = $23.56 and the Medicare deduction would be $380.00 x .0145 = $5.51.

5. Determine any state taxes and enter in the appropriate column.

6. Subtract all of the deductions from the employee's gross wages to determine the employee's net pay. Enter this figure in the final column and prepare the employee's paycheck using the deduction information from this sheet. Also prepare a check to your payroll tax bank account for a total of the Federal withholding amount and two times the Social Security and Medicare amounts. This includes your employer share of these taxes. The employer's share of Social Security and Medicare taxes is equal to the employee's share.

Employee Payroll Record

Employee:
Address:

Social Security #:
Number of Exemptions:
Rate of Pay: Overtime Rate:
Pay Period:

Date	Check #	Pay Period	Reg. Hours	OT Hours	Gross Pay	Fed. W/H	S/S Ded.	Medic. Ded.	State Taxes	Net Pay
Pay Period TOTAL										

Payroll Depository Record

You will be required to deposit taxes with the IRS on a monthly or quarterly basis (unless your total employment taxes totaled more than $50,000.00 for the previous year, in which case you should obviously consult an accountant). If your employment taxes total less than $2,500.00 per quarter, you may pay your payroll tax liability when you quarterly file your Federal Form 941: Employer's Quarterly Federal Tax Return. If your payroll tax liability is more than $2,500.00 per quarter, you must deposit your payroll taxes on a monthly basis with a bank using IRS Form 8109: Federal Tax Deposit Coupon. Copies of these two Federal forms are contained on the Forms-on-CD. To track your payroll tax liability, use the Payroll Depository Record which follows these instructions:

1. On a monthly basis, total each column on all of your Employee Payroll Records. This will give you a figure for each employee's Federal withholding, Social Security, and Medicare taxes for the month.

2. Total all of the Federal withholding taxes for all employees for the month and enter this figure in the appropriate column on the Payroll Depository Record.

3. Total Social Security and Medicare taxes for all of your employees for the entire month and enter this figure in the appropriate columns on the Payroll Depository Record. Note that "SS/EE" refers to Social Security/Employee's Share and that "MC/EE" refers to Medicare/Employee's Share.

4. Enter identical amounts in the SS/ER and MC/ER columns as you have entered in the SS/EE and MC/EE columns. "ER" refers to the employer's share. The employer's share of Social Security and Medicare is the same as the employee's share, but is not deducted from the employee's pay.

5. Total all of the deductions for the month. This is the amount of your total monthly Federal payroll tax liability. If necessary, write a check to your local bank for this amount and deposit it using IRS Form 8109: Federal Tax Deposit Coupon.

6. If you must file only quarterly, total all three of your monthly amounts on a quarterly basis and pay this amount when you file your IRS Form 941: Employer's Quarterly Federal Tax Return. On a yearly basis, total all of the quarterly columns to arrive at your total annual Federal payroll tax liability.

Payroll Depository Record

Month	Fed. W/H	SS/EE	SS/ER	MC/EE	MC/ER	Total
January						
February						
March						
1st Quarter						

1st Quarter Total Number of Employees: Total Wages Paid:

Month	Fed. W/H	SS/EE	SS/ER	MC/EE	MC/ER	Total
April						
May						
June						
2nd Quarter						

2nd Quarter Total Number of Employees: Total Wages Paid:

Month	Fed. W/H	SS/EE	SS/ER	MC/EE	MC/ER	Total
July						
August						
September						
3rd Quarter						

3rd Quarter Total Number of Employees: Total Wages Paid:

Month	Fed. W/H	SS/EE	SS/ER	MC/EE	MC/ER	Total
October						
November						
December						
4th Quarter						

4th Quarter Total Number of Employees: Total Wages Paid:

Yearly TOTAL						

Yearly Total Number of Employees: Total Wages Paid:

Annual Payroll Summary

The final payroll form is used to total all of the payroll amounts for all employees on a monthly, quarterly, and annual basis. Much of the information on this form is similar to the information that you compiled for the Payroll Depository Record. However, the purpose of this form is to provide you with a record of all of your payroll costs, including the payroll deduction costs. This form will be useful for both tax and planning purposes as you examine your business profitability on a quarterly and annual basis. Follow these directions to prepare this form:

1. For each month, total all of your employees' gross and net pay amounts from their individual Employee Payroll Records and transfer these totals to this form.

2. For each month, transfer the amounts for Federal withholding from the Payroll Depository Record to this form.

3 For each month, total both columns on your Payroll Depository Record for SS/EE ("Social Security/Employee") and SS/ER ("Social Security/Employer") and transfer this total to the "S/S Taxes" column on this summary. Total the MC/EE ("Medicare/Employee") and MC/ER ("Medicare/Employer") columns also and enter the total in the "Medicare Taxes" column on this form.

4. On a quarterly basis, total the columns to determine your quarterly payroll costs. Annually, total the quarterly amounts to determine your annual costs.

Annual Payroll Summary

	Gross Pay	Federal W/H	S/S Taxes	Medicare Taxes	State Taxes	Net Pay
January						
February						
March						
1st Quarter Total						
April						
May						
June						
2nd Quarter Total						
July						
August						
September						
3rd Quarter Total						
October						
November						
December						
4th Quarter Total						
Yearly TOTAL						

Chapter 15

Taxation of Businesses

A basic comprehension of the information required on federal tax forms will help you understand why certain financial records are necessary. Understanding tax reporting will also assist you as you decide how to organize your business financial records. A checklist of tax forms is provided that details which IRS forms are necessary for each type of business. In addition, various schedules of tax filing are also provided to assist you in keeping your tax reporting timely. Finally, a sample of each form is included on the Forms-on-CD. Taxation details for all five basic business entities follow:

Taxation of Sole Proprietorships

The taxation of sole proprietorships is a relatively easy concept to understand. The sole proprietorship is not considered a separate entity for federal tax purposes. Thus, all of the profits and losses of the business are simply reported as personal profits or losses of the sole owner. They are reported on IRS Schedule C: Profits or Losses of a Business or on IRS Schedule C-EZ: Net Profits of a Business and are included in the calculations for completing the owner's joint or single IRS Form 1040.

Please note that many of the tax forms in this chapter will only apply to a sole proprietorship that actually hires employees. Simply because a sole proprietorship business is owned by one owner does not in any way restrict the sole owner from hiring employees or independent contractors to assist in the operation of the business. In fact, there have been sole proprietorships that have operated with many, many employees and at different locations and even in many states.

Sole Proprietorship Tax Forms Checklist

☐ IRS Form 1040: U.S. Individual Income Tax Return

☐ IRS Schedule C: Profit or Loss From Business. Must be filed with IRS Form 1040 by all sole proprietorships, unless Schedule IRS Schedule C-EZ is filed

☐ IRS Schedule C-EZ: Net Profit From Business. May be filed if expenses are under $5,000 and other qualifications are met (See Schedule C-EZ)

☐ IRS Form 1040-SS: Self-Employment Tax. Required for any sole proprietor who shows $400 income from his or her business on IRS Schedule C or C-EZ

☐ IRS Form 1040-ES: Estimated Tax for Individuals. Must be used by all sole proprietors who expect to make a profit requiring estimated taxes

☐ IRS Form SS-4: Application for Employer Identification Number. Must be filed by all sole proprietors who will hire one or more employees

☐ IRS Form W-2: Wage and Tax Statement. Must be filed by all sole proprietors who have one or more employees

☐ IRS Form W-3: Transmittal of Wage and Tax Statement .Must be filed by all sole proprietors who have one or more employees

☐ IRS Form W-4: Employee's Withholding Allowance Certificate. Must be provided to employees of sole proprietors. Not filed with the IRS

☐ IRS Form 940: Employer's Annual Federal Unemployment Tax Return (FUTA). Must be filed by all sole proprietors who have employees

☐ IRS Form 941: Employer's Quarterly Federal Tax Return. Must be filed by all sole proprietors who have one or more employees

☐ IRS Form 8109: Federal Tax Deposit Coupon. Used by all employers with quarterly employee tax liability over $2,500.00 (Obtain from IRS)

☐ IRS Form 8829: Expenses for Business Use of Your Home. Filed with annual IRS Form 1040, if necessary

☐ Any required state and local income and sales tax forms

Sole Proprietorship Monthly Tax Schedule

❑ If you have employees, and your payroll tax liability is over $2,500.00 quarterly, you must make monthly tax payments using IRS Form 8109

❑ If required, file and pay any necessary state or local sales tax

Sole Proprietorship Quarterly Tax Schedule

❑ Pay any required estimated taxes using vouchers from IRS Form 1040-ES

❑ If you have employees, file IRS Form 941 and make any required payments of FICA and withholding taxes

❑ If you have employees and your unpaid FUTA tax liability is over $500.00, make FUTA deposit using IRS Form 8109

❑ If required, file and pay any necessary state or local sales tax

Sole Proprietorship Annual Tax Schedule

❑ If you have employees, prepare IRS Forms W-2 and provide to employees by January 31

❑ File IRS Form W-3 and copies of all IRS Forms W-2 with IRS by January 31

❑ If you have paid any independent contractors over $600 annually, prepare IRS Forms 1099 and provide to recipients by January 31; and file IRS Form 1096 and copies of all IRS Forms 1099 with IRS by January 31

❑ Make required unemployment tax payment and file IRS Form 940

❑ File IRS Form 1040-SS with your annual IRS Form 1040

❑ File IRS Schedule C and IRS Form 1040

❑ If you are required, file and pay any necessary state or local sales, income, or unemployment taxes

❑ File IRS Form 8829 with your annual IRS Form 1040, if necessary

Taxation of Partnerships

There may be certain tax advantages to the operation of a business as a partnership. The profits generated by a partnership may be distributed directly to the partners without incurring any "double" tax liability, as is the case with the distribution of corporate profits in the form of dividends to the shareholders. Income from a partnership is taxed at personal income tax rates. Note, however, that depending on the individual tax situation of each partner, this aspect could prove to be a disadvantage. The losses of a partnership are also distributed directly to each partner at the end of each fiscal year and may be written off as deductions by each individual partner. Tax credits are also handled in a similar fashion.

For detailed understanding about the individual tax consequences of operating your business as a partnership, a competent tax professional should be consulted. A basic comprehension of the information required on federal tax forms will help you understand why certain financial records are necessary. Understanding tax reporting will also assist you as you decide how to organize your business financial records.

A chart of tax forms is provided which details which IRS forms may be necessary. In addition, a schedule of tax filing is also provided to assist you in keeping your tax reporting timely. Finally, a sample of each form is presented on the Forms-on-CD that accompanied this book.

Partnership Tax Forms Checklist

☐ IRS Form 1040: U.S. Individual Income Tax Return .Must be filed by all partners. Do not use IRS Form 1040-A or IRS Form 1040-EZ

☐ IRS Form 1065: U.S. Partnership Return of Income .Must be completed by all partnerships

☐ IRS Form 1065 - Schedule K-1: Partner's Share of Income, Credit, Deductions, etc. Must be filed by all partners

☐ IRS Form 1040-SS: Self Employment Tax. Required for any partner who shows $400+ income from their business on Schedule K-1

☐ IRS Form W-2: Wage and Tax Statement. Must be filed by all partnerships who have one or more employees

☐ IRS Form 1040-ES: Estimated Tax for Individuals. Must be used by all partners who expect to make a profit requiring estimated taxes

☐ IRS Form SS-4: Application for Employer Identification Number. Must be filed by all partnerships who will hire one or more employees

☐ IRS Form W-3: Transmittal of Wage and Tax Statement. Must be filed by all partnerships who have one or more employees

☐ IRS Form W-4: Employee's Withholding Allowance Certificate. Must be provided to employees of partnerships. It is not filed with the IRS

☐ IRS Form 940: Employer's Annual Federal Unemployment Tax Return (FUTA). Must be filed by all partnerships with employees

☐ IRS Form 941: Employer's Quarterly Federal Tax Return. Must be filed by all partnerships who have one or more employees

☐ IRS Form 8109: Federal Tax Deposit Coupon. Must be filed by all partner ships with employees and a quarterly income tax liability over $2,500, or a quarterly federal unemployment liability of over $500.00

☐ Any required state and local income and sales tax forms. Please check with the appropriate tax authority for more information

Partnership Monthly Tax Schedule

☐ If you have employees, and your payroll tax liability is over $2,500 quarterly, you must make monthly tax payments using Form 8109

☐ If required, file and pay any necessary state or local sales tax

Partnership Quarterly Tax Schedule

☐ Pay any required estimated taxes using vouchers from IRS Form 1040-ES

☐ If you have employees: file IRS Form 941 and make any required payments of FICA and Withholding Taxes

☐ If you have employees and your unpaid FUTA tax liability is over $500 quarterly, make FUTA deposit using IRS Form 8109

☐ If required, file and pay any necessary state or local sales tax

Partnership Annual Tax Schedule

☐ If you have employees, prepare W-2 forms and provide to employees by January 31st and file Form W-3 and copies of all W-2 forms with IRS by January 31st

☐ If you have paid any independent contractors over $600 annually, prepare 1099 Forms and provide to recipient by January 31st and file Form 1096 and copies of all 1099 forms with IRS by January 31st

☐ Make required unemployment tax payment and file IRS Form 940

☐ File IRS Form 1040-SS with your annual 1040 Form

☐ If required, file and pay any necessary state or local sales, income, or unemployment tax

☐ File IRS Form 1065 and Schedule K-1. Also provide a copy of Schedule K-1 to each partner by January 31st

Taxation of Corporations

Corporations are a separate entity under the law and as such are subject to taxation at both the state and federal levels. In general corporations are subject to federal income tax on the annual profits in many ways similar to the tax on individual income. However, there are significant differences. The most important aspect is the "double" taxation on corporate income if it is distributed to the shareholders in the form of dividends. At the corporate level, corporate net income is subject to tax at the corporate level.

Corporate funds that are distributed to officers or directors in the form of salaries, expense reimbursements, or employee benefits may be used by a corporation as a legitimate business deduction against the income of the corporation. Corporate surplus funds that are paid out to shareholders in the form of dividends on their ownership of stock in the corporation, however, are not allowed to be used as a corporate deduction. Thus, any funds used in this manner have been subject to corporate income tax prior to distribution to the shareholders. The dividends are then also subject to taxation as income to the individual shareholder and so are subject to a "double" taxation.

S-corporations are taxed similarly to partnerships, with the corporation acting only as a conduit and all of the deductions and income passing to the individual shareholders where they are subject to income tax. Corporations may be used by businesses in many ways to actually lessen the federal and state income tax burdens. A competent tax professional should be consulted. A brief study of the federal tax forms your business will use will provide you with an overview of the method by which corporations are taxed. A basic comprehension of the information required on federal tax forms will help you understand why certain financial records are necessary. Understanding tax reporting will also assist you as you decide how to organize your business financial records.

A checklist of tax forms is provided detailing which IRS forms may be necessary. In addition, a schedule of tax filing is also provided to assist you in keeping your tax reporting timely. Finally, a sample of each IRS tax form mentioned is included on the enclosed Forms-on-CD.

Corporation Tax Forms Checklist

☐ IRS Form 1120: U.S. Corporation Income Tax Return. This forms must be filed by all corporations

☐ IRS Form 1120-W: Estimated Tax for Corporations. Must be completed by all corporations expecting a profit requiring estimated tax payments

☐ IRS Form W-4: Employee's Withholding Allowance Certificate. Must be provided to employees of corporations. It is not filed with the IRS

☐ IRS Form W-2: Wage and Tax Statement. Must be filed by all corporations

☐ IRS Form 1040, 1040-A, 1040-EZ: U. S. Individual Income Tax Return. One of these forms must be filed by all shareholders

☐ IRS Form SS-4: Application for Employer identification Number. Must be filed by all corporations

☐ IRS Form W-3: Transmittal of Wage and Tax Statements. Must be filed by all corporations

☐ IRS Form 940: Employer's Annual Federal Unemployment (FUTA) Tax Return Must be filed by all corporations. If the amount of FUTA tax due for any calendar quarter is over $500, the tax due must be deposited at a financial institution (using IRS Form 8190) within the month following the end of the quarter

☐ IRS Form 941: Employer's Quarterly Federal Tax Return. Must be filed by all corporations, within the month following the end of each quarter. When filed, the corporation must pay any income, social security, and Medicare taxes which are due and have not been deposited monthly using IRS Form 8109. You may pay these taxes quarterly with Form 941 if you total tax liability for the quarter is less than $2,500. If you deposited all taxes when due (using IRS Form 8109), you have 10 additional days from the normal due date to file Form 941

☐ IRS 8109: Federal Tax Deposit Coupon. Must be filed by all corporations with a quarterly income, social security and Medicare tax liability of over $2,500 or with a quarterly federal unemployment liability of over $500

☐ Any required state and local income and sales tax forms. Please check with the appropriate tax authority for more information

Corporation Monthly Tax Schedule

❑ If corporate payroll tax liability is over $2,500 quarterly, the corporation must make monthly tax payments using IRS Form 8109: Federal Tax Deposit Coupon

❑ If required: file and pay any necessary state or local sales tax

Corporation Quarterly Tax Schedule

❑ Pay any required corporate estimated taxes using IRS Form 8109

❑ File IRS Form 941: Employer's Quarterly Federal Tax Return and make any required payments of FICA and withholding taxes

❑ If corporate unpaid quarterly FUTA tax liability is over $500, make FUTA deposit using IRS Form 8109

❑ If required, file and pay any necessary state or local sales tax

Corporation Annual Tax Schedule

❑ Prepare IRS Form W-2: Wage and Tax Statement and provide to each employee by January 31st. Also file IRS Form W-3: Transmittal of Wage and Tax Statements for each employee and copies of all W-2 forms with the Social Security Administration by January 31st

❑ If corporation has paid any independent contractors over $600 annually, prepare IRS Form 1099-MISC: Miscellaneous Income and provide to recipients by January 31. Also file IRS Form 1096: Annual Summary and Transmittal of U.S. Information Returns and copies of all 1099 forms with IRS by January 31

❑ Make required unemployment tax payment and file IRS Form 940: Employer's Annual Federal Unemployment (FUTA) Tax Return

❑ File IRS Form 1120: U.S. Corporation Income Tax Return

❑ If required: file and pay any necessary state or local sales, income, or unemployment tax

Taxation of S-Corporations

Corporations are a separate entity under the law and as such are subject to taxation at both the state and federal levels. There are two types of corporations: C-corporations and S-corporations. The difference between the two is in the area of taxation. In general, C-corporations are subject to federal income tax on the annual profits in many ways similar to the tax on individual income. However, there are significant differences. The most important aspect is the "double" taxation on corporate income if it is distributed to the shareholders in the form of dividends. At the corporate level, corporate net income is subject to tax at the corporate level. Corporate funds that are distributed to officers or directors in the form of salaries, expense reimbursements, or employee benefits may be used by a corporation as a legitimate business deduction against the income of the corporation. Corporate surplus funds that are paid out to shareholders in the form of dividends on their ownership of stock in the corporation, however, are not allowed to be used as a corporate deduction. Thus, any funds used in this manner have been subject to corporate income tax prior to distribution to the shareholders. The dividends are then also subject to taxation as income to the individual shareholder and so are subject to a "double" taxation.

S-corporations are taxed similarly to partnerships, with the corporation acting only as a conduit and all of the deductions and income passing to the individual shareholders where they are subject to income tax. The S-corporation does not pay a corporate tax and files a different type of tax return than does a standard corporation. Taxation of the profits of the S-corporation falls to the individuals who own shares in the corporation. This also allows for each individual shareholder to personally deduct their share of any corporate losses. A competent tax professional should be consulted. A brief study of the federal tax forms your business will use will provide you with an overview of the method by which corporations are taxed. A basic comprehension of the information required on federal tax forms will help you understand why certain financial records are necessary. Understanding tax reporting will also assist you as you decide how to organize your business financial records.

A chart of tax forms is provided detailing which IRS forms may be necessary. In addition, a schedule of tax filing is also provided to assist you in keeping your tax reporting timely. Finally, a sample of each IRS tax form mentioned is included on the enclosed Forms-on-CD.

S-Corporation Tax Forms Checklist

☐ IRS Form 1040: Must be filed by all S-corporation shareholders. Do not use IRS form 1040-A or IRS form 1040-EZ

☐ IRS Form 2553: Election by a Small Business Corporation. Must be filed by all S-corporations

☐ IRS Form 1120-S: U.S. Income Tax Return for an S-Corporation. Must be filed by all S-corporations

☐ IRS Form 1120-S, Schedule K-1: Shareholder's Share of Income, Credit, Deductions, etc. Must be completed by all S-corporations

☐ IRS Form 1040-ES: Estimated Tax for Individuals. Must be used by all S-corporation shareholders who expect a profit requiring estimated taxes

☐ IRS Form SS-4: Application for Employer Identification Number. Must be filed by all S-corporations who will hire employees

☐ IRS Form W-2: Wage and Tax Statement. Must be filed by all S-corporations who have one or more employees

☐ IRS Form W-3: Transmittal of Wage and Tax Statement. Must be filed by all S-corporations who have one or more employees

☐ IRS Form W-4: Employee's Withholding Allowance Certificate. Must be provided to employees of S-corporations. It is not filed with the IRS

☐ IRS Form 940: Employer's Annual Federal Unemployment (FUTA) Tax Return. Must be filed by all S-corporation employers

☐ IRS Form 941: Employer's Quarterly Federal Tax Return. Must be filed by all S-corporations who have one or more employees

☐ IRS Form 8109: Federal Tax Deposit Coupon. Must be filed by all S-corporations with a quarterly income tax liability over $2,500.00 or a quarterly FUTA tax liability of over $500

☐ Any required State and Local Income and Sales Tax forms. Please check with the appropriate tax authority for more information

S-Corporation Monthly Tax Schedule

☐ If corporation has employees, and corporate payroll tax liability is over $2,500 quarterly, the corporation must make monthly tax payments using Form 8109: Federal Tax Deposit Coupon

☐ If required: file and pay any necessary state or local states tax

S-Corporation Quarterly Tax Schedule

☐ Pay any required estimated taxes using vouchers from IRS Form 1040-ES: Estimated Tax for Individuals

☐ If corporation has employees: file IRS Form 941 and make any required payments of FICA and Withholding Taxes

☐ If corporation has employees and corporate unpaid FUTA tax liability is over $500, make FUTA deposit using IRS Form 8109

☐ If required: file and pay any necessary state or local sales tax

S-Corporation Annual Tax Schedule

☐ Prepare IRS Form W-2: Wage and Tax Statement and provide to each employee by January 31st. Also file IRS Form W-3: Transmittal of Wage and Tax Statements for each employee and copies of all W-2 forms with the Social Security Administration by January 31st

☐ If corporation has paid any independent contractors over $600 annually, prepare IRS Form 1099-MISC: Miscellaneous Income and provide to recipients by January 31. Also file IRS Form 1096: Annual Summary and Transmittal of U.S. Information Returns and copies of all 1099 forms with IRS by January 31

☐ Make required unemployment tax payment and file IRS Form 940

☐ File IRS Form 1120-S and Schedule K-1 of IRS Form 1120-S. Also provide a copy of Schedule K-1 to each shareholder by January 31st

☐ If required: file and pay any necessary state or local sales, income, or unemployment taxes

Taxation of a Limited Liability Company

There may be certain tax advantages to the operation of a business as a limited liability company. There are three methods by which a limited liability company can be taxed at the federal level. The choice of method is, for the most part, up to the member(s) of the company. The checklists provided in this chapter are separated into these three general divisions.

LLC Taxation As a Partnership

All limited liability companies that have more than one member will be taxed at the federal level as a partnership, unless the members elect otherwise. The partnership taxation is automatic and does not require any election or filing of any form for the election. If, however, a limited liability company elects to be taxed as a regular corporation, the members must vote to make this election and they must file Internal Revenue Service Form 8832: Entity Classification Election. If corporate taxation is elected, see below under "Taxation As a Corporation."

If the limited liability company is to be taxed as a partnership, the profits generated by the limited liability company may be distributed directly to the members without incurring any "double" tax liability, as is the case with the distribution of corporate profits in the form of dividends to the shareholders. Income from a limited liability company is taxed at the personal income tax rate of each individual member. Note, however, that depending on the individual tax situation of each member, this aspect could prove to be a disadvantage. The losses of a limited liability company are also distributed directly to each member at the end of each fiscal year and may be written off as deductions by each individual member. Tax credits are also handled in a similar fashion. A list of necessary tax forms for limited liability companies being taxed as partnerships is included at the end of this chapter.

LLC Taxation As a Corporation

All limited liability companies, whether they have only one member or many, may elect to be taxed at the federal level as a corporation. This corporate taxation is not automatic and requires the filing of IRS Form 8832: Entity Classification Election. The company should complete this form, checking the box stating "Initial classification by a newly-formed entity (or change in current classification of an existing entity to take effect on January 1, 1997)." Under "Form of Entity" on this form, the limited liability company should check the box in front of the statement: "A domestic eligible entity electing to be classified as an association taxable as a corporation." This will cause the limited liability company to be taxed as a corporation.

If the limited liability company is to be taxed as a corporation, the profits generated by the limited liability company will not pass through directly to the member, as with taxation of sole proprietorships or partnerships. Indeed, taxation of corporations opens the company up to "double" tax liability, in that any corporate profits are first taxed at the corporate level, and then the distribution of corporate profits in the form of dividends to the shareholders (or members) is taxed at the individual level at the personal income tax rates of the members. Note, however, that depending on the individual tax situation of the member, this aspect could prove to be an advantage. For a limited liability company that elects to be taxed as a corporation, the business losses are also not distributed directly to the member as individual deductions, but rather serve as deductions only for the company against company income. Tax credits are also handled in a similar fashion. A list of necessary tax forms for limited liability companies being taxed as corporations is included at the end of this chapter.

LLC Taxation As Sole Proprietorship

All limited liability companies that have only one member will be taxed at the federal level as a sole proprietorship, unless the sole member elects otherwise. The sole proprietorship taxation requires the filing of IRS Form 8832: Entity Classification Election. The single-member company should complete this form, checking the box stating "Initial classification by a newly-formed entity (or change in current classification of an existing entity to take effect on January 1, 1997)." Under "Form of Entity" on this form, the single-member limited liability company should check the box in front of the statement: "A domestic eligible entity with a single owner electing to be disregarded as a separate entity." This will cause the single-member limited liability company to be taxed as a sole proprietorship. If, however, a single-member limited liability company elects to be taxed as a regular corporation, the member must also file IRS Form 8832: Entity Classification Election. If corporate taxation is elected, see above under "Taxation As a Corporation."

If the limited liability company is to be taxed as a sole proprietorship, the profits generated by the limited liability company pass through directly to the sole member without incurring any "double" tax liability, as is the case with the distribution of corporate profits in the form of dividends to the shareholders. Income from a limited liability company is taxed at the personal income tax rate of the sole member. Note, however, that depending on the individual tax situation of the member, this aspect could prove to be a disadvantage. The losses of a limited liability company are also distributed directly to the member as individual deductions. Tax credits are also handled in a similar fashion. A list of necessary tax forms for limited liability companies being taxed as sole proprietorships is included at the end of this chapter.

For a detailed understanding of the individual tax consequences of operating your business as a limited liability company, a competent tax professional should be consulted. The federal tax forms that are mentioned in this chapter are contained on the Forms-on-CD. A brief study of the tax forms will provide you with an overview of the method by which limited liability companies are taxed. A basic comprehension of the information required on federal tax forms will help you understand why certain financial records are necessary. Understanding tax reporting will also assist you as you decide how to organize your business financial records.

Various checklists of tax forms are provided that detail which IRS forms may be necessary for each method of taxation of limited liability companies. In addition, various schedules of tax filing are also provided to assist you in keeping your tax reporting timely.

Limited Liability Company Tax Forms Checklist
Taxed As a Sole Proprietorship

☐ IRS Form 8832: Entity Classification Election. This form must be completed and filed by all limited liability companies electing to be treated as a corporation

☐ IRS Form 1040: U.S. Individual Income Tax Return. Do not use IRS Form 1040A or IRS Form 1040EZ: Income Tax Return for Single and Joint Filers With No Dependents

☐ IRS Schedule C (Form 1040): Profit or Loss From Business (Sole Proprietorship) must be filed with IRS Form 1040 by all limited liability companies electing to be treated as sole proprietorships, unless Schedule IRS Schedule C-EZ: Net Profit From Business (Sole Proprietorship) is filed

☐ IRS Schedule C-EZ (Form 1040): Net Profit From Business (Sole Proprietorship) may be filed if expenses are under $5000 and other qualifications are met

☐ IRS Form 1040-SS: U.S. Self-Employment Tax Return. Required for any sole proprietor who shows $400+income from his or her limited liability company business on IRS Schedule C or IRS Schedule C-EZ

☐ IRS Form 1040-ES: Estimated Tax for Individuals must be used by all companies that expect to make a profit requiring estimated taxes

☐ IRS Form SS-4: Application for Employer Identification Number must be filed by all companies who will hire one or more employees

☐ IRS Form W-2: Wage and Tax Statement must be filed by all companies that have one or more employees

☐ IRS Form W-3: Transmittal of Wage and Tax Statements must be filed by all companies that have one or more employees

☐ IRS Form W-4: Employee's Withholding Allowance Certificate must be provided to employees of companies. Not filed with the IRS

☐ IRS Form 940: Employer's Annual Federal Unemployment (FUTA) Tax Return must be filed by all companies that have employees

☐ IRS Form 941: Employer's Quarterly Federal Tax Return must be filed by all companies that have one or more employees

☐ IRS Form 8109: Federal Tax Deposit Coupon. Used by all companies with quarterly employee tax liability over $2500. (Obtain from IRS)

☐ IRS Form 8829: Expenses for Business Use of Your Home. Filed with annual IRS Form 1040, if necessary

☐ Any required state and local income and sales tax forms

Limited Liability Company Tax Forms Checklist
Taxed As a Partnership

☐ IRS Form 1040: U.S. Individual Income Tax Return must be filed by all members. Do not use IRS Form 1040A or IRS Form 1040-EZ: Income Tax Return for Single and Joint Filers With No Dependents

☐ IRS Form 1065: U.S. Return of Partnership Income must be completed by all limited liability companies which are taxed as partnerships

☐ IRS Schedule K-1 (Form 1065): Partner's Share of Income, Credits, Deductions, etc. must be filed by all members

☐ IRS Form 1040-SS: U.S. Self-Employment Tax Return. Required for any member who shows $400+income from his or her business on Schedule K-1

☐ IRS Form 1040-ES: Estimated Tax for Individuals must be used by all members who expect to make a profit requiring estimated taxes

☐ IRS Form SS-4: Application for Employer Identification Number must be filed by all companies that will hire one or more employees

☐ IRS Form W-2: Wage and Tax Statement must be filed by all companies that have one or more employees

☐ IRS Form W-3: Transmittal of Wage and Tax Statements must be filed by all companies that have one or more employees

☐ IRS Form W-4: Employee's Withholding Allowance Certificate must be provided to employees of companies. Not filed with the IRS

☐ IRS Form 940: Employer's Annual Federal Unemployment (FUTA) Tax Return must be filed by all companies that have employees

☐ IRS Form 941: Employer's Quarterly Federal Tax Return must be filed by all partnerships that have one or more employees.

☐ IRS Form 8109: Federal Tax Deposit Coupon. Used by all companies with quarterly employee tax liability over $2500. (Obtain from IRS)

☐ Any required state and local income and sales tax forms. Please check with the appropriate tax authority for more information

Limited Liability Company Tax Forms Checklist
Taxed As a Corporation

☐ IRS Form 8832: Entity Classification Election. This form must be completed and filed by all limited liability companies electing to be treated as a corporation

☐ IRS Form 1040: U.S .Individual Income Tax Return must be filed by all members. Do not use IRS Form 1040A or IRS Form 1040EZ: Income Tax Return for Single and Joint Filers With No Dependents

☐ IRS Form 1120: U.S. Corporation Income Tax Return. This form must be filed by all limited liability companies electing to be treated as a corporation

☐ IRS Form 1120-W (Worksheet): Estimated Tax for Corporations must be completed by all limited liability companies expecting a profit requiring estimated tax payments

☐ IRS Form SS-4: Application for Employer Identification Number must be filed by all limited liability companies

☐ IRS Form W-2: Wage and Tax Statement must be filed by all limited liability companies

☐ IRS Form W-3: Transmittal of Wage and Tax Statements must be filed by all limited liability companies

☐ IRS Form W-4: Employee's Withholding Allowance Certificate must be provided to employees of limited liability companies. It is not filed with the IRS

☐ IRS Form 940: Employer's Annual Federal Unemployment (FUTA) Tax Return must be filed by all limited liability companies

☐ IRS Form 941: Employer's Quarterly Federal Tax Return must be filed by all limited liability companies

☐ IRS Form 8109: Federal Tax Deposit Coupon. Used by companies with quarterly employee tax liability over $2500. (Obtain from IRS)

☐ Any required state and local income and sales tax forms. Please check with the appropriate tax authority for more information

Limited Liability Company Monthly Tax Schedule

❑ If you have employees, and your payroll tax liability is over $2500 quarterly, you must make monthly tax payments using IRS Form 8109: Federal Tax Deposit Coupon

❑ If required, file and pay any necessary state or local sales tax Quarterly Tax Schedule

Limited Liability Company Quarterly Tax Schedule

❑ Pay any required estimated taxes using vouchers from IRS Form1040-ES: Estimated Tax for Individuals

❑ If you have employees, file IRS Form 941: Employer's Quarterly Federal Tax Return and make any required payments of FICA and withholding taxes

❑ If you have employees and your quarterly unpaid FUTA tax liability is over $500, make FUTA deposit using IRS Form 8109: Federal Tax Deposit Coupon

❑ If required, file and pay any necessary state or local sales tax Annual Tax Schedule

Limited Liability Company Annual Tax Schedule

❑ If you have employees, prepare IRS Form W-2: Wage and Tax Statement for each employee and provide to employees by January 31; and file IRS Form W-3: Transmittal of Wage and Tax Statements and copies of all W-2 Forms with IRS by January 31

❑ If you have paid any independent contractors over $600 annually, prepare IRS Form 1099-MISC: Miscellaneous Income and provide to recipient by January 31; and file IRS Form 1096: Annual Summary and Transmittal of U.S. Information Returns and copies of all 1099 Forms with IRS by January 31

❑ Make required unemployment tax payment and file IRS Form 940: Employer's Annual Federal Unemployment (FUTA) Tax Return

☐ File IRS Form 1040-SS: U.S. Self-Employment Tax Return with your annual IRS Form 1040: U.S. Individual Income Tax Return

☐ File IRS Form 1065: U.S. Return of Partnership Income and Schedule K-1 (Form 1065): Partner's Share of Income, Credits, Deductions, etc. (treatment as a partnership)

☐ File IRS Form 1120: U.S. Corporation Income Tax Return (treatment as a corporation)

☐ File IRS Schedule C (Form 1040): Profit or Loss From Business (Sole Proprietorship) and IRS Form 1040: U.S. Individual Income Tax Return (treatment as a sole proprietorship)

☐ If you are required, file and pay any necessary state or local sales, income, or unemployment taxes

Glossary

Account: A separate record of an asset, liability, income, or expense of a business.

Accounting: The process for recording, summarizing, and interpreting business financial records.

Accounting method: The method of recording income and expenses for a business; can be either accrual method or cash method.

Accounting period: A specific time period covered by the financial statements of a business.

Accounting system: The specific system of record-keeping used to set up the accounting records of a business. See also *single-entry accounting* or *double-entry accounting.*

Accounts payable: Money owed by a business to another for goods or services purchased on credit. Money that the business intends to pay to another.

Accounts receivable: Money owed to the business by another for goods or services sold on credit. Money that the business expects to receive.

Accrual method: Accounting method in which all income and expenses are counted when earned or incurred regardless of when the actual cash is received or paid.

Accrued expenses: Expenses that have been incurred but have not yet been paid.

Accrued income: Income that has been earned but has not yet been received.

ACRS: Accelerated Cost Recovery System. Generally, a method of depreciation used for assets purchased between 1980 and 1987.

Agent: A person who is authorized to act on behalf of another. A corporation acts only through its agents, whether they are directors, employees, or officers.

Aging: The method used to determine how long accounts receivable have been owed to a business.

Amend: To alter or change.

Articles of Incorporation: The charter of the corporation, the public filing with a state that requests that the corporation be allowed to exist. Along with the Corporate Bylaws, they provide details of the organization and structure of the business. They must be consistent with the laws of the state of incorporation.

Assets: Everything a business owns, including amounts of money that are owed to the business.

Assumed name: A name, other than the corporation's legal name as shown on the Articles of Incorporation, under which a corporation will conduct business. Most states require registration of the fictitious name if a company desires to conduct business under an assumed name. The corporation's legal name is not an assumed name.

Authorized stock: The number of shares of stock that a corporation is allowed to issue as stated in the Articles of Incorporation. All authorized shares need not be issued.

Balance sheet: The business financial statement that depicts the financial status of the business on a specific date by summarizing the assets and liabilities of the business.

Balance sheet accounts: Asset and liability accounts used to prepare business balance sheets.

Balance sheet equation: Assets = Liabilities + Equity, or Equity = Assets – Liabilities.

Board of directors: The group with control of the general supervision of the corporation. They are elected by the shareholders and the directors, in turn, appoint the officers of the corporation.

Bookkeeping: The actual process of recording the figures in accounting records. Business corporation laws: For each individual state, these provide the legal framework for the operation of corporations. The Articles of Incorporation and the Bylaws of a corporation must adhere to the specifics of state law.

Business liabilities: Business debts. Also the value of the owner's equity in his or her business.

Bylaws: The internal rules that govern the management of the corporation. They contain the procedures for holding meetings, appointments, elections and other management matters. If these conflict with the Articles of Incorporation, the provision in the Articles will be controlling.

C-corporation: A business entity owned by shareholders that is not an S-corporation. Subject to double taxation, unlike S-corporations.

Calendar year: Year consisting of 12 consecutive months ending on December 31st.

Capital: Initially, the actual money or property that shareholders transfer to the corporation to allow it to operate. Once in operation, capital also consists of accumulated profits. The net worth of the corporation, the owner's equity in a business, and/or the ownership value of the business.

Capital expense: An expense for the purchase of a fixed asset; an asset with a useful life of over one year. Generally, must be depreciated rather than deducted as a business expense.

Capital stock: See *authorized stock*.

Capital surplus: Corporation owner's equity. See also *retained capital*.

Cash: All currency, coins, and checks that a business has on hand or in a bank account.

Cash method: Accounting method in which income and expenses are not counted until the actual cash is received or paid.

Cash out: Cash paid out for business purposes, such as a refund.

Certificate of Incorporation: See Articles of Incorporation. Note, however, that some states will issue a Certificate of Incorporation after the filing of the Articles of Incorporation.

Chart of Accounts: A listing of the types and numbers of the various accounts that a business uses for its accounting records.

Check register: A running record of checks written, deposits made, and other transactions for a bank account.

Close corporation: Corporation with less than 50 shareholders that has elected to be treated as a close corporation. Not all states have close corporation statutes. (For information regarding close corporations, please consult a competent attorney.)

Closely held corporation: Not a specific state-sanctioned type of corporation, but rather a designation of any corporation in which the stock is held by a small group of people or entities and is not publicly traded.

Common stock: The standard stock of a corporation that includes the right to vote the shares and the right to proportionate dividends. See also *preferred stock.*

Consent Resolution: Any resolution signed by all of the directors or shareholders of a corporation authorizing an action, without the necessity of a meeting.

Corporate record book: Contains all the corporate records (except accounting records).

Corporate stock transfer book: Record of the issuance and transfer of stock certificates.

Corporation: A business entity owned by shareholders; can be a C-corporation or an S-corporation.

Cost basis: Total cost to a business of a fixed asset.

Cost of goods sold: The amount that a business has paid for the inventory that it has sold during a specific period. Calculated by adding beginning inventory and additions to inventory and then deducting the ending inventory value.

Credit: In double-entry accounting, an increase in liability or income accounts or a decrease in asset or expense accounts.

Cumulative voting: A voting right of shareholders that allows votes for directors to be spread among the various nominees. This right protects the voting strength of minority shareholders. The amount of votes in cumulative voting is based on the number of shares held times the number of director positions to be voted on. The shareholder can then allocate the total cumulative votes in any manner.

Current assets: Cash and any other assets that can be converted to cash or consumed by the business within one year.

Current debt: Debt that will normally be paid within one year.

Current liabilities: Debts of a business that must be paid within one year.

Current ratio: A method of determining the liquidity of a business. Calculated by dividing current assets by current liabilities.

Debit: In double-entry accounting, a decrease in liability or income accounts or an increase in asset or expense accounts.

Debt: The amount that a business owes to another. Also known as "liability."

Debt ratio: A method of determining the indebtedness of a business. Calculated by dividing total liabilities by total assets.

Depreciation: Cost of fixed asset deductible proportionately over time.

Dissolution: Methods by which a corporation concludes its business and liquidates. Dissolutions may be involuntary because of bankruptcy or credit problems or voluntary on the initiation of the directors or shareholders of a corporation.

Dividend: A distribution of money or property paid by the corporation to a shareholder based on the amount of shares held. A proportionate share of the net profits of a business that the board of directors has determined should be paid out to shareholders, rather than held as retained earnings. Dividends must be paid out of the corporation's net earnings and profits. The board of directors has the authority to declare or withhold dividends based on sound business discretion.

Domestic corporation: A corporation is a domestic corporation in the state in which it is incorporated. See also *foreign corporation.*

Double-entry accounting: An accounting system under which each transaction is recorded twice: as a credit and as a debit. A very difficult system of accounting to learn and understand.

Equity: Any debt that a business owes. It is owner's equity if owed to the business owners and liabilities if owed to others.

Expenses: The costs to a business of producing its income. Any money that it has paid or will pay out during a certain period.

FEIN: Federal Identification Number, used for tax purposes.

FICA: Federal Insurance Contributions Act. Taxes withheld from employees and paid by employers for Social Security and Medicare.

Fictitious name: See *assumed name.*

FIFO: First-in, first-out method of accounting for inventory. The inventory value is based on the cost of the latest items purchased.

Financial statements: Reports that summarize the finances of a business; generally a profit and loss statement and a balance sheet.

Fiscal year: A 12-month accounting period used by a business.

Fiscal-year reporting: For income tax purposes, reporting business taxes for any 12-month period that does not end on December 31 of each year.

Fixed assets: Assets of a business that will not be sold or consumed within one year. Generally, fixed assets (other than land) must be depreciated.

Foreign corporation: A corporation is referred to as a foreign corporation in all states other than the one in which it is actually incorporated. In order to conduct active business affairs in a different state, a foreign corporation must be registered with the other state for the authority to transact business and it must pay an annual fee for this privilege.

FUTA: Federal Unemployment Tax Act. Federal business unemployment taxes.

General journal: In double-entry accounting, used to record all of the transactions of a business in chronological order. Transactions are then posted (or transferred) to the appropriate accounts in the general ledger.

General ledger: In double-entry accounting, the central listing of all accounts of a business.

Gross pay: The total amount of an employee's compensation before the deduction of any taxes or benefits.

Gross profit: Gross sales minus the cost of goods sold.

Gross sales: The total amount received for goods and services during an accounting period.

Gross wages: The total amount of an employee's compensation before the deduction of any taxes or benefits.

Income: Any money that a business has received or will receive during a certain period.

Income statement: Financial statement that shows the income and expenses for a business. Also referred to as an "operating statement" or "profit and loss statement."

Incorporator: The person who signs the Articles of Incorporation. Usually a person, but some states allow a corporation or partnership to be an incorporator.

Indemnify: To reimburse or compensate. Directors and officers of corporations are often reimbursed or indemnified for all the expenses they may have incurred in incorporating.

Initial capital: The money or property that an owner or owners contribute to starting a business.

Intangible personal property: Generally, property not attached to land that you cannot hold or touch (for example: copyrights, business goodwill, etc.).

Inventory: Goods that are held by a business for sale to customers.

Invoice: A bill for the sale of goods or services that is sent to the buyer.

Issued shares: The number of authorized shares of stock that are actually transferred to shareholders of the corporation. Also referred to as outstanding shares. See also *treasury shares.*

Ledgers: The accounting books for a business. Generally, refers to the entire set of accounts for a business.

Liabilities: The debts of a business.

LIFO: Last-in, first-out method of valuing inventory. Total value is based on the cost of the earliest items purchased.

Liquidity: The ability of a company to convert its assets to cash and meet its obligations with that cash.

Long-term assets: The assets of a business that will be held for over one year. Those assets of a business that are subject to depreciation (except for land).

Long-term debts: Debts that will not be paid off in one year.

Long-term liabilities: The debts of a business that will not be due for over one year.

Long-term loans payable: Money due on a loan more than one year in the future.

Long-term notes payable: Money due more than one year in the future.

MACRS: Modified accelerated cost recovery system. A method of depreciation for use with assets purchased after January 1, 1987.

Managers: In a limited liability company, those persons selected by the members of the company to handle the management functions of the company. Managers of limited liability companies may or may not be members/owners of the company. Managers are roughly analogous to the officers of a corporation.

Members: In a limited liability company, those persons who have ownership interests (equivalent to shareholders in a corporation). Most states allow single-member limited liability companies.

Minutes: A written record of the activities of a meeting.

Net income: The amount of money that a business has after deducting the cost of goods sold and the cost of all expenses. Also referred to as "net profit."

Net loss: The amount by which a business has expenses and costs of goods sold greater than income.

Net pay: The amount of compensation that an employee actually will be paid after the deductions for taxes and benefits.

Net profit: The amount by which a business has income greater than expenses and cost of goods sold. Also referred to as "net income."

Net sales: The value of sales after deducting the cost of goods sold from gross sales.

Net wages: The amount of compensation that an employee will actually be paid after the deductions for taxes and benefits.

Net worth: The value of the owner's share in a business. The value of a business determined by deducting the debts of a business from the assets of a business. Also referred to as "owner's equity."

No-par value: Shares of stock that have no specific face value. The board of directors can assign a value to the shares for sale and can then allocate a portion of the sales price to the paid-in-capital account.

Nontaxable income: Income that is not subject to any state or local sales tax.

Not-for-profit corporation: A corporation formed under state law that exists for a socially worthwhile purpose. Profits are not distributed but retained and used for corporate purposes. May be tax-exempt. Also referred to as "nonprofit."

Officers: Manage the daily operations of a corporation. Generally consists of a president, vice president, secretary, and treasurer. Appointed by the board of directors.

Operating margin: Net sales divided by gross sales. The actual profit on goods sold, before deductions for expenses.

Operating statement: Financial statement that shows the income and expenses for a business. Also referred to as "income statement" or "profit and loss statement."

Owner's equity: The value of an owner's share in a business. Also referred to as "capital."

Par value: The face value assigned to shares of stock. Par-value stock must be sold for at least the stated value, but can be sold for more than the par value.

Partnership: An unincorporated business entity that is owed by two or more persons.

Payee: Person or business to whom a payment is made.

Payor: Person or business that makes a payment.

Perpetual duration: Existence of a corporation forever.

Personal property: All business property other than land and the buildings that are attached to the land.

Petty cash: Cash that a business has on hand for payment of minor expenses when use of a business check is not convenient. Not to be used for handling sales revenue.

Petty cash fund: A cash fund. Considered part of cash on hand.

Petty cash register: The sheet for recording petty cash transactions.

Physical inventory: The actual process of counting and valuing the inventory on hand at the end of an accounting period.

Piercing the corporate veil: A legal decision that allows a court to ignore the corporate entity and reach the assets of the shareholders, directors, or officers.

Plant assets: Long-term assets of a business. Those business assets that are subject to depreciation (other than land).

Posting: In double-entry accounting, the process of transferring data from journals to ledgers.

Pre-paid expenses: Expenses that are paid for before they are used (for example: insurance, rent, etc.).

Preemptive rights: A shareholder right that allows shareholders the opportunity to maintain their percentage of ownership of the corporation in the event that additional shares are offered for sale.

Preferred stock: Generally, stock that provides the shareholder with a preferential payment of dividends, but does not carry voting rights.

Profit and loss statement: Financial statement that shows the income and expenses for a business. Also referred to as an "income statement" or "operating statement."

Proxy: A written shareholder authorization to vote shares on behalf of another. Directors may never vote by proxy (except in some close corporations).

Quorum: The required number of persons necessary to officially conduct business at a meeting. Generally, a majority of the shareholders or directors constitutes a quorum.

Real property: Land and any buildings or improvements that are attached to the land.

Reconciliation: The process of bringing a bank statement into agreement with the business check register.

Recovery period: Specific time period for dividing up the cost into proportionate amounts.

Registered agent: The person designated in the Articles of Incorporation who will be available to receive service of process (summons, subpoena, etc.) on behalf of the corporation. A corporation must always have a registered agent.

Registered office: The actual physical location of the registered agent. Need not be the actual principal place of business of the corporation.

Resolution: A formal decision that has been adopted by either the shareholders or the board of directors of a corporation.

Retail price: The price for which a product is sold to the public.

Retained capital: Corporation owner's equity. See also capital surplus.

Retained earnings: In a corporation, the portion of the annual profits of a business that are kept and reinvested in the business, rather than paid to shareholders in the form of dividends.

Revenue: Income that a business brings in from the sale of goods or services or from investments.

S-corporation: A type of business corporation in which all of the expenses and profits are passed through to its shareholders to be accounted for at tax time individually in the manner of partnerships. A specific IRS designation that allows a corporation to be taxed similarly to a partnership, yet retain limited liability for its shareholders.

Salary: Fixed weekly, monthly, or annual compensation for an employee.

Sales: Money brought into a business from the sale of goods or services.

Sales income: Revenue derived from selling a product of some type.

Salvage value: The value of an asset after it has been fully depreciated.

Service income: Income derived from performing a service for someone.

Service of process: To accept subpoenas or summonses for a corporation.

Shareholder's equity: In a corporation, the owner's equity of a business divided by the number of outstanding shares.

Shareholders: Owners of issued stock of a corporation and, therefore, owners of an interest in the corporation. They elect the board of directors and vote on major corporate issues.

Short-term loans payable: Money due on a loan within one year.

Short-term notes payable: Money due within one year.

Single-entry accounting: A business recordkeeping system that generally tracks only income and expense accounts. Used generally by small businesses, it is much easier to use and understand than double-entry accounting.

Sole proprietorship: An unincorporated business entity in which one person owns the entire company.

Stock transfer book: The ledger book (or sheets) in which the registered owners of shares in the corporation are recorded.

Straight-line depreciation: Spreads the deductible amount equally over the recovery period.

Supplies: Materials used in conducting the day-to-day affairs of a business (as opposed to raw materials used in manufacturing).

Tangible personal property: Property not attached to land that you can hold and touch (for example:machinery, furniture, equipment).

Taxes payable: Total of all taxes due but not yet paid.

Treasury shares: Shares of stock that were issued, but later reacquired by the corporation and not canceled. May be issued as dividends to shareholders. They are issued, but not outstanding for terms of voting and quorums.

Trial balance: In double-entry accounting, a listing of all the balances in the general ledger in order to show that debits and credits balance.

Wages: Hourly compensation paid to employees, as opposed to salary.

Wages payable: Total of all wages and salaries due to employees but not yet paid out.

Wholesale price: The cost to a business of goods purchased for later sale to the public.

Working capital: The money available for immediate business operations. Current assets minus current liabilities.

Index